I0820818

BOOM TIMES IN CHILLIWACK

MERLIN BUNT

Boom Times in CHILLIWACK

MEMORIES FROM THE POST-WAR YEARS

HARBOUR PUBLISHING

1 2 3 4 5 — 29 28 27 26 25

HARBOUR PUBLISHING CO. LTD.
P.O. Box 219, Madeira Park, BC, V0N 2H0
www.harbourpublishing.com

EDITED by David Marsh
COVER AND TEXT DESIGN by Libris Simas Ferraz / Onça Publishing
INDEXED by Brittany Vesterback, Javelin Editorial Services
PRINTED AND BOUND in Canada

Canada Council for the Arts Conseil des arts du Canada

HARBOUR PUBLISHING acknowledges the support of the Canada Council for the Arts, the Government of Canada, and the Province of British Columbia through the BC Arts Council.

LIBRARY AND ARCHIVES CANADA CATALOGUING IN PUBLICATION

Title: Boom times in Chilliwack : memories from the post-war years / Merlin Bunt.
Names: Bunt, Merlin, author.
Description: Includes bibliographical references and index.
Identifiers: Canadiana (print) 20250238926 | Canadiana (ebook) 20250238985 | ISBN 9781998526369 (hardcover) | ISBN 9781998526376 (EPUB)
Subjects: LCSH: Chilliwack (B.C.)—History.
Classification: LCC FC3849.C55 B86 2025 | DDC 971.1/37—dc23

TABLE OF CONTENTS

INDIGENOUS LAND ACKNOWLEDGEMENT

IT IS AN INESCAPABLE TRUTH, BEYOND DEBATE, THAT THE STORIES behind the buildings, events and people profiled in *Boom Times in Chilliwack* unfolded on the traditional and unceded (some would say occupied and seized) territory of the Ts'elxwéyeqw and Pelólxw communities of the Stó:lō Nation. Specifically, the original stewards of the land upon which the city of Chilliwack is located were members of the communities of Aitchelitz (traditional name: Áthelets), Skowkale (Sq'ewqeyl), Skway (Shxwhá:y), Soowahlie (Th'ewá:li), Squiala (Sxwoyehálá), Tzeachten (Ch'íyáqtel), Yakweakwioose (Yeqwyeqwí:ws), Skwah (Sqwá), Cheam (Xwchíyò:m), and Kwaw-kwaw-a-pilt.

In 1860, the Preemption Act was introduced, enabling settlers/colonialists to homestead local land with no regard for who may have been there first, and with the Crown's sanction. In an ideal world, instead of this legislation prevailing, the affirmations of today's United Nations Declaration on the Rights of Indigenous Peoples and the spirit of the recommendations by the Truth and Reconciliation Commission would have been in place at that time. Of course, and unfortunately, this was not the case. Much has been spoken and written about the injustice of Indigenous Peoples' land status across the nation, including in the community of Chilliwack, and there is really little new that I can add here.

Nevertheless, it is important for me to make a positive and sincere statement about what happened and the reality that exists today. The extent to which *Boom Times in Chilliwack* stirs up pleasant memories in certain people of a twenty-five-year period during the twentieth century in no way minimizes, misstates, or otherwise ignores the reality of what happened to the Stó:lō Nation in the nineteenth century. I hope this land acknowledgement is a small step towards correcting the stories and practices that attempt to erase Indigenous Peoples' history and culture, as well as supporting the overall process of advancing Indigenous rights as they pertain to treaties, land, resources, cultures, and the environment. I also believe that acknowledging the realities of Chilliwack's land status can serve as a form of resistance against the continued erosion of Indigenous Peoples' rights.

Thus, I sincerely and respectfully acknowledge that the land upon which Chilliwack sits is the traditional, ancestral, and unceded territory of the Stó:lō Peoples, who stewarded it for myriad generations prior to the arrival of colonialists. I also recognize that many of their rights were stripped and denied using centuries of laws and policies based on legal doctrines such as *terra nullius*, which declared land empty despite the presence of Indigenous Peoples.

From a personal perspective, I grew up here as a descendant of a prominent Chilliwack pioneer, and I never heard the traditional names of the Indigenous communities, nor was I really aware of the politics, prejudice, and morality associated with the land's history. Indigenous people and how they were regarded were minimized, and in many cases talked about in the past tense. Historicizing their struggles and simply pretending they do not exist in no way eliminates their rights. With the admittedly modest platform of this book, I welcome the opportunity to shed some light on both what happened historically and the real progress that needs to unfold. The complexity and harmful legacy of colonialism, and how it continues to affect Indigenous lands, will simply not go away if it continues to be unacknowledged.

INTRODUCTION

I WAS BORN IN CHILLIWACK IN 1953 AND RAISED HERE, AND THUS I experienced first-hand much of the history covered in *Boom Times in Chilliwack*. And my memories of that special time ultimately led to the genesis of this book (although I did not know it at the time).

In 2006 I was living in Vancouver, and on a warm September weekend I drove to Chilliwack for an overnight visit with my parents. On the Saturday afternoon, I thought I would take a stroll downtown and revisit some fond memories from my youth. I also had with me my first, newly purchased digital camera. I had not been home in a long while, and I was astonished and saddened to see how the city was changing (forever impacting aspects of my formative years that were important to me). Some historic buildings were boarded up or gone, others were in disrepair, lots were empty, and long-time businesses had folded. I suddenly felt compelled to start taking photos of older structures and locations before they were gone or permanently changed—to in some sense preserve them, as well as perhaps start a rudimentary record of old Chilliwack. I had a vague idea that someday I might somehow use these images, as I did enjoy researching and writing as a pastime, and the older I got, the more nostalgic I became about earlier times in the city and in my life.

In 2012, I had more time on my hands as I was working for myself, and I started writing short stories about local history topics (illustrated with my earlier photos). I initially sent the articles just to my interested friends and family. However, when I finally joined Facebook in 2013, that opened up a whole new world in terms of like-minded history buffs and a broader audience. I started posting my stories on multiple Chilliwack-related sites, and they received an enthusiastic response. In 2014, I created the Chilliwack History Perspectives page on Facebook as a means to have all my history articles in one place—a repository that I could update with a new original piece every Sunday. This move proved successful and rewarding far beyond my expectations, eventually leading to why you currently have this book in your hands.

History books take us back to earlier times, allowing us to learn, perhaps enjoy a temporary escape to a happier period, and hopefully be entertained. I believe *Boom Times in Chilliwack* accomplishes these goals by celebrating the history of what to me and many others is a special place and time—Chilliwack and the dynamic quarter century following the end of World War II. During this era, the city and its culture experienced unprecedented growth and change, leading to lasting and largely positive memories for many. These changes in many ways affect the Chilliwack of today. Specifically, the book profiles a representative sample of major developments in Chilliwack life back in the day, including the new library and fire hall (1949), courthouse (1952), arena (1958), hospital (1959), Highway 1 (1960), and civic centre (1967). Also, the Paramount Theatre installed its iconic neon sign downtown in spring 1949, and the drive-in theatre on the edge of town opened the next summer. Meanwhile, the city's restaurant options, retail sector, elementary and secondary schools, and sporting scene all grew significantly, each producing unforgettable memories for its users.

I have written this book for a number of reasons. I had a happy childhood in Chilliwack, with many good memories of places, people, and events, and I love my hometown very much. And as aspects of its rich history have continued to change or be eliminated, I wanted to somehow get things down on paper to create a record of how things were that will endure long after I am gone. I am of the age where one straddles two different eras in recent North American history, which I describe as pre-digital and digital. I can thus relate to and integrate features of both older and newer Chilliwack life in my stories. I also have direct family connections to several prominent Chilliwack settlers, which is a motivating factor. And in my retirement years, researching and writing has become a satisfying pastime for me. Finally, it seems the more Chilliwack grows—the city's population exceeded 108,000 as of December 31, 2024—the more its residents want to learn about and preserve how it was (largely via documented accounts and images). Not surprisingly, I received many requests from followers of my Facebook page to produce a book as a logical next step in my pursuit of chronicling the community's history.

I feel I am well positioned to write this history not just because I lived through much of it, but because I in fact have a direct or indirect connection to virtually all of the forty-eight stories the book features. For example, in 1959, I was one of the young kids who sat on a little chair on the concrete platform at the CN train station on Nowell Street as Queen Elizabeth II walked three feet in front of me. In 1958, my mother and I listened to first-hand accounts of the big Royal Hotel fire on CHWK Radio 1270. In late December 1965, I was at the loud Chilliwack Coliseum when the local team won the city's first "A" Division championship in the annual Peewee Hockey Jamboree. And many times I would marvel at the yellow airplane on the roof of Brett's Garage, just a block from Five Corners. In the past dozen years, these and similar experiences have led me to write literally hundreds of stories on the community's history. I have posted these articles on a weekly basis on my Chilliwack History Perspectives site, and this book flows from that body of research, writing, and publishing.

Despite living in Chilliwack during most of its post-war boom period, there was still much I did not know about parts of its rich history. For instance, I spent many enjoyable evenings at the first Chilliwack Coliseum with no idea that before it was finally completed in 1958, it stood for almost a decade as an unfinished shell and visual blight due to funding shortfalls. Similarly, I was a bit too young to have been aware of (let alone attended) the Roy Orbison show at the old Agricultural Hall in 1963, after which his good friend, Johnny Cash, paid him a visit backstage. I was also too young to have appreciated the cultural significance of Chilliwack's modern bus depot opening in 1950, situated just fifteen metres from the old BCER rail terminal station (to be razed one week later), on the site of today's Salish Plaza. And I had no idea that Marilyn Monroe paid a short visit to the city the year I was born.

Although there are a number of books available on specific aspects of Chilliwack's history, none detail the community's post-war boom times to the extent this one does. The last publication dealing with diverse aspects of the community's history was *The Chilliwack Story*, from 2007, and it took a broader perspective. *Boom Times in Chilliwack* profiles topics that have for the most part not been addressed in print elsewhere. It captures the spirit of the times, transporting you back to when things were booming; it was a simpler time in Chilliwack and in life, one that we never tire of revisiting. Where appropriate, I have included images that tie in with the narrative, as I strongly subscribe to the old adage that a picture is worth a thousand words.

Those who read *Boom Times in Chilliwack* will likely fall into two groups. One includes those of a certain age who lived in Chilliwack during the period following the end of the war. They experienced the history covered in the book, and as they get older, they want to nostalgically relive their memories and learn more about the city of their youth. The other group encompasses people who were born or moved here in later years and are naturally curious to learn about how their town was back in the day (or about the house or neighbourhood they live in) and how that relates to today's city.

The cultural and physical shifts covered in the book—including the advent of fast-food drive-ins, subdivisions, and a burgeoning consumer culture—represent a microcosm of changes that were happening in communities across North America, but with a special local flavour. Through extensively researched stories and archival photos, *Boom Times in Chilliwack* captures the economic optimism of the 1950s and 1960s and chronicles the developments that laid the groundwork for the Chilliwack of today. It provides a portal to the post-war period that boomers recall fondly as the time of their youth, as well as the "time of their lives."

I sincerely believe that when you pick up this book, you will not soon want to put it down. You will discover some things about a dynamic period in Chilliwack's past that you were not aware of and which may surprise you. This goes for long-time locals who may be strolling down memory lane as well as relatively newer residents. I belong to the former group, and it was a nostalgic and revelatory experience for me putting this book together. I do hope you enjoy it.

Chapter 1
BUILDING TO MEET THE BOOM

AS ONE OF BRITISH COLUMBIA'S OLDEST MUNICIPALITIES, CHILLIWACK boasted many solid public buildings by the mid-twentieth century, among them a courthouse, fire hall, post office, hospital, and municipal offices. But the civic landscape was transformed in the post-war years amidst the ever-present sounds of demolition and construction. In step with a growing population and steadily increasing tax base, the city of Chilliwack (as well as the provincial and federal governments) undertook many key infrastructure projects in the 1950s and 1960s to meet the community's needs. Besides serving their intended purpose, these structures engendered many warm and enduring memories. Some of these buildings, such as the old brick post office and the skating arena, are now gone, while others—including the new fire hall and library, both built in 1949, and the 1952 courthouse—still exist in a modified fashion. This chapter focuses on several standout buildings that provide concrete evidence of the boom years: the fire hall, library, provincial courthouse, Chilliwack Coliseum, and post office.

A MODERN FIRE HALL, 1949–2004

Early in the twentieth century, the newly incorporated city of Chilliwack was in need of key public infrastructure. In 1908 the city acquired a site for its first fire hall, paying $175 for the lot behind the Royal Bank at the southeast corner of Main Street and Wellington Avenue. Taxpayers passed a $4,000 initiative with a 72 percent approval rate, and in 1909, the critical infrastructure was completed. In a contemporary context, Fire Hall No. 1 was located on what became the rear (south) portion of the Royal Hotel Pub. After thirty-five years the fire hall on Main Street would become obsolete, and on December 13, 1945, taxpayers again overwhelmingly (this time with 91 percent in favour) approved the spending of $45,000 to construct a new one. The city had earlier acquired a vacant lot at the southwest corner of Young Road North and Victoria Avenue West, and plans were drawn up to construct a state-of-the-art, 5,000-square-foot structure at this high-profile location only 100 metres north of Five Corners.

But it would be well over three years before Chilliwack's new fire hall became a reality. Tenders were first called in June 1946. By August 1947 the city had received only one bid, for $65,000, well in excess of what taxpayers had approved two years earlier. Plans were thus revised to meet the original budget, and by October construction of the project was well underway. City officials anticipated that the building would be ready for use by December. However, the continuing high cost of post-war building materials and rising labour costs resulted in numerous construction delays and further revisions to the plans, delaying completion by an additional eighteen months.

Finally, on June 22, 1949, Chilliwack's new Fire Hall No. 1 opened to much fanfare, with a crowd of five hundred attending the opening ceremony. The structure was described in the press as the "most modern firehall of its size in British Columbia" and "ultra-modern in appearance," its colour combination of light brown and cream considered a welcome break from the traditional red. The ground floor had space for three trucks, and the hall featured a recreation room upstairs for volunteer members. Dormitory space was provided for five firefighters. The 800-pound cast-iron bell from the original fire hall on Main Street was installed at the top of the new structure, eventually to be replaced by powerful sirens in the 1950s.

The township's fire department sometimes collaborates with the city's to battle major fires. In this shot from about 1949, the township's fire truck is between the city's two vehicles in front of the new fire hall. Chilliwack Fire Department Collection

The city's new fire hall opened only two weeks after the Paramount Theatre on Yale Road East (see chapter 5) and six months before the new city library on Wellington Avenue. These three structures heralded the start of a 1950s construction boom in downtown Chilliwack. Over the years, many young boys and girls received a tour of the city's fire hall, usually conducted by long-time fire chief George Strevens (1895–1977), either through a school outing or perhaps a Cubs or Scouts evening. If kids were out on their bicycles in the vicinity of the fire hall and heard the alarm or siren, they might pedal furiously to the corner and watch all the excitement as one, if not two, fire trucks headed off with their lights flashing and sirens blaring. Some tried to follow the trucks on their bike, but usually to no avail. And when the fire department was experiencing a quiet day, some youngsters enjoyed watching the firefighters clean their trucks until their fire-engine-red chassis shone like polished shoes.

On June 16, 1979, local voters approved a referendum to amalgamate the city of Chilliwack and the township of Chilliwhack, effective

January 1, 1980. As part of the process, the fire departments of the two municipal entities merged, but the 1949 fire hall on Young Road North retained its status as Chilliwack's Fire Hall No. 1. On April 30, 1998, the long-standing Buckerfield's farm supply store at the corner of Cheam Avenue and Young Road burned down in a spectacular fire. The city later acquired the vacant property of about one and a half acres as the site for a new fire hall / office building, and in June 2004, Chilliwack's newest Fire Hall No. 1 opened on the old Buckerfield's site (along with the offices of the Fraser Valley Regional District). After serving the city for over fifty years, the previous fire hall on Young Road was purchased in 2007 by an architectural firm, which went on to become a long-term tenant of the heritage structure. The new owner completely remodelled the old building to house its offices, preserving many features of what was a fine example of period architecture.

After the city's aging fire hall was sold and transformed to architectural offices, the new owners ensured that certain elements of the original structure were preserved. These included the hose-drying tower, evident to the right in this 2025 image, as well as the three "garage doors" on the facade, which were converted to tinted windows. Merlin Bunt Collection

A NEW PUBLIC LIBRARY, 1949–1982

Chilliwack did not have its first dedicated library facility until 1930. It was enabled by the largesse of the prominent philanthropist Andrew Carnegie, who funded a vast network of libraries around the world, including 125 across Canada (Vancouver's Carnegie Community Centre being part of this legacy). The location of Chilliwack's much-anticipated institution was the main floor of a two-decade-old building on the east side of Nowell Street South, between Yale Road East and Princess Avenue East, known as Hampton Court. On August 13, 1930, the city's new library opened at 12 Nowell Street South. At only 480 square feet, it was not a large facility.

By 1946, Chilliwack's present and future library needs had already outgrown the cramped space. On January 21, 1947, the Chilliwack Citizens' Library Committee moved that the city's library seek a new home as soon as possible. In 1948, the committee identified a central parcel of land at the northwest corner of Wellington Avenue and College Street as the preferred building site. At the time, this property accommodated City Park, which had served as the city's only park since 1936. On October 4, the city and township jointly approved construction of the new library on this site, next to the long-established Cooke's Presbyterian Church and only 250 metres west of Five Corners.

The plans called for a one-storey, 1,664-square-foot brick building, with a two-level roof separated by clerestory windows to maximize natural light in the main reading room. A crescent-shaped sidewalk led from two points on Wellington Avenue to the front entrance. Shelving accommodated 7,500 books—twice the capacity of the Nowell Street premises. Construction of the building started in early 1949, and the library officially opened at 115 Wellington Avenue on December 14. The *Chilliwack Progress* described it as "one of the finest small library buildings in Western Canada." Mayor T. T. McCammon of the city and Reeve W. T. Richardson of the township officiated at the opening ceremonies.

The city's "Public Library" (as it is referred to in signage over the entrance) has clerestory windows at the two-level break in the roof that maximizes natural light in its main reading room. Also evident in this photo, taken circa 1953, is the manicured lawn to the right (east) of the structure, which accommodated the library's major 1962 expansion. Chilliwack Museum and Archives

The new library was appreciated and well utilized during the 1950s, and as the population grew, so did the need for more space to accommodate rising membership levels and more books. To address these pressing space requirements, the library underwent a major expansion in 1962. Part of the new space was to accommodate the Chilliwack Museum, which had been situated in the city's police station on Nowell Street North since 1958. On November 8, with city council members and the public in attendance, Chilliwack's expanded library reopened. The space allotted to the museum was 700 square feet, in an L-shaped extension facing College Street.

Just eight years on, as the 1960s drew to a close, the library was increasingly voicing its need to take over the museum's space to accommodate its continuing growth. In 1970, some advocates suggested that the library relocate its entire operation to the recently vacated brick post office building, on Yale Road East near Five Corners. Then, it was proposed, the current library structure could become the permanent home of the Chilliwack Museum as well as a tourist information centre.

However, reconditioning the old post office building and other technical challenges made this proposal cost-prohibitive. The following year, on December 2, 1971, thanks to provincial centennial funding, the Wells Centennial Museum opened adjacent to Evergreen Hall, itself the product of federal centennial funding, and the Chilliwack Library gratefully took over the museum's vacated space.

By 1978, Chilliwack's population had more than doubled since the library on Wellington Avenue opened in 1949, and pressure on the undersized and aging facility continued to mount. Finally, on March 13, 1979, both councils approved a site at Salish Place for the community's new and larger library. Construction commenced in 1981 and on March 13, 1982, the city's third library opened, at 45680 First Avenue. The previous library structure subsequently housed a number of community groups, including Chilliwack Community Services and, starting in 1995, Family Place. Eventually the property was boarded up, and for

Chilliwack's brick library has aged gracefully over the years, and as illustrated in this 2018 image, in its current role as a youth support centre it integrates well with the city's evolving downtown area. Merlin Bunt Collection

a number of years its future remained uncertain. In 2014, a group called Cyrus Centre Chilliwack leased the former library building from the city, transforming it into a homeless youth shelter with four emergency beds while providing meals, clothing, advocacy, referrals, showers, laundry, life skills training, and employment coaching.

For thirty-three years, this facility provided information, education, and enjoyment to resident library users. For many, one fond and lasting memory associated with it is their interactions with the head librarian for many years, Mabel Fox (1919–1980). She was perceived as always kind and helpful to countless young people, but as many found out, she was intolerant of noise and any other behaviour inappropriate for "her" library. Now long removed from its original role, the building with the classic brick design still stands, accommodating other community purposes in addition to reminding locals of its vital public role in an earlier era.

THE BRICK COURTHOUSE, 1952–2002

Chilliwack has had only three courthouses in its history. Although the current facility, near Five Corners, is by far the most modern and efficient, it is the community's second—still standing at 9391 College Street—that was for half a century a mainstay in city life and remains the one many locals still identify with. In addition to judicial and related uses, the familiar brick structure accommodated numerous government services, such that citizens had multiple reasons to visit it in the course of their everyday lives. This courthouse was another result of strong post-war growth, replacing the city's first one, built in 1894 at the northwest corner of Victoria Avenue West and Young Road North, which had become woefully inadequate for the community's needs.

By 1949, various government services were scattered in multiple locations around the downtown area. At a meeting on March 10, the city's board of trade stressed that development of a new provincial government building was paramount. Seven months later, this urgent need only increased when the aging and already deteriorating courthouse suffered a fire in the early hours of October 30, greatly damaging the structure and destroying some equipment and a number of records. The government in Victoria decided not to incur costly repairs given the building's age, inadequate space, and poor functionality, but decisions lagged on funding and site selection for a new courthouse. By December, three locations were identified, but none of these sites was chosen. On April 11, 1950, the BC government finally announced its approval of funding for Chilliwack's new provincial building and indicated that construction would start relatively soon. The Board of Trade then chose a half-acre site, comprising two lots, at the southwest corner of College Street and Victoria Avenue West—property owned by the city.

On December 14, 1949, the community's new brick library had opened on the site, also designated as a public park. In response to citizens' unfavourable reaction to the city's only park being developed, council earlier moved that the remaining portion of the site be improved with a children's playground, as opposed to being sold for commercial or government building projects. Council was committed to following through on its planned playground, but when reminded of the site's proximity to a liquor store, a funeral home, and a library, it changed its position. On June 13, 1950, it approved sale of the property to the provincial government, provided that the land be properly landscaped and that the new structure "conform architecturally to the nearby library building, thereby creating unity within the area." Here, "unity" referred to the library's brick construction, a popular trend in Chilliwack at the time.

On June 20, council set the price for the land at $15,000. A subsequent appraisal commissioned by the provincial government placed the value of the two lots at $12,000. On August 21, council accepted this lower offer and sold the land to the province. As a result, City Park was destined to be just a memory. Tenders for the city's new courthouse were called in April 1951, and construction started in July. By early

August, pile driving was complete and concrete was being poured for the $275,000 structure. Not long after, on December 30, a devastating fire completely gutted the first courthouse. Within a few weeks, the site was razed, and the remains of the building were sold for scrap. Since the city's new courthouse was still under construction, all legal proceedings and civic functions had to be relocated to temporary quarters in the downtown area.

Plans for the new courthouse called for a two-storey, L-shaped, sixty-one-room structure, with 118 feet of frontage on College Street and 150 feet down Victoria Avenue West. A rotunda soared the full interior height of the building, framed in stainless steel, with a wide expanse of glass that allowed much sunlight. On July 8, 1952, some second-floor tenants started moving into the building. Eleven different government offices that were previously dispersed around the city would now be consolidated in one centre. Tenants not related to the justice sector included the registrar of voters, motor licensing office, game warden, public health services, hospital insurance offices, social welfare branch, district agriculturalist, electrical inspector, and school inspector. The official opening of the courthouse, at 77 College Street, took place on September 17. Two prominent BC government cabinet ministers took part in the ceremony—Attorney General Robert Bonner and Agriculture Minister (and local MLA) Ken Kiernan—along with BC Chief Justice W. B. Farris. The public was also invited to inspect this latest addition to the city's mid-century urban landscape.

In the ensuing years, the second courthouse became a part of many local people's lives. For example, early every year it was the place to obtain one's new licence plates. It was also the base for written learners' licence tests and final road tests, the latter usually ending with the dreaded parallel-parking challenge beside the courthouse, on Victoria Avenue.

In 1997, the BC government deemed that the useful life of the forty-five-year-old brick courthouse was near an end and decided to terminate Chilliwack's court services—which had been in place for over a century.

The city's new courthouse was required to be of brick construction with appropriate landscaping to match the new library directly to the south. Prior to its opening in 1952, the land upon which it stands was part of the city's only park. Chilliwack Museum and Archives

An action committee called the Coalition for Justice was struck to lobby against the closure. The provincial government later announced that it would pause and reconsider its plans, and in the fall of 1999, it officially reversed its decision, keeping Chilliwack's court services in place. It was also prepared to spend $5 million to undertake necessary repairs and upgrades to the aging courthouse. However, the government later agreed to apply this money to construction of a new court facility, rather than investing in a structure that would never be sufficient for the community's needs. Thus, the old courthouse remained in use for several more years, and the community retained its court services for the long-term future. Chilliwack's third (and current) courthouse complex was constructed near Five Corners, officially opening on May 31, 2002.

After the new courthouse opened, the College Street structure was no longer occupied. For more than a decade it sat idle, in a state of neglect and disrepair, eventually becoming a boarded-up abandoned building with an uncertain future—a symbol of what many viewed as the questionable state of downtown Chilliwack. In 2013, the property was purchased by a religious group that had ambitious plans to refurbish the building while adding a partial third storey. The church

By June 2015, redevelopment of the brick courthouse was well underway, with a third storey to follow. This two-year process increased the structure's gross leasable area to about 9,500 square feet. Merlin Bunt Collection

While transformation of the city's brick courthouse was finished in 2016, it would be a further seven years before a tenant was secured for the main floor. The partial third floor serves as a sanctuary for the structure's owner, a religious group. Merlin Bunt Collection

envisioned the first two floors housing commercial tenants, and the top floor would accommodate its sanctuary. Starting in 2014, the new owners gutted the interior while adding the third floor towards the front of the structure. Although the project was completed in the latter part of 2016, the refurbished building struggled to attract commercial tenants, and for several years For Lease signage was a constant.

Ultimately, prospects for the old courthouse property changed for the positive, a result partly attributed to other redevelopment projects in the city's downtown core. In March 2023, the available commercial space in the historic building was leased. For many locals, their memories of this classic mid-century brick structure on College Street involve legal, civic, and administrative matters, some local but most provincial in nature. The renovated building integrates well with the ongoing resurgence of the downtown area, and this prominent example of Chilliwack's mid-century public architecture and infrastructure continues to thrive.

THE CHILLIWACK COLISEUM, 1958–2004

Of the numerous buildings that are no longer part of Chilliwack's landscape, most were unremarkable, but a few resonated with the entire community, serving multiple generations and taking on iconic status in the local context. One beloved example is the original Chilliwack Coliseum. As compelling as the memories it created during its lengthy run as the city's largest entertainment venue is the story of how it came about: a decade-long saga marked by the unwavering determination of its proponents, the skepticism of many community ratepayers, escalating costs, repeated disappointments, and numerous delays. It is also a cautionary tale of how unbridled optimism and community spirit can get the better of fiscal prudence and fundamental due diligence.

In 1945, with the end of World War II approaching, a priority for city council was for Chilliwack to develop its own community centre.

This initiative involved the relocation of the city's popular baseball park, then situated on Young Road South. The general thinking at the time was to move the ballpark to the fairgrounds on Corbould Street. However, some felt that the public would not go down to this area, which was considered to be on the outskirts of the city and too far to travel. Nevertheless, at a council meeting on November 5, the city ended months of strenuous debate by formally designating the fairgrounds as the location for the city's new community centre.

Development plans included an arena, grandstand, and baseball park. After some debate, the site selected for the arena was only sixty metres directly south of the existing Agricultural Hall (opened in 1936). By early 1946, the arena was being referred to as the Memorial Centre, in respect to those Chilliwack citizens who had served in the recently concluded war. (In subsequent years, the name was changed to the Memorial Arena, then the Chilliwack Recreational Centre, and finally the Chilliwack Coliseum.) Council soon struck a Memorial Centre Committee (MCC), comprised of representatives from thirty-seven organizations, and it immediately busied itself with inspecting other arenas in BC, gathering data on capital cost, revenues, operations, dimensions, maintenance costs, management, potential uses, and so on.

On December 11, 1946, the MCC approved ambitious plans for construction, financing, and administration of the community's new ice arena. The cost of the project was set at $200,000. The committee envisioned that this large capital expenditure would be financed by issuing bonds to local citizens and business entities, along with soliciting donations from supporters. As the *Chilliwack Progress* editorialized, "The building itself will be a proud addition to our community. The whole venture is a 'reinvestment in ourselves.'" At no time were public funds (that is, ratepayer property tax revenues) mentioned as a potential financing source. In January 1947, the MCC launched an official funding campaign. Initially there was enthusiastic support from the community, and donations and bond subscriptions came in at a strong rate. This early positive reaction greatly encouraged the MCC, causing it to believe that the funding goal would easily be reached on schedule. Buoyed by its optimism, the MCC started placing orders with construction suppliers. However, by March only 28 percent of the necessary financing had been secured, causing some concern about the true extent of community support.

Regardless, residents appeared keen and enthusiastic about the initiative, displaying much pride, energy, and engagement. Each week the *Progress* provided a funding status update. And for the first time, the project's catchy slogan, "Let's Skate in '48," started to be used in advertising, financing campaigns, signage, and more. Yet by December, funding on hand had reached only $97,000—less than half of the projected cost. Also, the $200,000 figure the MCC had set in 1946 did not allow for any significant cost increases. Despite these portents, on January 27, 1948, the MCC formally approved plans to proceed with construction of the new ice arena. The committee believed this announcement would spur more bond purchases and donations, such that the troubling shortfall would soon be addressed.

In April 1948, Lem Hay, the project's new superintendent, announced that construction was set to begin in May. At that point, after more than a year of intensive fundraising, still only about half of the budget had been secured. Construction progressed until early June, when that year's disastrous Fraser River flood postponed the work. At that point only the foundation had been laid. Although the project's supply chain was affected somewhat by the flood, delays were not lengthy, and the bigger concern continued to be insufficient financing. By late July, construction was proceeding ahead of expectations, with reinforced concrete pillars being erected. Despite the devasting effects of the flood elsewhere in the valley, no material shortages had been experienced on the arena project. However, more significantly, costs were rising and the project was still more than $100,000 short of its total budget. By October, the arena was essentially just half completed.

The entity now in charge of the arena's construction, the Chilliwack Recreational Center Association (CRCA), then made a direct plea to local residents and businesses. It clearly stated why it made common sense to finish the project, the sooner the better, and to make that happen, the public would have to either purchase bonds or make outright cash donations. At its meeting on January 28, 1949, the CRCA officially suggested that Chilliwack ratepayers could make up the project's $120,000 funding shortfall by way of a bylaw vote. Obviously the "Skate in '48" vision was not going to be realized, and the slogan ceased to be used in fundraising campaign efforts. In September, for the first time, the *Chilliwack Progress* referred to the half-finished arena as the city's "white elephant."

During a meeting at city hall on September 27, 1949, the CRCA moved that a delegation approach the provincial government for a grant to finish the project, but this step resulted in no further financing. Also at this meeting, a member of council said the city was "losing face" with the large, unfinished structure, and that it was "bad advertising, hurts business." Council further noted that the $100,000 investment in the project to date had been useless, and that without a roof and walls, the structure, such as it was, would deteriorate. By summer of 1950, construction remained halted, as did progress on reducing the budget shortfall.

The CRCA's earlier proposal to put a Memorial Centre bylaw vote to ratepayers, as a means to use public funds to get the arena completed, went ahead in 1950, but it was rejected—as were similar votes in 1953 and 1955. (Most of the opposition was in the township, as city ratepayers were largely in favour). Being forced to look at the half-built arena every day for several years resulted in a rising level of resentment among some members of the community, and after the first bylaw defeat, terms such as "derelict," "ugly," and "skeleton" were being bandied about. A renewed fundraising campaign was launched, and in August 1951, Collins-Macken Lumber Co. donated lumber for completion of the roof. On September 12, fuelled by much volunteer labour, the final remaining sheet of aluminum was placed on the roof. The next steps would be erection of the walls and installation of the seats, and these critical milestones depended on cash flow and more volunteer labour.

For several years, slow but incremental progress continued. On February 1, 1955, construction of the seating finally started, utilizing 75,000 board feet of lumber that had been purchased. Donations continued coming in and much volunteer labour was being supplied, which allowed seating for 2,700 spectators to be completed by early spring. In March, the slogan "Skate in '58" was first mentioned—not seriously at the time, but it would turn out to be prophetic. In April 1955, the upper portions of the structure's two sides were finished. At that point, enough of the work had been completed for the CRCA to feel the venue was ready to host its first public event. Seating and electricity were in place, and there was a roof overhead, although the two ends were still exposed to the elements. The arena's first official function was held on Friday, May 13, at 8:00 p.m.—a gala band concert and variety show attended by 1,800 curious citizens (tickets fifty cents). There was a damp chill in the air throughout the official opening gala, likely contributing to a less-than-full house, but first-nighters who did attend brought blankets, as advised. The next step was to close off the arena's north and south ends to keep the weather out.

The Chilliwack Coliseum's first official function was held in 1955 before 1,800 curious and chilly citizens, despite the arena being very much unfinished. By late 1957, after nine years of sporadic progress, the venue was a year away from completion. Chilliwack Museum and Archives

The following year, a funding opportunity came to light that gave realistic hope of a foreseeable end to the ongoing, eight-year debacle of completing the arena. On July 10, 1956, the CRCA learned that federal grant funds could be available, providing they "contribute to the holding of agricultural shows." Since the agricultural angle, as opposed to the arena's hockey or entertainment use, might secure senior government grants, the go-forward strategy changed accordingly. To better support pursuit of this critical financing source, officials decided to formally transfer control of the arena project to the Chilliwack Agricultural Association (CAA), at least from an optics perspective. The parties also agreed that when the final funding was in place and the project completed, control of the facility would revert from the CAA to the city. Securing this vital funding took two years to finalize, ultimately requiring the coordinated efforts of the city, the township, and the CAA.

Meanwhile, construction continued. In November 1956, the gravel parking area surrounding the Ag Hall, curling rink, and new arena was paved, providing capacity for 275 cars. By January 1957, locals had started using "Chilliwack Coliseum" to refer to the structure. And during a cold snap that month, the unfinished arena was flooded to allow skating for the first time, with approximately 1,500 locals enjoying the experience.

Renewed appeals to the provincial and local governments for funding were also made in 1957. Ultimately, the campaign to bridge the final funding gap involved obtaining grants from the federal government, provincial government, and, to a lesser extent, both the city and township governments (after the three earlier bylaw defeats). By March, the CAA had applied for a grant of $50,000 from Ottawa and $50,000 from Victoria to complete "an 'all-weather coliseum' for agricultural purposes." Earlier in the year, agricultural association officials also observed that the completed coliseum offered "excellent shelter against atomic fall-out," reflecting the tenor of the era. All references to the structure during grant negotiations continued to be "Agricultural Coliseum," to stay onside with grant stipulations governing agriculture facilities. At the end of November, the CAA formally announced that it had enough funding in place to finish the arena and issued requests for proposals for the remaining work. In June 1958, after thirteen kilometres of plastic pipe to carry the refrigerant for the ice surface was laid, the cement floor was poured.

On November 1, 1958, the Chilliwack Coliseum hosted the first of literally thousands of hockey games to be played there. Before 1,200 fans, the Chilliwack Flamingos and Nanaimo Clippers played to a 7–7 draw. The vision of "Let's Skate in '48" had finally became a reality—in *1958*. On December 27, after ten long years, the new pride of Chilliwack officially opened, with a standing-room-only crowd celebrating the successful conclusion of what for some had been a long, bad dream. The next year, the coliseum started hosting what quickly became a popular and lasting staple of the Christmas holiday season—the annual Peewee Hockey Jamboree (see chapter 10). For the following forty-five years, the building was a part of everyday community life, hosting countless events: hockey games at all levels, concerts, curling bonspiels, agricultural exhibitions, religious gatherings, lacrosse games, circuses, and annual fall fair festivities. At the popular public skating sessions, some locals met their future spouses.

By the early 2000s, the coliseum was still drawing decent crowds for junior hockey and other events, but only because the new venue—Prospera Place, approximately 300 metres to the southwest—was not yet open. Scott Taylor

At the start of the twenty-first century, the growth of Chilliwack—combined with the aging condition and limited size of the coliseum—underscored the need for an up-to-date and considerably larger arena complex. Plans were soon finalized for building a new facility (initially referred to as a "multiplex," with two sheets of ice), also on the fairgrounds. Construction of the new arena commenced in April 2003. To the dismay of many, there would soon be no need to retain the coliseum. Ultimately, the land upon which it sat was destined for a "higher and better use" as part of the growing entertainment complex on the old fairgrounds site. The last regular-season hockey game at the old arena took place on February 28, 2004, when the Chilliwack Chiefs concluded their home schedule, falling 5–3 to South Surrey in front of 2,585 fans. In September, the new arena, which would be known as the Prospera Centre for fifteen years due to a sponsorship arrangement

The coliseum was demolished in June 2005, and nostalgic fans of the "Old Barn on Corbould" set up chairs and brought picnic baskets to pay homage to the arena and the many cherished memories they associated with it. Chilliwack Museum and Archives

with the Prospera Credit Union, opened its doors to the public. And in June 2005, the venerable Chilliwack Coliseum was demolished, to the sadness of many locals who associated it with countless memories of great times over the years. For many, it was an integral part of their youth.

On September 25, 2010, five years after the coliseum was taken down, the new Chilliwack Cultural Centre opened on the same site. On September 3, 2019, in homage to its historic and fondly remembered predecessor, the Prospera Centre was renamed the Chilliwack Coliseum. After a prolonged, contentious, and often discouraging ten-year construction period, the first Chilliwack Coliseum became a long-term source of pride and affection for the community. What was often lovingly referred to as the "Old Barn on Corbould" will live on in the memories of those who experienced it.

THE OLD BRICK POST OFFICE, 1913–1970

On the short list of Chilliwack's historic buildings of distinction is the city's brick post office, which stood for six decades on Yale Road East, near Five Corners. This local landmark was a source of pride—the visual appeal of its classic design and rich, rust-coloured masonry being complemented by its role as a social centre of sorts. Not only was it a place to pick up and drop off mail; here citizens could also be updated on relevant local, provincial, and national issues. The post office also served as a central spot to meet friends before heading off to other destinations around town. Because it served the community during the mid-twentieth century and was upgraded at that time, it rates a mention in this chapter.

In 1910, the city's first dedicated post office building, which had only twelve square feet of space to accommodate the public, was deemed outdated and too small. In response, the federal government, recognizing the city's rapid growth and future potential, approved construction

Work on the city's long-awaited concrete-and-brick post office took over a year. It immediately became a social and business anchor for downtown Chilliwack. Chilliwack Museum and Archives

of a new, bigger, and modern post office to be constructed on the same site—the north side of Yale Road East between Five Corners and Nowell Street North. The imminent arrival of the BC Electric Railway in October 1910 and its associated growth implications for the community was a significant factor in this decision. In July 1911 the government called for tenders for the project, a concrete-and-brick, two-storey structure with a basement, and the construction contract was awarded in December. The building would have sixty-five feet of frontage on Yale Road East, a depth of fifty feet, and a seventeen-foot driveway at the rear to receive incoming mail. In addition to being the city's postal station, the building would serve as a customs house and include living quarters on the upper floor.

Construction of the new post office commenced on February 23, 1912. Some fifteen months later, on May 5, 1913, this grand addition to Chilliwack's infrastructure officially opened at what became 31 Yale

Road East. The "gift of the Borden Government," as some citizens called it, was an immediate hit. Its immediate neighbour to the east, the *Chilliwack Progress*, referred to it as a "fine large and commodious building," among other accolades. Besides serving an important communications role in the community, the structure became a social and business anchor for downtown Chilliwack. By the latter 1940s, the city's population had surpassed 5,000, far beyond the 1,675 residents on hand in 1913 when its brick post office opened. In 1949, door-to-door mail delivery was slated to start in the city, and this significant change in postal operations would put further pressure on the existing space. Consequently, a major expansion of the post office was undertaken in 1948, extending its footprint thirty-seven feet farther north towards the alley, as well as widening it to the extent that there was only three feet of clearance between it and the *Progress* building.

Chilliwack's post-war growth required the post office to expand, and the large undeveloped land to its rear (evident in this 1948 aerial shot) accommodates a thirty-seven-foot extension north towards the alley. This new space was also needed for door-to-door mail delivery, which started in 1949. Chilliwack Board of Trade

For the next two decades, Chilliwack continued to grow, and towards the end of the 1960s, the federal government decided that its aging brick post office was obsolete and too small to serve the city for the remainder of the twentieth century and beyond. Ottawa acquired land on the northeast corner of Yale Road East and Nowell Street North (100 metres east of the existing post office) for development of a new, modern federal building, which would include a bigger and more functional postal station. Construction of the new building at 46229 Yale Road started in August 1969. The $700,000 grey brick structure, which some characterized as brutalist architecture, would accommodate the new post office, a Canada Customs and Revenue office, a Canada Manpower Centre, and five other government agencies. The new postal station, Chilliwack's ninth, was officially opened on May 15, 1970.

Before the new facility was even complete, debate began on the fate of its predecessor structure. Heritage enthusiasts were keen for the building to be preserved and repurposed. Possible uses put forward included a museum or a unified police station for the city and township. Another potential option that was seriously considered was relocating the city's library. However, all stakeholders eventually acknowledged that the cost of repairs and renovations involved in transitioning the aging structure to another viable use, along with other technical challenges, made any such proposals unfeasible. And since there was no obvious future use for the beloved building, which had served several generations of citizens, it became destined for demolition. The city envisioned the site being redeveloped with a large, modern commercial structure, and it eventually acquired the property from the federal government for this purpose. As the city was motivated to undertake this initiative in the near term, plans unfolded quickly.

On January 5, 1972, demolition of Chilliwack's renowned brick post office started, a process that took about four months to complete. Demolition crews estimated there were 40,000 bricks in the pre–World War I structure, of which 30,000 were salvageable and sold to local buyers. After demolition, more than three years lapsed before redevelopment

The building that replaced the brick post office, the Chilliwack Business Centre (originally the Zen Building), opened in 1976 but was structurally condemned by the city within just a few years. Remediation of the issues was a slow process in the recession of the early 1980s, and at one point it had no tenants. Merlin Bunt Collection

began on the high-profile downtown site, with the vacant lot at one time being used for a farmers' market. On September 23, 1975, construction commenced on a three-storey commercial/retail structure on the site, at a cost in excess of $1 million. In May 1976, the new Zen Building (named after the developer, Giovanni Zen Construction) was complete and welcoming tenants. When it opened, this addition to the city's downtown was criticized by citizens (in particular heritage advocates) for adding nothing of any aesthetic value, particularly in comparison to the structure it replaced—the classically designed brick post office.

Because the 1913 building served the community in the 1950s and 1960s, many current and former residents have warm memories associated with it. Some recall sunning themselves during lunch hours on the stone ledge flanking two staircases at the front of the structure.

Such was its prominence, shoppers identified the location of a store in downtown Chilliwack by its proximity to the post office. Others remember walking up the front steps and entering the brightly lit public area on the main level, with its floor of small, black-and-white mosaic tiles, leading to two metal-barred wickets where one lined up to buy stamps and transact other business. Notices of public interest were regularly posted on the east wall. And on Wednesday afternoons, *Chilliwack Progress* carriers received their allotment of papers at the rear of the building, next door to the newspaper.

Due to the building's central location near Five Corners, many twentieth-century photographs of downtown Chilliwack show this popular landmark. Its distinctive design and brick construction differentiated it from its neighbours and have inspired a number of nostalgic artistic tributes. Today there is no tangible commemoration at the historic post office's old location on Yale Road East, where it stood from 1913 to 1972. However, although it has been gone for decades, this integral aspect of an earlier era in the community's history will not be forgotten. Had finances, vision, and priorities been different, the structure might still be standing today, and it would have likely integrated well as part of District 1881, the downtown renaissance project scheduled for completion in 2025. Instead, patrons of the various establishments on the south side of Yale Road who look across the street can only imagine how it once was.

Chapter 2

SHIFTING GEARS IN TRANSPORTATION

AS CHILLIWACK'S ECONOMY AND POPULATION EXPANDED AFTER WORLD War II, the community's transportation needs and patterns also changed. The car culture was revving up, and many people sought the relative freedom that vehicle ownership offered. Plus, local travel by bus would soon be available. The BC Electric Railway made its last run to the city on September 30, 1950, marking the end of an era and a shift to a new mode of regional transportation. Ten days later, residents could board a Pacific Stage Lines coach bound for Vancouver at the newly constructed bus depot. A decade later, the modern Highway 1 opened, a four-lane freeway bypassing the previous east–west route along Yale Road and forming part of the Trans-Canada Highway. This chapter discusses these momentous changes in transportation, on the ground and also in the air.

THE CHILLIWACK AIRPORT, 1946

From early on, residents of Chilliwack were fascinated with the growing field of aviation, eager to both watch and participate in the new industry and pastime. On July 1, 1914, as part of that year's Dominion Day celebrations, the first plane to ever land in the area—a Curtiss biplane piloted by Billy Stark of Vancouver—touched down in the oval at the fairgrounds, thrilling the large crowd that turned out for the event. As the *Chilliwack Progress* reported:

> The wind was gusty and with difficulty Mr. Stark arose and flew over the town and field shortly after two o'clock and at eight o'clock he made another flight, a beautiful one, soaring away to the south and around over the town at the rate of about 60 miles an hour. It was a graceful sight to see the daring aviator . . . soaring through the air like a huge bird and alighting in almost the identical spot from which he had ascended.

When World War I broke out later that month, local interest in aviation was quieted for the duration. But in early 1919, it was announced that plans were being finalized for an airplane to make an appearance in Chilliwack. This news created a sense of excitement and expectation, since the advancing technology of flying machines coincided with the upbeat post-war mood. On June 27, 1919, two flying aces from World War I circled the oval at the fairgrounds several times before making a perfect landing on the infield grass, to the incredulous cheers of a throng of aviation enthusiasts. The pilots' appearance was part of the burgeoning aeronautics industry's first attempt to fly an airplane across BC.

By 1930, aviation had become more entrenched in a rapidly changing world, and interest remained high in Chilliwack. To that point, relatively fragile airplanes had been landing at the fairgrounds or at rural open fields. But it became clear that a dedicated local landing facility was required.

Very soon, three rudimentary airfields would be built in the area to accommodate the growing demand. The first was laid out in 1930 on the Evans family farm, about 1.2 kilometres east of Lickman Road and south of the Trans-Canada Highway. Evans Field was used for approximately two years before reverting to farming purposes. On June 3, 1931, a more formal facility opened in Greendale (then known as Sumas), at the southeast corner of South Sumas Road and Chadsey Road. Known as Chadsey Field, the venue was at first described as an aerodrome, for there were several aviation-related structures on the site. Chadsey Field remained in use to varying degrees until 1939, when World War II broke out. In 1932, Chilliwack's third "airport" was established, a private facility in East Chilliwack on property owned by Earl Brett, a local aviation pioneer. Brett's Field was an eighty-acre site at the northeast corner of Upper Prairie Road and Patterson Road, in the shadow of Elk Mountain. This facility became the centre of flying activities in the community for the rest of the 1930s, ultimately being discontinued in 1941.

Restrictions associated with the outbreak of World War II significantly curtailed the flying scene in Chilliwack. But after the war, North America experienced a boom in aviation, both private and commercial, since many pilots had concluded their military service and there was a good supply of inexpensive yet serviceable war-surplus aircraft available. This boom rekindled an interest in flying in Chilliwack, with people buying planes and obtaining their pilot licences. The city and township councils faced mounting pressure to establish a proper, regulated airport; citizens suggested it would be highly inappropriate to ask returning air force veterans to take off and land airplanes in what were essentially pastures. On May 17, 1945, at an overflow meeting at city hall, the Chilliwack Flying Club was formed, with a membership of 150. This group had access to planes, so now all it needed was an appropriate base for flying and storing them. A campaign to develop a modern airport soon began. Proponents touted direct benefits such as increased tourism, employment opportunities, passenger and freight service, and faster communication.

The club had identified a potential location for the new airport south of the city immediately east of Young Road South, just over a mile from Five Corners. Airport advocates preferred this eighty-acre site because it was flat, was close to the urban centre and transportation lines, and could accommodate a runway of sufficient length. The

Airport Road, visible behind the terminal building in this 1948 aerial shot, opened on July 1, 1946, extending east from Young Road. At that time the airport had no paved runway. Chilliwack Board of Trade

two municipal councils arranged for an airport purchase bylaw vote to take place on August 23, 1945, in which ratepayers would be asked to authorize spending $40,000 for the facility. The initiative passed easily and the land purchase was finalized. Development activities soon commenced, with surveying, grading, and levelling of the main runway getting underway on October 4.

But as was often the case with Chilliwack infrastructure development during the twentieth century, optimism had exceeded pragmatic reality. The planning for the new airport had underestimated the land requirement. Thus, on October 15, a twenty-eight-acre land parcel adjacent to the future landing strip was leased to allow future construction of further hangars and an administration building. In February 1946, construction began on the first building, a combination workshop and hangar. The target date for the airport's overall completion was May 1.

Chilliwack Airport's octagonal terminal building, with its welcoming window flower boxes, became a long-time and familiar symbol of both the airport and the community. Chilliwack Museum and Archives

However, wet weather delayed construction, pushing back the airport's opening while increasing costs. Although the facility was still unfinished, the first plane landed on the airport's new runway on April 1, carrying two people as part of advance testing.

The Chilliwack Airport received its official licence on May 27, 1946, and on July 1 a new street extending east from Young Road South to give access to the airport was opened; appropriately it was called Airport Road. On February 1, 1947, the new airport suffered a significant setback when gale-force winds blew down the Chilliwack Flying Club hangar, the largest building in the complex, destroying three planes and damaging a fourth. The entire structure of 120 by 32 feet was blown back 15 feet from its original foundations and reduced to a shambles. Such was community spirit and pride in the new airport that citizens of the community, along with members of the Canadian Military Engineers and the Chilliwack Flying Club, banded together to rapidly rebuild the demolished hangar.

On May 11, 1947, the Chilliwack Airport's new and larger terminal building was officially opened. Built largely by volunteer labour, it was an eight-sided structure with space for numerous aircraft, a coffee shop, an office area, and a club room. The place name Chilliwack was painted in white capital letters on the terminal's roof for the benefit of incoming pilots. To commemorate the building's opening, officials staged an all-day celebration at the airport, starting with a "breakfast flight" by a twenty-seven-plane fleet from Vancouver. Hundreds of locals made their way to the airport that day, taking the opportunity to inspect the attractive new building.

As the decades passed and the 1980s unfolded, Chilliwack was growing and the level of activity at the airport had greatly increased. The existing wood-frame terminal building, whose distinctive design was a familiar symbol of both the airport and Chilliwack, was nearing forty years of age and had become inadequate for the airport's needs. By 1985, plans for a bigger, modern building of brick and metal were well underway. The comprehensive, $1.25 million airport expansion project included extension of the runway with a turnaround area and new asphalt overlay. On July 5, 1986, the Chilliwack Airport's new terminal and extended runway officially opened, and a large crowd listened to congratulatory messages from numerous politicians and dignitaries.

The new structure was built only ten metres east of the original one, and this limited separation came close to being a disastrous decision. After work had started on slowly dismantling the aging wooden terminal, on October 29, 1986, a fire burned the former terminal to the ground (it was believed to have been arson). Given the proximity of the old and new structures, had it not been for a strong easterly wind the new terminal might have been significantly impacted by the fire.

Today's Chilliwack Municipal Airport, at 46244 Airport Road, is far removed from its beginnings in the 1940s as essentially a field with a few markings and several rudimentary buildings. It covers 130 acres (52.6 hectares) and has almost 4,000 feet (1,219 metres) of paved and lit runway, including a parallel taxiway. Chilliwack's airport is considered one of the most attractive in BC by those who use it. Some locals still recall the formative days of aviation in the area, when the new airport, although basic and unsophisticated, nevertheless put Chilliwack on

The fire that burned the thirty-nine-year-old wooden terminal structure to the ground in 1986 would likely have impacted the new terminal had a different wind prevailed. Chilliwack Museum and Archives

BC's aviation map. In those earlier times the passion that people had for flying, and all it represented, fuelled development of the city's airport. And one particular aspect of the airport's history that people fondly recall is the octagonal terminal building that welcomed pilots and passengers for four decades.

A MODERN BUS DEPOT, 1950–1984

In the 1950s, prior to the dominance of air travel—and in response to the declining preference for using fixed rail routes to get around the country—travel by bus gained a prominent position in the North American travel and social scene, a much bigger role than it has today. Chilliwack residents, like many others, sought the mobility and choices associated

In May 1950, the final design for Chilliwack's new bus depot building was released, closely matching the finished facility that opened six months later. *Chilliwack Progress* Archive

with bus travel. Accordingly, a number of bus services started up and were soon flourishing. The advertising campaigns of carriers such as Greyhound and Pacific Stage Lines (PSL) suggested it was fashionable to take bus trips, emphasizing their excitement, low cost, dependability, mobility and flexibility compared to trains, and the fact that there was someone else at the wheel. Hollywood reinforced this image by incorporating bus travel in its films—many movies presented the bus station as a place of drama, opportunity, intrigue, and romance.

Chilliwack has had several bus depots over the years, but one stands out historically due to its location, its design, and the era in which it flourished. Located only 200 metres south of Five Corners, the city's most memorable bus depot opened at the dawn of the prosperous 1950s.

The British Columbia Electric Railway (BCER) provided the main mode of transportation between Chilliwack and the coast from 1910. However, as the midpoint of the twentieth century approached, the railway was experiencing a large and permanent decline in ridership. In response, BCER's parent company, BC Electric, decided to terminate the Chilliwack Line run, setting a target date of early fall 1950. At the same time, the company strategically incorporated the PSL bus service to capitalize on consumer trends. Since BC Electric owned the site of the downtown Chilliwack BCER terminal (along with much adjoining land that accommodated the rail line and ancillary buildings), the company chose to build its new PSL bus depot essentially where the train station stood for four decades, fronting Young Road South. More precisely, the new bus depot would be fifteen metres north of the train terminal, a structure that at one time was a showpiece of the city's downtown. Two storeys high and decorated with walkways and gardens, and with a stylish glass canopy over the tracks, the old terminal had beautiful sweeping lines that impressed visitors and locals alike over the years. Plans called for construction of the new building to be undertaken concurrently with the train station's operations during its final days. After the railway station's demolition, the site of the razed building would be used for the new depot's paved bus bays.

In May 1949, BC Electric announced preliminary plans for its new Chilliwack bus depot—one of several it planned to build in the Fraser Valley to meet increasing demand for bus service, including new facilities in Mission, Abbotsford, Haney, and Langley. A dual-purpose structure was envisioned: The southerly portion would serve as the

Construction of Chilliwack's new bus depot progressed through the summer months of 1950, just metres from the BCER rail terminal to the south, which was still functioning at the time. New bus parking stalls soon replaced the aging railway station. *Chilliwack Progress* Archive

bus depot, while the other part would be office space occupied by BC Electric (to become BC Hydro in 1961). Of the total $75,000 budgeted cost, $52,000 was allocated for the building and the remainder for yard paving and interior fitting. In April 1950, plans for Chilliwack's new bus station were finalized, characterized as "simple but distinctly modern in design." Tenders were soon called and the contract awarded, and construction started in early July.

Ultimately, the last run of the BCER tram from Chilliwack occurred on September 30, 1950, almost forty years to the day after the first train arrived to much fanfare. Similar to the BCER's inaugural trip back in 1910, the solitary passenger coach was decorated with banners for its final journey that Saturday. Ceremonies marking the changeover from interurban rail to bus service took place in Langley; fittingly, it was reported that "the Chilliwack party returned from Langley by bus." By October 7, a mere week after the last train had departed, the city's one-time showpiece BCER terminal station was torn down to make way for the driveway and parking bays of the new PSL bus depot. Two weeks earlier BCE had moved into its office space in the new structure, relocating from Yale Road East. On October 10, Chilliwack's new bus depot, at 137 Young Road South, was officially opened, with Mayor T. T. McCammon snipping a ceremonial ribbon in front of a crowd of two hundred.

A distinguishing feature of the terminal's design was a vertical element in the middle of the structure that sliced through the roof plane, serving as a marquee of sorts. PSL's logo of Pegasus, the flying horse, at the top of this feature was clearly visible from points around town, a mid-century modern architectural detail that differentiated the depot from other downtown buildings. Another feature of the immediately busy facility was its restaurant, which became known as the Bus Depot Lunch, regularly offering businessmen's lunch specials. By 1960, the restaurant was discontinued due to lack of demand by the travelling public, and the vacated space was taken over by BC Electric. However, the popular candy counter and newsstand remained, along with coffee and doughnut service. As part of a major renovation in 1960, automatic

The bus station's vertical marquee, featuring Pegasus, the flying horse, was visible from points around town, adding a distinctive architectural detail to the urban core. Royal BC Museum and Archives

exterior neon lighting was installed, lighting up the entire area around the structure at night.

During the 1980s, Chilliwack was undergoing social, demographic, and transportation changes. The imminent development of Salish Plaza (a retail complex that included the bus depot real estate), along with a trend to locate bus depots near major highways as opposed to urban centres, would both contribute to changes downtown. In 1984, Greyhound was leasing the aging bus depot on a month-to-month basis from BC Hydro as it actively pursued new premises away from the increasingly congested downtown core. The city's bus depot ultimately relocated to an existing building just west of Chilliwack Mall, on the south side of Luckakuck Way, opening on October 29. Greyhound chose this location due to better traffic manoeuvrability as well as its significantly shorter distance to Highway 1.

The old bus depot, at 9205 Young Road South, was subsequently renovated to accommodate commercial tenants, despite the comprehensive development of the new Salish Plaza that was about to proceed all around it. On May 1, 1985, Hurndall's Insurance Agencies and Uniglobe Travel set up shop there. But in 1990, after being a downtown landmark for forty years, Chilliwack's iconic bus depot was torn down, to be replaced by a retail structure forming part of the new shopping mall.

The role and romance of bus travel is now much less than in earlier times, exemplified by Chilliwack no longer having an actual bus depot—although later there was a form of a "bus terminal," as buses did stop at a service station in Sardis to pick up and drop off passengers on selected routes. Nevertheless, to this day many of a certain age, when looking south on Young Road from Five Corners, still see in their mind's eye the distinctive vertical marquee that signified the downtown bus depot, representing the community's popular link to destinations afar. For thirty-five years, locals knew the excitement of picking up or dropping off someone at the terminal, or perhaps taking a journey themselves, and memories of bus travel and the city's classic bus depot will endure.

THE OPENING OF HIGHWAY 1, 1960

Completion in 1960 of the separated four-lane freeway known as Highway 1 brought a number of major changes to life in Chilliwack. Prior to this transformative event, the drive to and from Vancouver was a much different, longer journey. Although it took the provincial Highway 1 name in 1941, it also represented the BC portion of Canada's national thoroughfare, the Trans-Canada Highway (TCH). Yale Road East and West formed part of the TCH, coursing through the city's downtown core and connecting it not just to Vancouver but points eastward, such as Toronto, Montreal, and beyond.

In the mid-twentieth century, the trip from Chilliwack to Vancouver on what was then the Trans-Canada encompassed a scenic tour through several valley communities. Driving to the coast took well over two hours on a sometimes narrow two-lane roadway. Starting on Yale Road West, motorists headed past the Chilliwack Drive-In Theatre and on towards the Vedder Canal Bridge (passing the impressive white Barrow house on the left, shortly before the span). Just west of Abbotsford, the two-lane TCH veered south, travelling through Aldergrove on what became the Fraser Highway, and then on to Langley, passing the community's airport on the right. From there, the route made its way through Surrey, eventually heading north on King George Boulevard and then across the Pattullo Bridge (which was less harrowing then, at two lanes, than in later years). Entering New Westminster, the TCH headed west on McBride Boulevard, up 10th Avenue to Kingsway, and then along Kingsway directly into Vancouver.

With the opening of the Pattullo in 1937, this was the route most locals took to Vancouver for almost three decades, until the opening of the Port Mann Bridge. Since almost all of it was just two lanes, the route often featured a lengthy lineup of impatient motorists following a slow vehicle, along with dangerous passing attempts.

After World War II, the Lower Mainland's population was growing quickly, and it became apparent that the aging two-lane national highway through the Fraser Valley would soon be inadequate. As early as 1953, plans were underway for a wider and more efficient stretch of the TCH through the region. In February of that year, the first survey team arrived in Chilliwack to map out a potential route, and within a few years the community's new segment of the TCH was determined: Dubbed the Chilliwack Bypass, it would stretch 31 kilometres from Bridal Falls to the Vedder Canal and form part of a 122-kilometre four-lane highway straight through to West Vancouver. On December 12, 1956, after much land assembly and logistical preparation, work began on the first section of the new freeway—west of the city near Bowman's Mill, next to the Fraser River at the foot of Chilliwack Mountain.

By early 1959, construction of Chilliwack's portion of the new Highway 1 was progressing. The new interchange/cloverleaf was in place, while the four lanes of the freeway were yet to be paved. The future locations of shopping malls in Sardis were agricultural land at this point. Chilliwack Museum and Archives / Norman Williams, photographer

The Chilliwack Bypass took almost four years to complete, prolonged periods of rain having wreaked havoc with paving schedules. Finally, on August 1, 1960, the community's new $8 million highway project opened. It included the integral cloverleaf at Cottonwood Corners, also referred to as the "interchange" or "overpass." An elaborate and well-attended celebration that included provincial cabinet ministers Phil Gaglardi and Ken Kiernan marked the watershed event. A crowd of spectators stood on the cloverleaf and looked down while the ribbon was cut and the ceremonial first car drove the "luxurious" new roadway. At the time the bypass opened, officials expected the new Port Mann Bridge to be open by 1962, thus completing the so-called superhighway, but in the end this critical span across the Fraser River was not finished until 1964.

The new highway's descriptor "bypass" proved to be apt, as that is what it clearly did—it bypassed downtown Chilliwack. This new reality was met with mixed reactions from locals. Although merchants feared a significant loss of business—particularly owners of motor inns, gas stations, and restaurants—the bypass reduced traffic congestion in downtown Chilliwack, and the city's budget for road maintenance became more manageable. Once the local segment of the TCH was integrated with the subsequent portions of the highway to Vancouver, and economic uncertainties had been addressed, the term "bypass" was phased out. Overall, users were quite pleased with the wide, straight, and separated four-lane thoroughfare that delivered them to and from Vancouver in approximately half the time the trip took previously, and in safer fashion.

When the new Highway 1 opened in Chilliwack on August 1, 1960, the district's MLA, Ken Kiernan, picked a random child from the crowd for the honour of cutting the ceremonial ribbon. Using the same scissors that opened the Agassiz-Rosedale Bridge four years earlier, six-year-old Gwen Wickham of Greendale cuts the blue ribbon stretched across the sparkling new four-lane throughway. *Chilliwack Progress* Archive

Chapter 3
LANDMARK STRUCTURES

ALONGSIDE THE IMPORTANT INFRASTRUCTURE PROJECTS COMPLETED during Chilliwack's post-war boom years (see chapter 1), a number of beloved buildings went up in the community during that period, including some that would become iconic. A few of them still stand today, but many have long since disappeared from the local landscape. Noteworthy structures of the post-war era that resonate with locals, past and present, include the Royal Bank Building at Five Corners, the Pringle Hatcheries complex on the old Trans-Canada Highway, and the civic centre known as the Ag Hall / Evergreen Hall (a 1967 centennial project). Not a building per se but certainly a landmark, there is also the airplane that sat atop a downtown building for almost three decades, inspiring much local fascination. This chapter begins with a look back at an earlier building, the fondly remembered CN train station, that continued to play a key role in the 1950s and 1960s.

THE CN TRAIN STATION, 1915–1984

Train travel was an integral part of life during much of the twentieth century, but as the 1950s unfolded, the public's preference for fixed rail routes as a means of transportation was declining. And although automobile culture eventually took over, the romance of the rails from an earlier era remained popular in Chilliwack and residents continued to

After purchasing their tickets inside the station, passengers excitedly wait on the 256-foot concrete platform, straining to see the train's light or hear its horn to the east or west. Soon they will be whisked off to an adventure somewhere in Canada. Chilliwack Museum & Archives

rely on the service. One of the community's most aesthetically pleasing landmarks was its CN train station at the south foot of Nowell Street, at Railway Avenue. For many who boarded or disembarked at the station, saw someone off, or greeted a loved one upon their arrival, this building and location still hold special memories. Eventually, passenger rail service to Chilliwack ended, and the treasured station's demise was sudden and unexpected, shrouded in murky circumstances.

In 1914, Canada had three national railway lines, but none passed through Chilliwack. However, the country's third intercontinental railway, the Canadian Northern Railway, was working on the BC portion of its national line, and by early 1915 it had laid tracks through the Fraser Valley. At that time, small towns in Canada very much wanted to be on a national railway line, as this brought a sense of prestige and also enhanced the local economy. On May 24, the local stretch of Canada's newest railway opened—but accommodating only regional service, three times per week between Port Mann and Hope. It was a further three months before the first transcontinental train roared through town. On August 27, a train that had left Toronto for Vancouver four days earlier passed through at 10:00 p.m. without stopping, a journey that ultimately took 106 hours. This event—although fleeting, in darkness, and with few witnesses—signified the start of a new era in Chilliwack.

At the time of this important milestone in the city's history, its much-anticipated train station had yet to be built. Grading work on the site of the rail terminal started on October 16, 1915. Fast-tracked construction of the station structure was soon underway, and the building was completed in less than six weeks. On December 1, the new train terminal opened at 557 Nowell Street South. It was designed by one of Canada's pre-eminent rail architects of the time, John Schofield. Although he primarily worked in Manitoba and central Canada, he did design three special stations in what was then considered the frontier West: identical terminals in Chilliwack and Hope in BC and Estevan in Saskatchewan. Each was categorized as a third-class station, a design often reserved for small rural towns, and identified by its living quarters for the station agent on the second floor. As such, the structure somewhat resembled a house, distinguished by its pyramidal/hipped roof. The dimensions of the Chilliwack station were 24 feet by 70 feet, and the concrete platform in front of it extended 256 feet.

Many locals have numerous memories (mostly pleasant, some otherwise) associated with the city's train station. Royal train tours stopped in Chilliwack in 1939, 1951, and 1959, and in each case the area around the station and its concrete platform played an integral role in the spectacle, enabling the royals' walkabout and other festivities. Over the years, several Hollywood luminaries stopped at the CN station, usually on their way to vacation in BC or Alberta. In particular, on July 24, 1953, Marilyn Monroe spent ten minutes at the terminal, during which she gave a recent local high school graduate the distinction of being the first man she kissed in Canada (see chapter 7). On

February 2, 1967, the six-car Confederation Train arrived at the station for two days as part of its cross-country 331-day, 83-stop observance of the nation's centennial. And in the early morning hours of May 12, 1984, part of a 110-car westbound freight train derailed in front of the terminal, spilling much of its cargo of copper ore concentrate and wood chips. Miraculously, the station structure escaped the accident unscathed, with derailed freight cars literally a few feet from its front door (which by then had a new address, 8955 Nowell Street, due to the city–township amalgamation).

The 110-car freight train derailment in front of the CN station in 1984 was caused by a station wagon missing the right turn onto Railway Avenue and skidding onto the railway tracks—avoiding the train station building by just two metres. Unbeknownst to the motorist (or anyone else at the time), this seemingly minor incident would knock the train tracks out of alignment just enough to cause the derailment. Later that year, a barrier was installed to prevent southbound cars from driving onto the tracks. Hank Suderman Collection

At the time of the May 1984 derailment, Chilliwack's train station was sitting empty, as Via Rail was no longer stopping to pick up passengers in the city. This loss of service, which was poorly received by the community, was part of a CN business consolidation initiative. Further, CN no longer wanted its aging train station building. It offered the historic structure to the city for one dollar, provided that it be relocated, but city council declined to proceed. It had determined the proposal was not financially viable, nor could a suitable long-term land lease be secured.

Within a few months, the future of the city's cherished train station would no longer be in doubt. On September 22, 1984, the Chilliwack Fire Department responded to a 4:34 a.m. call reporting a fire at the station, and it took firefighters three hours to contain the blaze. Arson was strongly suspected since there was no heat or electricity in the vacant building. The station's interior was gutted by the fire, and officials initially believed that the structural integrity of the building had been greatly compromised. After the police completed their investigation, CN assured local officials as late as October 5 that the possible demolition of the station would be delayed to allow sufficient time to determine whether the heritage building could be restored. However, a demolition permit had been applied for on October 3, and the city had issued it on October 10. Suddenly, on October 15, with no announcement and before the viability of restoration had been ascertained, the city's venerable train station was summarily razed, replaced by a level patch of sand and gravel. During the demolition process, the contractor noted that much of the building was "completely rotten," which likely precluded any restoration plans.

Thus, after sixty-nine years, Chilliwack's one-time symbol of its national relevance was abruptly gone. There was an outcry from the city's heritage enthusiasts about both the historic station's sudden demise and the ambiguous communications from CN. In June 1985, Via Rail service through the city returned, as the community had been designated as a regular daily stop for the *Super Continental* rail service.

Occasionally some nostalgia-minded motorists drive down to the old train station site and are struck by the lack of any indication that an important part of the city's history stood here for decades. The only remnant of what had been a staple of Chilliwack life for almost seventy years is a lengthy portion of the 256-foot concrete platform, which is partially overgrown with weeds. Merlin Bunt Collection

Via Rail also erected a modest passenger shelter to replace the departed CN train station. However, this daily service was later cut back to Via Rail's passenger train *The Canadian*, which stopped in Chilliwack three times per week on a flag-stop basis (with forty-eight hours' advance notice required). With the passenger shelter eventually gone, the city's "train station" then consisted solely of a signpost and a paved platform on the north side of the CN railway tracks at Nowell Street—the very site where the actual train station sat for decades.

With its classic appearance and prominent role in Chilliwack life, the CN train station left its mark on the community's transportation and cultural history. Over the years, thousands of locals boarded there, taking the first step in their journey to higher education, business meetings, family visits, travel adventures, or wartime service. Few motorists head to the southern point of Nowell Street anymore, and those who do are often struck by the emptiness of the area. The only remnant of the station is a significant portion of the concrete platform. Although no plaque or monument commemorates what once was, numerous photographs of the station exist, as well as some nostalgic artistic tributes. Many current and former residents still recall the thrill of waiting on the platform and finally hearing the horn of the train that would soon whisk them off to elsewhere.

THE ROYAL BANK BUILDING AT FIVE CORNERS, 1950

One historically significant and aesthetically pleasing structure built downtown as the 1950s began was the Royal Bank Building. Its high-profile location at the northwest corner of Wellington Avenue and Young Road made it a vital constituent of the urban core over the years. Although the Royal Bank of Canada was the first chartered bank to open its doors in the city, it was the last to locate at Five Corners—long regarded as the centre of business in the Fraser Valley.

Although much of Chilliwack's townsite was laid out in 1881 and its combined city and township population had reached 3,600 by 1900, not until 1903 did a major Canadian bank consider it a community with a future worthy of capital investment. On May 27, the *Chilliwack Progress* announced that the Royal Bank of Canada would soon be opening a branch in the city. Within a month, the bank had commenced operations in the Driscoll Block, a wood-frame structure built in 1895 at the northeast corner of Young Road North and Yale Road East. When it opened, the Royal Bank branch was just the seventh in BC (including only two in Vancouver and one in Victoria). As the city grew in the early days of the new century, so did the Royal Bank, and soon its cramped space and relatively pedestrian design (for a bank), although well located, were not sufficient for its purposes. Thus, in 1905 the bank decided to develop its own building, purchasing a vacant lot at the southeast corner of Wellington Avenue and Main Street, just two blocks west of its current location. Excavation of the site started in May 1906, and in October, the Royal Bank moved into its stately new building. Locals were most impressed with the design, detail, and quality of the new bank, said to be equal to that of any in a big city.

The Royal Bank operated from its new home for the next four decades, a period during which Chilliwack—and the world in general—underwent tremendous growth and change. As the midpoint of the twentieth century approached, the bank realized its premises had become somewhat old, too small, and outdated. In 1949, to respond to the changing times and its own operational needs, the bank again acquired a downtown site for a new, modern home: a choice Five Corners property that was then accommodating the Langley Greenhouses florist business. On October 4, the florist shop relocated next to the city's new fire hall on Young Road North (see chapter 1). Its previous home was demolished shortly thereafter to allow construction to start on the new Royal Bank Building.

Plans for the bank's new, $46,000 building called for a mid-century modern structure, longish and relatively narrow, essentially one and a half storeys in height. Its entrance was finished in aluminum and the facade was red brick trimmed in Haddington Island stone. One of the building's interior features was the first soundproof bank ceiling in the city. As the *Chilliwack Progress* announced prior to construction, "Bringing the depositor and [bank] clerk closer together will be the long low counters and unobtrusive screens, making the high ugly tellers' cages and standing on tiptoe to reach the cheques and blanks a thing of the past." On July 10, 1950, the Royal Bank opened the doors of its new premises, at 1 Wellington Avenue. This made four chartered banks then located at Five Corners: Nearby were branches of the Bank of Montreal, the Canadian Bank of Commerce, and the Bank of Nova Scotia.

For the next twenty-three years, the Royal Bank, in its handsome brick building, was a constant in the business world of downtown Chilliwack. However, in the early 1970s, as the community's needs continued to grow, it once again sought a bigger and more modern space. In

For the quarter century following its completion, the Royal Bank at 1 Wellington Avenue was a staple of the Five Corners business scene. PicClick

1971, the bank purchased a redevelopment property at the southeast corner of Main Street and Princess Avenue West. Chilliwack Tire had been located on the site for several years; the building was soon demolished and the property levelled in advance of the bank constructing its new home. On September 10, 1973, after being at Five Corners since 1950, the Royal Bank opened its new main branch at 9296 Main Street with much fanfare. The 5,500-square-foot, single-storey structure was almost twice the size of its previous facility. The bank had a staff of thirty-one and featured two entrances, the city's first drive-through teller service, and parking for twenty-one cars. Its exterior was again of stylish brick, and the bank's interior design, very much of its time, featured "the latest in color-coordinated decor in oranges, golds, red, coral and exposed brick."

The Royal Bank's vacated premises at Five Corners soon had another chartered bank as its tenant, albeit for a short period. The Bank of Montreal had been patiently waiting for the Royal to vacate its long-time home, which was just fifteen metres across the street from its own branch at the northeast corner of Yale Road East and Young Road North. In 1973, the Bank of Montreal announced plans to build a much larger, two-storey, $1 million bank building to occupy its current site and that of the Barber Block next door. The first step in the bank's redevelopment process occurred in October when the Barber Block (formerly the Driscoll Block) was torn down. Then, at 5:30 a.m. on Sunday, December 2, Bank of Montreal staff, accompanied by RCMP officers, relocated across the street to the 1950 brick building that, until three months earlier, had been the home of the Royal Bank. This move allowed the Bank of Montreal's former facility, built in 1912, to be demolished. The bank operated from the 1950 building for most of the next three years, until July 24, 1976, when its new main branch officially opened.

Over the years, structural alterations to the rear of the Royal Bank Building changed its external appearance, but it still retains its classic mid-century look and charm. Inside, the whole vibe is different, having transformed from stately bank to sports bar/restaurant.
Merlin Bunt Collection

With the departure of the Bank of Montreal, Canada Permanent Trust (a.k.a. The Permanent) signed a lease for the coveted space. In November 1976, the Permanent took out a building permit for renovations to its new home. In keeping with city council's vision that new premises downtown incorporate a turn-of-the-century look, the renovated space featured "a winding staircase with solid oak railings, murals of early Chilliwack and parts of BC, and the extensive use of plants." The Permanent opened its doors at Five Corners in February 1977. By that time, the exterior of the brick bank building had also changed, having been somewhat transformed with a canopy along Wellington Avenue (part of a coordinated city initiative to improve the downtown shopping experience), wooden signage, and awnings. In 1986, the Permanent merged with Canada Trust, the latter becoming the new tenant of the heritage structure.

In 1993, the land accommodating the Royal Bank Building was rezoned from Town Centre Commercial to Nightclub/Neighbourhood Pub. This paved the way for hospitality-type tenants. In 1994, after seventeen years, Canada Trust ended its tenancy at Five Corners, moving to the Chilliwack Mall, which had opened in 1981. For the next four years, the former bank mostly remained vacant, waiting for an entrepreneur to capitalize on the entertainment zoning now in place. In 1998, the landmark structure welcomed the first of a succession of restaurant-related enterprises.

The Royal Bank Building, at 45975 Wellington Avenue, remains an integral part of the downtown core, and of Five Corners—a historic locale and reborn hub, proximate to the District 1881 development. The building's exterior appearance has not changed materially, but the internal decor and layout of the conservative bank days have been replaced by a more relaxed entertainment motif. Locals have always appreciated the structure's signature brick exterior, for its colour and its permanence. They also value that this building is still part of the downtown landscape while representing a welcome link to the community's post-war past.

PRINGLE ELECTRIC HATCHERIES, 1941–2018

As motorists approached Chilliwack from the east or west, familiar buildings signalled they were getting close to their destination. One such structure, situated three kilometres east of Five Corners, was a fixture on Yale Road East for over seventy years. Pringle Electric Hatcheries, later known as Pringle Hatcheries, represented a landmark for locals and was also a prominent community business, owned by the Pringle family. They built the hatchery in 1941 after the parent company's success with two other hatcheries in Alberta. As these operations approached capacity, the family expanded west, selecting Chilliwack due to the "availability of excellent breeding stock" along with its warmer climate, which naturally enhanced the hatching process. Also in the early 1940s, the rising importance of the poultry industry in the Fraser Valley was bolstered by the government offering subsidies and moving to stabilize the egg market. Egg prices were at an all-time high, and there was also a program to export eggs to England during the war years. These factors resulted in a steadily increasing demand for quality chicks and a growing chick hatchery industry in the region.

The Pringles purchased five acres on the north side of Yale Road East at Prest Road. Construction commenced in mid-1941, and in November the hatchery building, in gleaming white, opened for business at 179 Trans-Canada Highway East. The original structure was 1,440 square feet, relatively small compared to the complex it eventually became. Most of the new building was devoted to a state-of-the-art incubator room with capacity for up to 200,000 eggs. A small office was attached to the main building. Several other hatcheries operated in the community in the early 1940s, but Pringle Hatcheries was the dominant one. The competitiveness of the industry compelled the business to advertise frequently, primarily in the *Chilliwack Progress*. In 1942, officials anticipated that between 400,000 and 500,000 chicks would be hatched in the district, a record to that point, and by 1943 the Pringle Hatcheries operation had doubled production.

In 1941, the new Pringle Electric Hatcheries plant opened its doors. It was considerably smaller than it would become after later expansions responding to growth in the company and the industry. *Chilliwack Progress* Archive

The driving force behind the plant was M. E. "Jerry" Pringle (1910–1991). In addition to building and subsequently managing the hatchery for a number of years, he was a high-profile participant in the Fraser Valley food processing industry and served as the community's member of Parliament from 1968 to 1972. After leaving politics, Pringle was a consultant to the federal Department of Agriculture, after which he became chair of the Canadian Egg Marketing Agency. He was also an aviator, flying his own plane for both personal and business purposes. By the late 1940s, the success of Pringle Hatcheries was such that it was exporting live chicks to the Prairies. When the company asked Trans-Canada Air Lines to fly them over the Rockies, the airline declined, citing the perceived risk that the live cargo would not survive the trip due to lack of oxygen. As the *Chilliwack Progress* reported in a mid-1945 article about transporting local farm products, "Air transport would move the chicks in a small fraction of the time now taken by railways, and this would be a definite advantage to hatcherymen." But no commercial carrier was willing to take the chicks, so Pringle flew them himself, taking off from the Chilliwack Airport and becoming the first "poultryman" to successfully fly baby chicks across the Rockies to the Prairie market.

By the late 1940s, the novelty of electricity as an integral aspect of the chick hatching industry had worn off, and what had initially been known as Pringle Electric Hatcheries became Pringle Baby Chicks and Pringle Hatcheries Ltd. In 1953, the business continued to utilize more of its five-acre site by undergoing a 6,250-square-foot expansion. The new space housed the Lower Mainland's first commercial egg production operation, accommodating 5,000 egg-laying hens, a capacity that was doubled the following year when the building expanded again. The Pringle business continued to grow, and by 1965 it was hatching approximately 5.2 million chicks per year. Due to its distinctive appearance, visitors to the area often mistook the hatchery structure for a well-maintained, expansive house.

By 1948, the enlarged all-white Pringle building on the Trans-Canada Highway/Yale Road East had become a landmark for motorists leaving or approaching the city, as well as a prominent part of the community's mid-twentieth-century economy. Chilliwack Board of Trade

In the mid- to late 1970s, the poultry operation that had thrived on the Pringle property for over three decades gradually wound down. Eventually the building was vacated, and in the ensuing years it deteriorated. By 2017, the aging structure, then at 47339 Yale Road, had been partially damaged by fire, and in 2018 the building was razed and the site levelled. In 2020, construction commenced on a sixteen-unit residential subdivision on the site of Pringle Hatcheries as well as land farther east along Yale Road. Today, there is no physical recognition of the former hatchery building, which was nestled beside Little Mountain. For decades it signified to many that they would soon be entering Chilliwack, or, if travelling east, approaching Little Mountain, Meadowlands Golf and Country Club, or the village of Rosedale. More than that, in its heyday Pringle Hatcheries gave Chilliwack, and in particular Jerry Pringle, prominence in the poultry industry both provincially and nationally.

After being damaged by fire and demolished in 2018, the site of Pringle Electric Hatcheries became part of a sixteen-lot subdivision, completed in 2021. Merlin Bunt Collection

THE AGRICULTURAL HALL, 1936–1967

In the post-war years, one of Chilliwack's more popular venues was its third agricultural hall (commonly referred to as the Ag Hall), situated at the southwest corner of Spadina Avenue and Corbould Street on the city's second fairgrounds. This critical piece of civic infrastructure spanned four notable eras in the community's history—the Depression years, the war years, the prosperous and growth-oriented 1950s, and the transformational 1960s. It hosted countless civic, entertainment, and sporting events as well as agricultural presentations.

This Ag Hall replaced the community's second one, which was built in 1909 but collapsed during the week of January 21, 1935, in the throes of that year's severe ice storm. It could not be rebuilt, paving

In addition to countless dances, performances, sports competitions, and agricultural displays, over the years the Agricultural Hall hosted diverse events such as badminton tournaments, new auto shows, religious rallies, fashion shows, rummage sales, bingo events, and magic shows. Chilliwack Museum & Archives and *Chilliwack Progress*

the way for a new, modern facility. Efforts to secure funding for the new structure were soon underway, with the community's MP, Harry Barber, successfully lobbying his colleagues in Parliament to have Ottawa pay its entire cost.

On September 23, 1935, a construction contract was awarded. One of the conditions of the federal grant was that the new facility be of sufficient size for widespread use by the community's various athletic groups. Thus, it was designed to serve as both a gymnasium and an entertainment venue. On April 24, 1936, with the nation still in the grip of the Great Depression, the new Ag Hall opened with a gala dance featuring a ten-piece orchestra, attended by 850 impressed citizens. The structure for the most part stood by itself on the largely undeveloped fairgrounds—the coliseum, curling rink, grandstand at the oval, and Monarch Park baseball diamonds (see chapter 10) were still years away from being built. The hall's entrance was only 200 feet from the corner of Corbould and Spadina, and fronting it was a circular driveway and grass, later replaced by a paved parking lot.

During the war years, a dance took place most every Saturday night at the Ag Hall, except when it was occupied with war-related commitments. As World War II drew to an end, the hall hosted a large Victory in Europe (V-E) celebration dance on May 7, 1945, presaging many well-attended dances it would host in the ensuing years. With the conclusion of the war came a new air of optimism and energy, and Chilliwack's citizens increasingly wanted to get out of the house for recreation in the form of sports, entertainment, socializing, and dancing. Consequently, there was a renewed interest in the hall for these pursuits. On the sporting front, basketball was prominently featured, and in 1946, professional wrestling became a regular event when the Vancouver circuit expanded to Chilliwack.

A few years on, in late 1950, civic officials took stock of the Ag Hall and realized it had yet to realize its potential as a true community centre. The building's acoustics were poor, the interior was drab and unpleasant to look at, and it was expensive to heat. Accordingly, a concert shell

In the late 1940s, the Agricultural Hall stood essentially by itself on the city's largely undeveloped fairgrounds. This changed in the 1950s with development of the coliseum, curling rink, Monarch Park, and other facilities. Royal BC Museum and Archives

was constructed on the hall's stage, the ceiling was repaired, and its interior was painted. Local service organizations and individuals volunteered their time to complete these improvement projects. Soon the building began hosting a range of community functions, along with the athletic, cultural, and agricultural events that had dominated its earlier years. However, by 1956, Chilliwack Senior High School's four-year-old gymnasium was significantly cutting into the hall's rental bookings. The school's gym was larger, less expensive to rent, and had a bigger stage, although the Ag Hall's acoustics were superior. Civic officials approached the school board requesting that rental rates be made more equitable, but nothing substantial resulted.

As early as 1961, talks were underway to modify or replace the Ag Hall, as the need for a true and up-to-date civic centre in Chilliwack had been clearly identified and prioritized. Locals felt that with the recently completed coliseum in full operation (see chapter 1), a new civic centre would integrate well with the growing development of the fairgrounds.

On February 6, the Civic Properties Commission advised council that the structure was quickly becoming obsolete and, in its current condition, would likely be dismantled in several years' time. Until then, it would have to get by on minimal upkeep until a new centre was in place. Six years passed before this vision became a reality, as financing of the ambitious undertaking became a critical issue. In the October 17 edition of the *Chilliwack Progress*, the paper editorialized with remarkable prescience that it might make financial sense to keep most of the current Ag Hall and integrate it into a new civic centre. The Civic Properties Commission also strongly advocated converting the Ag Hall to a new civic centre. Its members reasoned that this approach was cheaper than building a new facility, and that although the appearance and equipment of the Ag Hall were outdated, the structure had been well built and was structurally sound.

In 1965, a new civic centre was chosen as Chilliwack's national centennial project, but its scope and financing continued to be unresolved. After gaining consensus that integrating most of the existing Ag Hall into the new centre was the optimal approach, officials estimated that the city's and township's shares of the project's cost were $103,000 each, and that taxpayers had to approve these expenditures. The proposal was passed in both municipalities on December 11, and on the following May 2, preliminary plans for the new civic centre were approved at a joint council meeting. The plans officially confirmed that the core of the Ag Hall would be retained as the gymnasium/auditorium portion of the new structure. However, by that time the estimated budget for the project had risen 21 percent above what had been passed by taxpayers five months earlier. By November, city council was seriously considering not granting approval for the centennial project to proceed, as it did not have the taxpayer mandate to spend more than had been approved.

On November 14, a scaled-down version of the civic centre was presented to council for its consideration. This proposal was not well received; Mayor Alan Holder felt it would result in a "refurbished Ag Hall with a few trimmings added on the side." Council nevertheless decided to seek competitive tenders to gauge what the ultimate construction cost might be. On March 17, 1967, when the three sealed tenders were opened, the least expensive one came in at $74,000 in excess of the approved budget. In the midst of Canada's centennial celebration, the status of the community's centennial project (and ultimately the fate of the aging Ag Hall) was still very much up in the air. Township and city councils were faced with the prospect of either scrapping the project or finding ways to make up the significant shortfall. At a joint council meeting on April 3, councillors voted 8–4 to carry on with the new civic centre project and seek other funding sources. Officials feared that further delays would compromise available centennial grants that were being counted upon. Also, there was no appetite to spend thousands of dollars to recondition the old Ag Hall. Ultimately, on April 17, it took Mayor Holder's tie-breaking vote for the city to approve proceeding with the project, and work started the following week.

To ensure it would be completed during Canada's centennial year, work on the new civic centre was fast-tracked. In October 1967, as the building neared completion, the Chilliwack Centennial Committee held a contest, seeking "a distinctive name" for the new centre. The committee chose Evergreen Hall from among the two hundred entries. This name initially met with some public criticism, but the committee unanimously agreed to retain it. Finally, on December 15, after years of planning, negotiations, and meetings, the city's centennial project, incorporating much of the existing Ag Hall, opened to positive reviews. In a weekend full of celebratory ceremonies for the new civic centre, approximately 5,000 people attended the three days of events, starting with a crowd of 700 at Friday afternoon's official opening.

The diversity of events and attractions that took place at the original Ag Hall over its thirty-plus years was considerable. A non-exhaustive list includes countless dances, concerts, dramatic productions, sports competitions, carnivals, festivals, fairs, political rallies, town meetings, and remembrance services. The building that dominated the fairgrounds for so long still largely exists, physically forming a major part

Chilliwack's 1967 centennial project, the conversion of the Agricultural Hall to Evergreen Hall, almost didn't happen due to funding issues. Many today do not realize it is still largely with us, physically forming a large part of Evergreen Hall. Chilliwack Museum & Archives and *Chilliwack Progress*

of Evergreen Hall. Back in a time when the city was smaller, and the culture of the day was decidedly different, construction of this facility represented a huge step forward for the growing district, and the Ag Hall ultimately played a significant role in the everyday life of many Chilliwack citizens.

THE YELLOW AIRPLANE ON BRETT'S GARAGE, 1951–1977

Mid-century Chilliwack had a number of downtown landmarks, some quite unusual. One was the yellow airplane that sat on the roof of Brett's Garage (part of Brett's Ltd.), facing Hope Street. That each of the airplane, building, business, and street are long gone reflects how the city

A scene repeated many times over the years was children being taken downtown to see the yellow airplane on the roof of a building. In this photo, the adult is actually Earl Brett, the owner of the plane and founder of Brett's Ltd., posing with one of his grandkids. Chilliwack Museum & Archives

has changed over the years, but it has also inspired efforts to recapture these features of its urban past.

The man behind the curious downtown beacon was Earl Brett (1896–1988), one of the community's aviation pioneers (see chapter 2). An airplane sitting on top of Brett's automobile garage in his hometown represented well the passions of Earl Brett's life—flying, the automotive industry, and Chilliwack. As his interest in flying developed, along with an increasing fascination with the mechanical workings of aircraft, Brett acquired his first airplane in 1927. He flew it for 450 hours before legally obtaining his flying licence, something he was finally forced to do when Vancouver authorities seized his aircraft and held it until he passed his exam. In 1929, Brett built the Brett's Garage complex on Yale Road West at Princess Avenue West. The following year, Brett's Ltd. became a General Motors automobile dealership, an affiliation that lasted decades.

As his commercial interests grew, flying became a standard business practice for Earl Brett, who usually preferred to fly somewhere instead of taking a car. He served as president of the BC Aviation Council, which had its origins in Chilliwack, and was a founding member of the Chilliwack Flying Club. The highly visible yellow plane atop his garage was a Fairchild Cornell model, acquired by Brett in the late 1940s. It was the second Fairchild Cornell that he'd owned, having crashed his first one at Powell River in 1944, the sunken airplane being a total write-off.

The yellow aircraft on the roof of Brett's on Hope Street was less than two blocks from Five Corners, and with its elevated position it became a popular downtown Chilliwack landmark. *Chilliwack Progress* Archive

By 1950, Brett's Ltd. was a prominent city business, occupying the entire block of Princess Avenue West between Hope Street and Yale Road West, as well as fifty metres along Yale Road West. The company also owned undeveloped property on Hope Street, directly to the southwest of its large garage. In 1951, Brett's Ltd. built a new building on its Hope Street property to accommodate the garage's expanded machine and tire shop facilities. The addition was a separate structure, connected to the garage by adjacent doors. By this time, Earl Brett was no longer flying his second Fairchild Cornell airplane, and when construction on the garage addition was complete, he had the yellow aircraft placed on top of the building, forever a reminder to him of the joy he had flying it around Chilliwack and other parts of BC.

After looking out over downtown Chilliwack for twenty-seven years, in 1977 Earl Brett's yellow Fairchild Cornell aircraft was taken down and placed on a flatbed truck to be transported to the Pacific Aviation Museum in Richmond. Its whereabouts today are uncertain. Chilliwack Museum & Archives and *Chilliwack Progress*

For the next quarter century, the yellow airplane was a prominent feature of the city's downtown as well as a source of fascination to many of the community's kids. They often asked their parents to take them to Hope Street so that they could see the plane up close. They also wanted to know how an airplane could possibly be on the roof of a building, only two blocks from Five Corners.

By the mid-1970s, Brett's Ltd. was being managed by Earl Brett's son, Doug Brett. The combination of ongoing changes downtown, the business's aging premises, and what the younger Brett viewed as "prohibitive taxes . . . [and] unreasonable one-way streets" motivated him to relocate Brett's Garage and automotive dealership. The move's first phase took place on November 6, 1975, when Brett's Ltd. sold one acre of its downtown real estate to the Canadian Imperial Bank of Commerce for future development of its new flagship branch (opened in 1982). Terms of the deal included Brett's having to vacate its premises by the start of 1978. As a result, on June 20, 1977, the familiar yellow airplane that had looked out over downtown since 1951 was carefully taken down from its lofty station with personnel and equipment borrowed from Canadian Forces Base Chilliwack. Transported on a flatbed truck to the Pacific Aviation Museum in Richmond, it was later transferred to a hangar somewhere in Metro Vancouver, waiting to possibly be restored someday.

In 2019, as part of the ongoing revitalization of downtown Chilliwack, the owner of Salish Plaza—where Brett's Garage stood for more than half a century—commissioned a public art project to pay homage to Earl Brett's yellow Fairchild Cornell. Christened the *Golden Eagle*, the sculpture by Lucien Durey is seven feet high and twenty feet wide, following the outline of the original airplane. The neon-lit artwork was placed on the roof of the government liquor store in Salish Plaza on November 17, 2020, about thirty-five metres northeast of where the airplane sat on the roof of Brett's Garage. Similar to its predecessor, due to its elevated position (and its neon) the *Golden Eagle* is visible from many downtown vantage points and particularly stands out after dark.

For twenty-seven years, Earl Brett's plane atop his garage on Hope Street kept Chilliwack's aviation sector in the forefront of people's minds, while affording Brett quiet and enduring satisfaction of one of his life's passions. He miraculously (and perhaps fatefully) survived a number of airplane crashes over the years with no serious injuries. He continued flying until he was in his late fifties, when he had to stop for health reasons—years earlier than he'd wanted to. His popular yellow airplane has been gone from the downtown scene for decades, but thanks to the civic-minded owners of the site where it once sat, the *Golden Eagle* serves to inform current residents and remind old-timers of a distinctive urban landmark from an earlier era.

Chapter 4

HOUSING THE BABY BOOM

IN THE POST-WAR ERA, THE LARGE NUMBER OF VETERANS RETURNING to the community combined with a significant spike in the birth rate to cause Chilliwack an immediate and growing need for housing—both single-family detached homes and apartment-style rentals. This chapter examines the history of two important and popular residential developments from this period, the Menzies and Berkeley Subdivisions. These substantial planned neighbourhoods, to the east and north of downtown, provided much-needed housing stock for young parents and their children, the baby boomer generation. The chapter also discusses a pair of multi-unit buildings from mid-century: the Shangri-La Apartments (Chilliwack's "Pink Palace") and the deluxe Solange Apartments. In addition, it profiles a single-family residence, the Fredrickson house, that gained national notoriety in 1966 for allegedly being haunted.

THE MENZIES SUBDIVISION, 1948

Chilliwack responded to the accelerated post-war demand for affordable family housing by expanding its residential neighbourhoods into what was then referred to as the East End, a large tract of undeveloped land north of Yale Road East and east of Williams Street North. Several subdivisions of varying sizes were built, and these were often named after noted local citizens. The Menzies Subdivision, about one kilometre northeast of Five Corners, stood out due to its size, its location, and the number of young families it eventually accommodated.

Both the Menzies Subdivision and (later) Menzies Street were named after the Menzies family, which owned considerable real estate in the northeast sector of the city. Its members had served on city council, run for the BC legislature, held the offices of president of the Chilliwack Agricultural Society and president of the Chilliwack Board of Trade, and served as a Chilliwack school board trustee. One prominent member of the family, Fred A. Menzies, ran Menzies Hardware, immediately west of the future Eaton's building on Wellington Avenue, from 1912 to 1933.

AT LAST!

Yes, we are now proud to announce that the 69 choice high lots known as the Menzies Subdivision are for sale. The ground is all level, there are good wide streets, wide alleys, and no fear of water in your basement. Please call at this office for further particulars.

We also have good acreages close to city limits for sale.

COLIN C. JOHNSTON
INSURANCE AGENCY
14 Young Street South
Chilliwack, B.C.
Phone 2616

The first advertisement for the new Menzies Subdivision, from 1946, notes that the initial sixty-nine lots are on high ground—an important consideration in earlier Chilliwack, given the uncertain capabilities of its dikes and a major flood two years later. Lot prices at that time are equivalent to $13,100 in 2025 value. *Chilliwack Progress* Archive

In August 1946, after much anticipation ("At Last!" exclaimed an advertisement in the *Chilliwack Progress*), developers announced the imminent start of the city's newest housing development. The same early ad stressed that the initial sixty-nine lots were on high ground ("no fear of water in your basement")—an important consideration given the history of problems associated with the community's dikes. Another real estate ad stated:

> This subdivision has been carefully planned and surveyed with a view to appealing to the careful buyer wanting to locate in

a first class residential section. The lots are large, facing on a 66-ft. street and backing on a 25-ft. lane. A few of the lots have water frontage on Hope River. Prices range from $750 per lot up.

The 900-square-foot homes would be built on lots measuring 8,800 square feet. Construction of the first ten units started in March 1948, with costs (including land) ranging from $5,850 for a house with no basement up to $6,900 for one with a full basement. Fireplaces were an additional option.

Construction proceeded under a federal-municipal arrangement called the integrated housing scheme (later changed to the National Housing Act construction plan), with war veterans given top priority for the new units. Homes built in the first phase sprang up on the north side of Portage Avenue. The first house was completed on July 25 at 531 Portage Avenue (known as 46577 Portage Avenue after 1979), fifty-five metres west of Wells Street North. So proud were the developers of

In summer 1948, the first house in the new Menzies Subdivision was completed. It still stands today at 46577 Portage Avenue and has been noticeably improved and expanded over the years. *Chilliwack Progress* Archive

their progress, they had this model home furnished by David Spencer Ltd. and opened it for public inspection on August 14. The modest four-room house was described in Spencer's ad as "attractive . . . pleasant, and comfortable." Work on the second set of ten homes was delayed by

From an aerial perspective in 1954, the Menzies Subdivision appears fully defined and developed, including Mayfair Avenue, which was built in 1948 to connect Hazel Street North and Wells Street North. City of Chilliwack

the 1948 flood, which impacted builders' supply chains. Subsequently, these homes were made available to everyone, with prices ranging from $6,850 to $7,750.

Development of the Menzies Subdivision included construction of a new street called Mayfair Avenue. At 335 metres in length, it connected Wells Street North and Hazel Street North, midway between Riverside Drive and Portage Avenue. In 1951, a religious organization applied to build a small (1,800-square-foot) church within the subdivision on the west side of Wells Street North, near Riverside Drive. Final approval was never granted, as at a council meeting on April 23, angry ratepayers made it clear that they did not want a non-residential structure in their subdivision, potentially impairing the value of their investment. In 1953, the few remaining undeveloped lots were being advertised for sale from $775 to $1,150. By 1954, almost every lot within the development had been improved with a single-family residence.

In 1961, properties within the Menzies Subdivision and the Berkeley Subdivision farther west were described as "premium areas" in Chilliwack in terms of residential land value. It has been many years since the Menzies Subdivision has been referred to by its official name, but it played a major role in the city's growth after the end of the war, ultimately spurring completion of both Little Mountain Elementary School and Portage Park while serving as a welcome neighbourhood for young families.

THE BERKELEY SUBDIVISION, 1948

Demand for new housing in Chilliwack continued into the 1960s, driven by the burgeoning baby boomer generation. But the supply of real estate available for development dwindled. Although total land within the city's boundaries amounted to 1,040 acres, only 100 acres were still available for future development (residential, commercial, or industrial) after completion of the Menzies Subdivision in 1953.

And only one large tract of city land remained for residential development—a twenty-two-acre property one kilometre north of Five Corners that was bordered by Hope River to the north, Young Road North to the east, Corbould Street to the west, and Henley Avenue to the south. The city acquired the lot via a tax sale in the 1930s, when the landowner had defaulted on their property taxes. In the ensuing years, council occasionally allowed hay to be grown and harvested there for nominal revenue. In 1941, Chilliwack High School agricultural students were permitted to farm the land for a "combined experimental and commercial project." But despite the city's continuing growth and increasing demand for housing, almost ten years elapsed between initial planning stages and the full development of the large parcel with single-family residences.

That planning had begun by 1946. In June, in a complicated deal that involved a property swap with an adjacent landowner, the city obtained sixty-six feet of land that it planned to use as an allowance for the development's main road. The street would head east–west through the subdivision, and although it was not built until the early 1950s, council voted on August 19, 1946, to name the new roadway Berkeley

This 1948 aerial photo shows the future Berkeley Subdivision, still undeveloped and being used as the last existing hayfield within city limits. Henley Avenue, although built that year, would not start accommodating new housing until 1950. Royal BC Museum and Archives

Avenue after Chilliwack pioneer C. Berkeley Reeves (1859–1941). On November 17, 1947, council also approved the new Henley Avenue to form the southern border of the new residential subdivision, naming it after long-time citizen John T. Henley (1872–1961). Henley Avenue was laid out in 1948, but housing was not developed on it until 1950. And despite the approval of these two new and integral streets, seven more years passed before subdivision development proceeded in earnest, by which time it officially became the Berkeley Subdivision, harmonizing with the name of its main thoroughfare.

All told, six new streets were created within the Berkeley Subdivision—the forenamed two in the 1940s and four more in 1953. And because the development was oriented to families, plans included a 1.7-acre park. On November 23, 1953, council agreed on names for the four new streets; similar to the approach taken several years earlier, these honoured notable pioneers and politicians. Barber Drive recognized Harry J. Barber (1875–1959), one of the city's most illustrious citizens, who left an extensive, varied, and lasting legacy in the community. This street surrounded the subdivision's park, which was accordingly named Barber Park. Harrison Street honoured one of the city's higher-profile female pioneers, Matilda Harrison (1840–1925). Cawley Street celebrated Samuel A. Cawley Jr. (1858–1947), the only person to ever serve as both reeve of the township and mayor of the city. And Munro Street memorialized local politician James Munro (1863–1934). (As part of the 1980 municipal amalgamation, Munro Street was renamed Candow Street to avoid duplication of names.)

By 1953, bulldozers levelled the land within the subdivision, and gravelling of street rights-of-way started. On September 12, council and the city's planning commission met to finalize details on making the new subdivision a "model residential area." The agenda that evening included regulations governing the sale of lots and what types of house construction would be allowed. One notable resolution read, "That council reserve the right to refuse to sell a lot to any person without giving reasons." On September 28, council spent three hours debating lot prices. Members did agree that if the roads were paved and curbs installed, the lots would sell more quickly. On October 9 they set the prices for the subdivision's eighty-six lots to range from $1,300 to $1,550 depending on their size and location. Council had already received requests for six lots, such was the interest in this new and long-awaited residential development. The city's finance committee projected that sale of the property would net the city $80,000, which it could use to finish the stalled Chilliwack Coliseum project, then in its sixth year of construction due to funding shortfalls (see chapter 1).

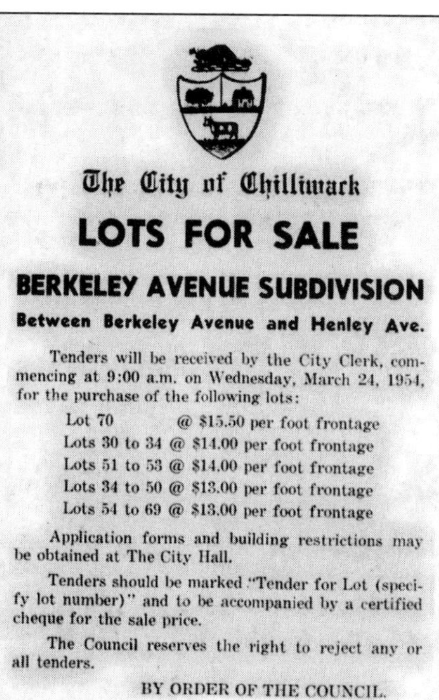

In late 1953 council set the prices for the Berkeley Subdivision's eighty-six lots, and the first advertisement for their sale ran in March 1954. Expressed in 2025 value, their prices ranged from $14,900 to $17,700 based on their size and location. *Chilliwack Progress* Archive

In early 1954, roads and laneways were roughed out. The lots went on sale March 24, but by July 31 only eleven of eighty-six had been sold. In May 1955, the city leased land north of Berkeley Avenue (fronting Hope River, immediately to the west of the Young Road Bridge where the river splits in two) for the purpose of creating a second park for residents of the subdivision. By September, sixty-six of the eighty-six lots had been sold, the two new parks had been seeded, and streetlights had been installed on the new roadways. By January 1956, all lots within the Berkeley Subdivision had been purchased, and most of them were built up with new housing. All of the homes were ranch style or split-level, designs somewhat more sophisticated and modern than the Menzies Subdivision homes, and cost between $10,000 and $13,000.

Over the years, the Berkeley Subdivision aged gracefully, remaining one of the city's more desirable residential areas due to its location and the relatively sound condition of its housing. Berkeley Avenue continues to be the main street in the area, spanning 550 metres between Young Road and Corbould Street. For sixty-five years, virtually no redevelopment of existing residential properties occurred on the main street. However, the status quo gradually started to change, and three new residences were built in 2021 on what was previously a single large lot. This new development initially met much opposition from local

By the fall of 1955 construction of new housing in the Berkeley Subdivision, heading from east to west, was well underway, with sixty-six of the development's eighty-six lots having sold. The 1.7-acre Barber Park and new roads such as Cawley Street and Munro Street were also in place. *Chilliwack Progress* Archive

residents, who cited concerns about traffic, neighbourhood heritage preservation, height of the structures, potential impact on the Hope River, and parking issues. The project was ultimately approved when the developer agreed to limit the houses' height to two storeys.

The City of Chilliwack now encompasses in excess of 26,100 hectares (64,500 acres). Much of that terrain is in the Agricultural Land Reserve, but undeveloped land remains available for future residential construction. This contrasts with the situation at the midpoint of the twentieth century, when land for housing in the city was becoming increasingly scarce. The future Berkeley Subdivision was then just a large hayfield north of town, the last within city limits, but it soon become integral to longer-term housing plans. Today it represents the last major residential development in the city prior to amalgamation.

THE SHANGRI-LA APARTMENTS, 1944–1967

Residents of Chilliwack prior to 1968—and in particular those who were students at Chilliwack Junior Secondary School—may recall an unusual apartment building on the east side of Williams Street North, approximately 100 metres from Yale Road East. Known as the Shangri-La Apartments, this structure stood out for two reasons—its design and its striking pink colour. The building had been constructed as a large single-family residence in the 1920s. By the beginning of the 1940s, the property's owner was attempting to either rent or sell the ten-room house, but had no takers. Eventually, they decided to convert the structure into a ten-unit apartment block, including ground-floor and basement suites. By 1944, renovations were complete (including the addition of a penthouse), and the Shangri-La Apartments were christened at 20 Williams Street North. As the demand for rental accommodation rose, the Shangri-La rarely experienced vacancies.

The city's newest apartment complex had a large, landscaped front lawn, and a semicircular sidewalk around the lawn led to a ten-step

This painting from circa 1960–1961 captures the view that daydreaming students at Chilliwack Junior Secondary School would take in. Both the Dari-Lou (prior to installation of its canopy in 1962) and the looming Shangri-La Apartments (complete with its fire escape stairway at the rear) dominate the vista. The Shangri-La's striking pink colour earned it the nickname "Pink Palace." Original painting by Neil Anderson

staircase and two front doors. The structure also featured a multi-vehicle carport just to the north. Since the building had no elevator, renters accessed their units via a central staircase. The Shangri-La was an immediate hit with the city's newlyweds, and during the next two decades, many couples began their married life in one of its affordable, centrally located (albeit smallish) rental units. In 1960, a three-room unit rented for $55 per month. During the 1950s, the Shangri-La was painted a distinctive shade of pink that made it stand out in the city's eastern sector and resulted in it being affectionately referred to as the "Pink Palace." Due to its eye-catching colour, and because it was the tallest building in the vicinity, it stood out to passing motorists as well as students in the north-facing classrooms within the junior high school, representing a welcome visual diversion from a tedious class. The Shangri-La's striking presence was also on view for patrons of the Dari-Lou drive-in restaurant across from the junior high, as well as drivers and their passengers making yet another pass through the drive-in as part of the time-honoured ritual of cruising Chilliwack's loop (see chapter 6).

Like many of Chilliwack's earlier wooden structures, the Shangri-La Apartments met its end in a spectacular fire. On Sunday morning, October 29, 1967, a fire broke out in a basement suite when a tenant unknowingly put a pillow on top of a lit oil lamp. Flames shot up the structure quickly, and the Shangri-La was soon fully involved. Although the $40,000 blaze resulted in no injuries, it left the apartment building's ten tenants homeless and destroyed most of their furnishings and personal possessions. A large crowd of onlookers gathered to watch the fire and was criticized for impeding firefighters' efforts, ignoring their warnings, and potentially causing further

A 1963 aerial perspective illustrates the Shangri-La Apartments' proximity to Yale Road East, as well as other departed neighbourhood landmarks such as Chilliwack Junior Secondary School and the Dari-Lou. City of Chilliwack

damage and possible injury. There was even one reported case of attempted looting. This contrasted sharply with the Royal Hotel fire in the summer of 1958 (see chapter 7), which occurred when the city was smaller and the times and culture were different. In that case, the more tightly knit community was praised for how it co-operatively pitched in to deal with the hotel's calamity.

As the Shangri-La burns to the ground in the 1967 fire, smoke is visible all over Chilliwack. The large crowd of onlookers would impede firefighters' efforts, ignoring their warnings and in one case attempting to loot the building. Chilliwack Museum & Archives and *Chilliwack Progress*

Soon after the fire, the remnants of the Shangri-La Apartments were razed, and on December 4 the property's owners formally applied to council to construct a new, modern apartment building. Initial plans called for a sixty-four-unit structure, ultimately reduced to forty-eight units. After due process, including rezoning of property south of the site, the new Shangri-La Apartments opened on August 29, 1969, less than two years after the devastating fire. Described as a "luxury apartment," Chilliwack's newest rental building boasted features such as wall-to-wall carpeting, coloured refrigerators, and natural gas ranges. Also proudly showcased was the new Shangri-La's status as the first apartment block in the community "to offer you the modern convenience of underground parking." In 1987, the second Shangri-La Apartments, whose address by that time had changed to

9482 Williams Street, was renamed Canterbury Court and in 1997 became the Mountain Village Apartments.

It has been several decades since the original Shangri-La Apartments, Chilliwack's Pink Palace, ceased to be a part of the city's urban landscape. Many locals are not aware of its existence, as it was gone before they happened upon the scene, but it was a constant in mid-twentieth-century Chilliwack for a quarter century and remains a vivid memory to that era's residents.

THE SOLANGE APARTMENTS, 1955

One high-profile rental structure from the 1950s—familiar to many by virtue of its location, uncommonly attractive design, and longevity—is the Solange Apartments. When it opened mid-decade, the city's newest apartment block turned heads, becoming instantly popular. Developing the Solange was the vision of a local man named Fred Janicki (1917–2007). After fourteen years as a logger, he decided to embark on a career in real estate development and construction, reasoning that this line of work, although not as lucrative as logging, was safer and less strenuous. He planned to specialize in houses and apartment buildings in and around the city. After first building his own home at the northeast corner of Corbould Street and Hodgins Avenue, as well as two others, he turned his sights towards constructing his first apartment block.

In 1954 Janicki purchased the vacant lot at the southeast corner of Yale Road East and Williams Street South, just under half an acre, with a view to developing Chilliwack's most modern apartment building. In April 1955, after Janicki secured a $60,000 building permit for a twelve-unit, two-storey structure, construction started. He planned to name the building the Solange Apartments after his wife, Gilberte Solange Janicki (1918–2003). For several months in early 1955, the building's uncommon name led to some confusion in the community as the *Chilliwack Progress* repeatedly misspelled it, substituting an *e* for the *a*.

The site of the future Solange Apartments is just an empty lot covered in vegetation in this 1954 aerial shot. Owner Fred Janicki would be issued a $60,000 building permit the following April to start construction. City of Chilliwack

After Janicki advised the paper of its error several times, the *Progress* finally corrected the spelling in future articles. The apartment block was scheduled to open in August, but due to several weather-related delays, as well as a fire caused by a plumber's torch, it was not completed until November. However, ten of the twelve units in the Solange were rented by early October, and three tenants had already moved in by that time.

When it opened at 2 Williams Street South, the Solange Apartments block was described as "ultra-modern" and "deluxe." Built of wood with vertical cedar siding and a stucco exterior, it included a four-car garage to the south of the property as well as a circular paved driveway with two entryways, all part of the landscaped grounds. The suites boasted a number of modern features, including a "private telephone," refrigerator, electric stove, and aluminum-frame windows with venetian blinds. They were also promoted as being soundproof. The generously sized units included four two-bedroom suites (990 square

As the Solange Apartments neared completion in the summer of 1955, there was a buzz around town due to the appealing appearance and location of the much-needed residential project. Its look changed dramatically seven years later with the addition of two penthouses. *Chilliwack Progress* Archive

feet), seven one-bedroom suites (850 square feet), and a single bachelor unit (600 square feet). One special feature emphasized in the pre-opening marketing campaign was an "intercom doorbell system."

Given its newness, modern features, and central location, the Solange was considered a highly desirable residence. Accordingly, it was fully occupied upon its opening, and vacancies were subsequently few and far between. One notable early tenant was John Spencer (1927–2008), scion of the Spencer's department store family, future Chilliwhack councillor, and prominent local nut farmer. Upon his marriage in June 1956, Spencer and his bride moved to Chilliwack, choosing to reside in the Solange before eventually relocating to their farm on the Trans-Canada Highway in Rosedale. In 1961, Fred Janicki sold the Solange Apartments to J. J. Krahn, who had immediate plans to expand it. In April 1962, he was issued a $12,000 building permit to add a partial third floor comprising two penthouse units on top of the seven-year-old structure, and they were completed by the end of the year. The penthouse additions, set back from the perimeter of the original two-storey structure, resulted in a distinctive look for the Solange, one still in place today.

After the 1980 amalgamation of the city and township, much development of the area south of Highway 1 occurred, changing the nature of downtown Chilliwack. With the construction of newer and more modern apartment blocks, the prominence of the Solange Apartments gradually lessened. Nevertheless, due to its favourable location and affordable rental rates, it remained relevant, undergoing a major upgrade in 2003 along with a change in management—changes that were heavily advertised in the *Chilliwack Progress*. Years later, residents of the Solange directly experienced further urban renewal when a six-storey, fifty-eight-unit apartment complex called Yaletown Living opened immediately to the east in 2022. Suddenly the "tall" three-storey building that had dominated the corner of Williams Street and Yale Road for so long was dwarfed by the new structure behind it.

The Solange Apartments block, at 9398 Williams Street, continues to thrive as a fully occupied rental building in "old" Chilliwack. At seventy years old, it remains the lone historic constant in its neighbourhood, since many other long-time landmarks are now gone.

For decades the Solange dominated the corner of Yale Road and Williams Street. Today, while it remains the lone historic constant in its neighbourhood, it also stands in the shadow of a newer six-storey apartment structure. Merlin Bunt Collection

Such contemporaries included Chilliwack Junior Secondary School, Chilliwack Senior Secondary School, the Dari-Lou, the Collegiate, the Cue-Ball Billiards Lounge, the Twin Peaks Restaurant, Orchard Park corner store, the Shangri-La Apartments, and the Galley 'n Gallery Dinner Theatre, as well as the three gas stations with which the apartment block shared its corner. It is most likely that someday a combination of factors—the Solange's desirable location, the building's age, and ongoing downtown renewal—will tip the scales in favour of the site's redevelopment, and the venerable structure will be taken down. Until that time, locals can appreciate the link to Chilliwack in the 1950s, when the Solange Apartments represented the newest and most desirable rental residence in the city.

THE FREDRICKSON HAUNTED HOUSE, 1966

In the mid-1960s, Chilliwack was still a relatively small and quiet town, rarely making news on a provincial level, let alone nationally or internationally. But in 1966, a timeless topic of universal intrigue—a haunted house with ghostly activity—gave the community a fleeting measure of recognition far beyond the usual.

When the three-storey house at 342 Williams Street North was built by George Bradwin in 1909, it was considered one of the city's statelier residences, highlighted by a corner turret that was topped off by what some viewed as a witch's-hat roof. The fourteen-room structure (including six bedrooms) was situated on a deep lot precisely where Williams Street North makes a fifty-metre, ninety-degree turn to the west before resuming its orientation north towards the Hope River. Being set back a distance from the road and surrounded by mature trees, the residence made for an impressive tableau in the fall of each year. For its first half century, other than a few sensational rumours, it led a normal, quiet existence. But this changed in 1965 after the house was purchased by Hetty Fredrickson (1921–1994).

The Fredrickson Haunted House, notorious in 1966, was later occupied by a group of musicians who rehearsed in the basement, along with various budding artists and writers working on their crafts elsewhere in the structure. The house burned down in 1975 and was replaced in 1977 by a large residence set far back from the road, similar to its predecessor. Chilliwack Museum and Archives

At well over six feet, Fredrickson was an exceptionally tall woman, and until she was in her mid-forties, she led an exotic life. Born in Java, Indonesia, she and her family lived in a dozen different countries before she turned fifteen. During the last two years of World War II, she was a member of the Dutch Resistance as well as the Netherlands' secret service and national forces. After the war, now living in The Hague, Hetty married, had two children, and started to indulge her love and talent for painting. In the early 1960s, she moved to Canada with her two sons.

In 1965, she moved to Chilliwack with her new husband, Douglas, and their children. Needing sufficient space for a combined family that now included five kids, the Fredricksons purchased the large house on Williams Street North at Portage Avenue, taking occupancy in December. The structure immediately appealed to Hetty, as she thought it looked like a castle, and she was confident her passion for painting would thrive there. Soon after her arrival, she gained a reputation as a "wonderfully eccentric artist": She drove a car with faces painted on log slices mounted on its sides, carried a two-foot-long cigarette holder, and organized mural-painting contests.

Soon, however, Fredrickson became aware that not all seemed normal. Footsteps were heard going up the stairs and walking around in one of the empty bedrooms on the top floor. She and Douglas often heard noises that sounded like the old iron bed and a chest of drawers were being moved around in the empty room. She then started to have a recurring and disturbing dream in which a distressed, mummified woman, with a strong scent of perfume and wearing a red cotton dress with yellow flowers, was lying in some unknown room. Soon after the dreams started, while she and Douglas were renovating the house, they discovered a hidden room that was blocked off with a false wall—a room that, according to Hetty, exactly matched the one in her dreams about the distressed woman. Shortly thereafter, an apparition appeared before her—a glowing mist that eventually took the general shape of a human body—and would do so several more times after that, always leaving behind a scent of perfume. Fredrickson believed she could even hear the ghost's breathing.

As an artist, Fredrickson felt compelled to paint the woman she saw in her dreams. For further inspiration, she sat alone in the newly discovered bedroom for several nights, and one evening the apparition of the distressed woman appeared, again with the strong perfume fragrance. She then started on her painting, and as she made progress, Hetty observed that subtle changes were being made to it, and not by her own hand. What had started out as a female face with a frightened expression was gradually transforming such that half the face was that of a male with a threatening demeanour. Also, she had included a book in the background of her painting, and of their own accord the words "Thou God Bless Love" appeared on its cover.

Fredrickson's troubling painting was adding a new dimension to the mysteries surrounding her house. Each day she added to the painting of the unknown woman, and while she slept at night, it would change somewhat, looking more and more like a man. One morning Fredrickson awoke to find the face in her painting had grown a moustache. The moustache then started to slowly disappear, to be replaced by the outline of a beard.

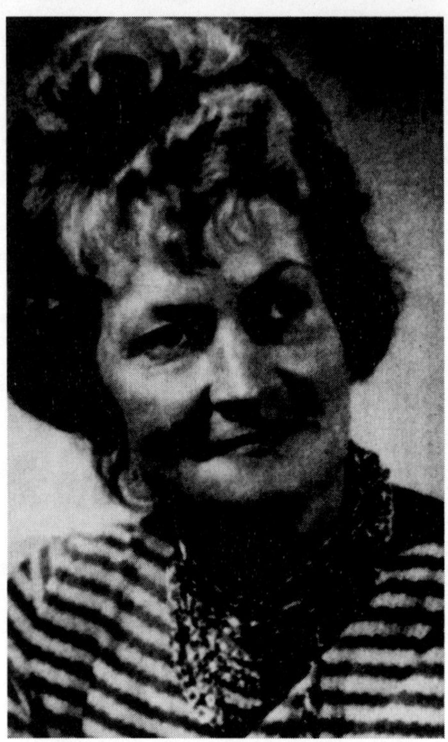

In 1966, Hetty Fredrickson was much talked about in Chilliwack. Her dynamic "ghost painting" was eventually donated it for a charity fundraiser. The painting's whereabouts became unknown, and she later relocated to Vancouver Island. *Chilliwack Progress* Archive

Fredrickson then conducted some research on her home and learned that in 1956, a man had apparently committed suicide in the house. Another rumour, this one more lurid, was that a woman was murdered there and her killer disposed of the remains by cementing them in the chimney. At this point, the general public was not aware of all the strange goings-on at the Fredrickson house, but that was soon to change. The *Chilliwack Progress* ran a regular feature called Community Portrait that profiled a local resident, and on May 18, 1966, Fredrickson was the subject—under the provocative headline "She Likes Living in a 'Haunted House.'" In the interview, she said that she "would not mind to have a logical explanation for those mysterious footsteps and for the dresser drawers that slide out during the night." Various media outlets immediately took notice of Fredrickson's claims and the sensational story snowballed, such was the allure of this subject matter. For the following month, most everyone in the community was talking about the haunted house on Williams Street North.

The *Vancouver Sun*, the *Province*, and the Canadian Press news agency ran a series of stories on the various phenomena allegedly occurring at the turreted Fredrickson house in Chilliwack, which just compounded the frenzy. Some international news outlets also took up the story—magazines in Brazil and Japan reported on the house—giving the city more global exposure than it likely had ever had before. Initially Fredrickson welcomed all the publicity, believing it might draw out the ghost more or help her find out what was happening and why. She even invited two reporters, from the *Vancouver Sun* and the *Province*, to spend one night in the mysterious bedroom in the hope they would observe what she had and then report it to the world. The two reporters did take up Fredrickson's offer, and although there were no ghostly sightings during the night, they did hear some noises they were unable to explain, and a piece of linoleum appeared to have moved on its own. On May 30, 1966, the *Province* ran a story on Fredrickson's changing painting with the headline "Portrait of a Ghost," which added to the mounting hoopla. More and more people wanted a tour of the Fredrickson haunted house—particularly to view the bedroom believed to be haunted by a ghost—and Hetty was inclined to accommodate them all. In fact, on Sunday, June 5, 1966, she welcomed (by her count) seven hundred visitors to her house.

Soon, though, Hetty Fredrickson had had enough of the mounting attention and intrusion in her life. She became weary of the whole subject of ghosts and requested that casual visitors stop coming to her door requesting a tour. She also told a *Progress* reporter that she would not be granting any more interviews until the ghostly phenomena were explained. Yet the very next month, Fredrickson applied to the city for a "haunted house" business licence. Council turned down her request due to zoning and neighbourhood concerns. Interest in the haunted Fredrickson house continued through the early summer of 1966, to the extent that Hetty found it impossible to continue living peacefully in the house she had once loved so much. When her husband accepted a job offer on Vancouver Island, Fredrickson decided to escape to Holland and visit her parents, taking her ghost painting with her. While there, she arranged for a renowned professor in parapsychology to examine the artwork. Although the professor believed "extraordinary spiritual influences" were in play, he could shed no definitive light on the matter.

Upon her return to Canada, Fredrickson joined her husband on Vancouver Island, never again to live in her high-profile home on Williams Street North. At first she let the house stand empty, but it became subject to vandalism. She then rented it to several tenants, some of whom did report unusual ghostlike encounters similar to those Hetty had reported, but they were given less attention. In 1972, she sold the property, and the new owners had a brush with disaster late in the year when the chimney caught fire. Luckily, the fire department was quick to respond. The purchasers resided in the house for only one year before listing it for sale—never disclosing why they chose to sell it so quickly. The subsequent sales campaign embraced the house's history by incorporating the concept of a "very old ghost." This unusual real estate marketing angle was also picked up by the Canadian Press, and its subsequent story perpetuated the saga of Chilliwack's haunted house. The Fredrickson house eventually met an untimely demise, eight years after Fredrickson had moved out. In the early hours of June 12, 1975, a large fire caused by a faulty hot-water heater completely gutted the early-twentieth-century structure.

Fredrickson lived the rest of her life on Vancouver Island, where she indulged her love of painting, passing away in 1994 at the age of seventy-three. Regarding her well-publicized "ghost painting," she received many offers to purchase it but did not want to part with something that had greatly defined her life for several years. She eventually donated the artwork to a Vancouver radio station as part of a haunted house exhibit and charity fundraiser, after which its whereabouts became unknown. The site of her notorious house was levelled, and in 1977 a new house went up on the lot, also set relatively far back from the road.

It has been decades since the spring of 1966, when one of the biggest news stories to emerge from Chilliwack was an active ghost said to be residing in an old house on Williams Street, and Hetty Fredrickson's attempts to make sense of it all. The mysteriously changing painting that she was working on well symbolized the sometimes bizarre narrative. Though the Fredrickson haunted house spent a limited time in the limelight, it certainly left its mark upon Chilliwack's anecdotal history.

Chapter 5

ENTERTAINMENT AND RECREATION

SOCIAL CHANGE WAS UNDERWAY IN THE 1950S, AND A NEW PROSPERITY and consumer culture took hold. As Chilliwack's post-war economy developed, residents enjoyed rising levels of disposable income, more free time, and, thanks to the increasingly prominent role of automobiles in society, greater mobility. More and more, people wanted to get out and have fun after weathering the grim war years. Catering to this need, numerous venues and events sprang up—some new, some revived—that afforded opportunities for letting loose and socializing, from movie theatres, dance clubs, and nightclubs to the agricultural fair, annual carnivals, and parades. This chapter profiles several popular sources of entertainment and recreation in the 1950s and 1960s, beginning with a classic swimming hole.

DAYTON'S POOL, FAIRFIELD ISLAND, 1956–1965

In the mid-twentieth century, many small towns in North America still had an undeveloped swimming hole, often a favourite of local kids. Chilliwack was no different; it had a number of natural swimming spots. Arguably the most beloved was Dayton's Pool on Fairfield Island, a flat, diked farming area less than three miles northeast of downtown, near Skwahla Indian Reserve No. 2. Settlers had arrived in 1871 and transformed the landscape, clearing trees, improving drainage, and roughing

Children swim in the "kiddies' pool" (right) at Dayton's Pool on August 8, 1960, a day when the temperature reached 35° Celsius. At this point it was known that the water was unsafe and polluted, but this was not a concern to most of the swimming hole's users. *Chilliwack Progress* Archive

out some rudimentary roads. Gradually a quiet farming community developed, and by 1892, the district's first schoolhouse was constructed. Dayton's Pool would be situated at the point where Hope River Road, Camp River Road, and Kitchen Road meet.

Dayton's Pool was named after the Dayton family—Bert Dayton (1881–1949), his wife Barbara Dayton (1890–1959), and their four children. The family had moved from Kamloops to Fairfield Island in 1926, purchasing a twenty-acre dairy farm near the northeast corner of Camp River Road and Kitchen Road, with the Gravelly Slough forming the property's western border. The slough was also known as Hope River, Hope Slough, or, to the local First Nations, Sqwa:la. Circa 1929, the township of Chilliwhack undertook a small in-channel excavation of

Gravelly Slough, adjacent to the Daytons' farm, to dredge gravel for use in the construction of a nearby bridge on Camp River Road. The excavation resulted in a body of water that could viably and safely be used for swimming.

With the population of Fairfield Island growing, word of mouth quickly spread about the new swimming spot, and it soon attracted local swimmers. Bert Dayton later completed some improvements to the small-scale, unsophisticated swimming hole. For the next two decades, the pool remained underdeveloped, appealing primarily to kids who lived nearby. But as the 1950s unfolded, this scenario would change significantly.

P. A. "Tony" Jesperson was the long-time guardian and champion of Dayton's Pool. He used his thirteen years on township council to ensure the swimming hole was regularly maintained and improved. *Chilliwack Progress* Archive

P. A. "Tony" Jesperson (1887–1966) was a lifelong resident of Fairfield Island, born on his family's farm on Jesperson Road. He had a fierce love of all things Fairfield Island, and in particular the community's youth. Jesperson also held a seat on the township council from 1948 to 1961. Leveraging this platform, he decided to make the improvement and ongoing maintenance of Dayton's Pool his pet project. He became its guardian and champion, devoting many hours to caring for the swimming hole.

In 1956, Jesperson spearheaded an initiative to enlarge, deepen, and generally improve Dayton's Pool and the area around it. Upon completion of the project, the swimming hole's popularity skyrocketed, and it became well known south of Hope River in the city of Chilliwack. This sudden popularity came with a price, however. On a typical sunny summer day, people would flock to the pool and over one hundred youngsters could be in the water at a time, with no supervision, and they left much litter scattered about. Safe parking was in short supply, and the pool had no toilets, change rooms, or garbage cans.

Soon the large crowds caught the attention of the police, which advised council about the risks associated with the lack of facilities and supervision. The RCMP recommended that conditions be improved, and by 1957 the township had installed boys' and girls' "changing shacks," widened Dayton Bridge to allow a safe walkway alongside the road, and added trash receptacles. In 1958, the township further improved the pool by installing two diving boards. In addition, it raised and expanded the perimeter gravel paths while also transforming the area directly below Kitchen Road into something of a beach, which gave swimmers a safe place to lounge when not in the water. The township also built an enclosed, wooden wading pool for younger children to the east of the main pool area, often referred to as the "kiddies' pool." Many younger kids, forced by their parents to stay in this shallow enclosure, would gaze towards the deeper, open waters of Dayton's Pool, longing to be with the older boys and girls.

The improved Dayton's Pool continued to draw bigger and bigger crowds. Such was its popularity that in 1958, the township received an application for a concession booth to sell pop, candy bars, and the like. However, council rejected this initiative due to concerns about broken glass from pop bottles resulting in lacerations to bare feet.

Although youngsters would enjoy the swimming hole earlier in the year, the Victoria Day long weekend generally marked the opening of the season for Dayton's Pool. Until well after Labour Day, it would be packed with happy families swimming, suntanning, picnicking, and visiting. On the last day of school in June (assuming the weather co-operated), many students from Central School, Little Mountain School, and

Strathcona School would hop on their bikes and head off to the pool for celebratory fun. (Dayton's Pool was just two miles away once the city kids hit the Wells Street Bridge.)

As in 1956, the 1958 improvements to the pool created a couple of unanticipated concerns. Automobile traffic greatly increased, resulting in some pedestrian safety issues, and there were now far more unsupervised young swimmers, raising the spectre of potential drownings and related liability risks. In response, the township secured parking for up to one hundred vehicles in an area off Camp River Road, southeast of Dayton Bridge, and employed a part-time lifeguard. Eventually, instructors offered swimming lessons at the pool. But another problem arose in 1958 that would ultimately lead to the demise of Dayton's Pool.

It had been known for some time that the swimming hole's water was less than pristine, and in June 1958 a number of swimmers reported contracting swimmer's itch, a harbinger of a more serious and long-term concern. The first formal recognition of a controversial and chronic water-quality issue came at the end of the year, when BC's director of health engineering ominously suggested that Dayton's Pool was "bacteriologically contaminated." A jolting headline in the year-end edition of the *Chilliwack Progress* newspaper read, "Ban Dayton Pool, 'Polluted, Unsafe.'" At the start of 1959, local authorities condemned the pool due to pollution. They cited seepage from nearby septic fields, along with manure from cattle having access to upstream water, as sources of the contamination.

Council vowed to investigate the viability and cost of chlorination as a means to ensure the pool met public health standards for swimming, but in May 1959, they determined that the water could not be chlorinated as it would then be toxic to fish. The increasingly frequent official warnings about risks to swimmers' health led some parents (and a few kids) to begin to seriously worry about the quality of the water. However, the majority of young people did not seem overly concerned and continued to use the pool.

By the summer of 1959, four signs had been erected at the swimming hole on the authority of the medical health officer. The notices warned that Dayton's Pool was condemned for health reasons, and that any swimmers entering the water would be doing so at their own risk. Despite the signs, over 500 swimmers frolicked in Dayton's Pool on a hot Sunday, July 19, 1959 (at a time when the combined population of the city and township was only about 25,000).

In May 1960, Tony Jesperson reported that Dayton's Pool was "spruced up and ready for the swimming season ahead." The bottom of Gravelly Slough had been cleaned off by a tractor, so the pool's water now ran over clean gravel. Dense brush had been removed upstream to allow more sunshine on the shallow water. The kiddies' pool had been

On Sunday, June 4, 1961, Dayton's Pool was again in full use on a warm weekend, still with no apparent concerns about the water's quality. Cars are parked on both sides of Camp River Road, despite the township earlier securing parking for up to 100 vehicles in the area across the road. Chilliwack Museum & Archives and *Chilliwack Progress*

sanded and a pipe added to aid circulation, while north of Dayton's Pool, a fence was under construction to keep cattle out of the water.

On November 13, 1961, through a decree from township council, Dayton's Pool officially became known as Jesperson Pool, in honour of Tony Jesperson and his tireless efforts to maintain the swimming hole for the people of Chilliwack in general and Fairfield Island in particular. For the next several years, bacterial count readings at Jesperson Pool ranged from barely acceptable to dangerously high, and regular warnings from the medical health officer continued. Sometimes the public heeded the warnings, while most other times people enjoyed the swimming hole as they had for years. However, when Jesperson died in 1966, Jesperson Pool lost its advocate and biggest booster. His passing, combined with the increasingly negative perception of the swimming hole as seriously polluted, decreased funding and maintenance, and the availability of safer swimming options in the community, resulted in the pool's rapid deterioration.

As the 1970s progressed, township council inevitably decided to tear down the pool's public infrastructure, and the end of the old swimming hole, an integral part of Chilliwack's post-war summer recreation history, was imminent. With Tony Jesperson gone and Jesperson Pool ceasing to exist as it once had, after some time the site's name unofficially reverted to Dayton's Pool, since that was the name the public remembered it most fondly by.

Although Dayton's Pool technically existed for four decades, the ten-year period from 1956 to 1966 was considered its heyday. The upgrading and expansion of the swimming hole in the 1950s, along with Tony Jesperson's dedicated oversight, meant that many young people spent those carefree years mostly disregarding the unhealthy water risk and flocking to the spot. From a young person's perspective, Dayton's Pool had many appealing features. It was well located, the water was generally warm, the pool was open at all hours, it was free, there was minimal supervision, and many other young people would be there.

After the turn of the twenty-first century, the City of Chilliwack formally recognized the significance of Dayton's Pool to the community's history by erecting an information sign to the south side of the bridge on Camp River Road. Today, the former swimming hole is largely overgrown with vegetation and has little water left. Other than the city's signage, there is nothing to indicate what once went on at this now quiet location. But those who regularly visited Dayton's Pool in the 1950s and 1960s can still clearly recall the energy of the spot; visualize the diving boards, the slide, and the kiddies' pool as well as the cars parked everywhere; and hear the sounds of happy chatter, music from transistor radios, and splashing. To those young people, it seemed like summer would never end, and school in September would never arrive.

THE CHILLIWACK DRIVE-IN THEATRE, 1950–1983

Drive-in theatres, which had their start during the Depression, could be found in most towns in North America by the mid-twentieth century, when low-cost land was abundant but entertainment options were not. And in regard to this community staple, Chilliwack was a frontrunner. In the summer of 1950, the Chilliwack Drive-In Theatre opened two and a half miles southwest of Five Corners on Yale Road West. It would become a beloved and classic symbol of Chilliwack—for over three decades an integral part of community life.

The theatre had its beginnings in 1949, when township council received two competing applications to develop Chilliwack's first drive-in movie venue. One involved a location on Young Road South near Brooks Avenue, and the other a twenty-two-acre site on the north side of Yale Road West, just west of Evans Road. Council chose the Yale Road West proposal, and by January 1950, the project's developers had purchased modern drive-in theatre equipment. They were then forced to wait for the winter weather to break before they could start construction.

By 1954, the entrance to the Chilliwack Drive-In Theatre on the Trans-Canada Highway had become a familiar and welcome sight to locals. Ralph Clarke took over operations management of the facility that year. Norman Williams

The new property was relatively isolated, and it would be the only development in the immediate area until the 1980s. Its layout included a long driveway heading north from Yale Road West to a large, fan-shaped area with ten groomed contours that could accommodate a total of 481 automobiles. A tall wooden fence surrounded the property, and the snack bar / projection hut was situated in the middle of the viewing area, straddling the second to fourth contours. Each automobile spot had a metal pole holding a speaker, which could be hung inside the car's window. The new drive-in's dominant feature was its imposing north-east-facing movie screen, visible from various vantage points next to the Trans-Canada Highway. The 1,748-square-foot screen comprised 110 sheets of plywood, all painted white—a simple approach that worked for the first nine years. The wooden screen was replaced in 1959 with a steel-fabricated screen double the size.

After a number of weather-related delays resulting from a wet spring, on July 1, Dominion Day, the community's newest entertainment venue finally opened (thirteen months after the Paramount Theatre opened its doors downtown). Chilliwack's new drive-in—just the second in all of BC—was an immediate hit, as many people delighted in watching a colour movie on a big screen from the comfort and privacy of their own automobile on a warm summer evening.

In 1954, Ralph Clarke (1928–2012), along with his father, G. Harold Clarke (one of the original partners in the project's development), assumed joint ownership of the drive-in, with Ralph taking over operations management. Several years later, he purchased his father's share of the business, becoming its sole owner. Clarke would be closely associated with the venue until its closure. During the drive-in's early years, he staged various family-oriented events, including corn roasts, farmers' and loggers' nights, even dances on a portable stage. Throughout his long tenure as owner-manager, Clarke was hands-on in all aspects of the facility's operation, including running the projectors himself when needed.

Ralph Clarke (1928–2012) was owner-operator of the Chilliwack Drive-In Theatre for three decades. During its early years he staged numerous family-oriented events while overseeing all facets of the drive-in's operation. *Chilliwack Progress* Archive

In the 1950s and 1960s, the prime years of the Chilliwack Drive-In, many local residents enjoyed movies and other special events there on a regular basis. While the Paramount Theatre was generally the venue for debuting first-run films in the community, the drive-in would later screen high-profile movies such as *The Graduate* for those who either missed them the first time or wanted to see them again. In its earlier years, the drive-in's season was generally nine months, stretching from early March until late November, but in the 1970s it would gradually contract to about six months.

With the opening of drive-in food outlets such as the Dari-Lou (1956) and later the A&W (1961) and Dog n Suds (1965), along with the subsequent formalization of Chilliwack's cruising loop (see chapter 6), "drive-in night" was on. Young people and families could have dinner at one of these restaurants and then head farther west to take in a double feature at the drive-in theatre, which was less than a mile beyond the A&W.

Chilliwack's drive-in had a number of features that appealed to all members of the family. The highly popular snack bar would not only satisfy one's thirst and hunger that had been stimulated by the colourful advertisements shown before and between the evening's movies, it was also a place to meet one's like-minded friends in attendance that night. In front of the drive-in's large white screen was a fenced playground that included swings and teeter-totters. If children arrived early enough with their parents, they could safely play there before the feature. It was all an exciting adventure for kids—movies, a playground, and maybe some treats like a Coke or a bag of popcorn. Because of the late hour, the youngest would often be in their pyjamas before leaving the house and be sound asleep when they got back, and their parents would put them straight to bed.

For many older teenagers, going to the drive-in became a rite of passage during their dating years. The term "passion pit" was commonly understood, and hardly restricted to just Chilliwack. A Monday-morning ritual was the "high school confidential" gossip about who had been seen with whom at the drive-in the previous Saturday night.

With the opening of Highway 1 in 1960, Chilliwack's drive-in theatre became a nighttime beacon for automobiles passing by at high speed, their passengers fleetingly viewing the movie on the large bright screen. And, despite a decrease in traffic on Yale Road West because of the new Trans-Canada Highway, the drive-in remained popular. However, as the 1970s turned into the 1980s, the appeal of such venues began to wane. The advent of home-based entertainment options such as VCR players for movie videos, video games, and cable TV made going to the drive-in a lower entertainment priority. The demise of drive-in theatres was also linked to rising land values—as more people and businesses relocated to the suburbs, the real estate upon which a drive-in sat became too valuable to accommodate a venture that was closed for six months of the year.

By the early 1980s, the aging Chilliwack Drive-In Theatre was rapidly losing its functional and financial viability. Over its life, staffing levels had ranged from three to fifteen employees and its patronage had varied from just a few cars on the grounds some nights to being completely full with over 1,200 viewers. Faced with the physical deterioration of the complex, the worsening quality of movies he was forced to show, and the emergence of other entertainment options, Ralph Clarke decided to permanently close his drive-in theatre in late 1983.

Although already shut down at the time, the theatre was to have one more moment in the spotlight. Vancouver's emerging superstar musician Bryan Adams was slated to release what would become his biggest album, *Reckless*, and in the spring of 1984 a video for one of its hits, "Summer of '69," was filmed at Chilliwack's dormant drive-in theatre. In some of the video's scenes, Adams is pictured painting the drive-in's large movie screen. This YouTube video is perhaps the only known footage of the old Chilliwack Drive-In Theatre, albeit in its final days.

By late 1984, Clarke had sold his drive-in property, and the theatre was slated for demolition to enable a comprehensive development plan for the area. On Sunday, December 16, 1984, at 11:00 a.m., the huge screen was brought down by a crane, and the kiosk / marquee, ticket booth / entrance, and snack bar / projection hut were similarly

After thirty-four years on Yale Road West, the Chilliwack Drive-in Theatre was torn down on December 16, 1984, its landmark movie screen ending up on its side. Today the silo tanks of an industrial complex at 44955 Yale Road occupy the spot where the screen once stood. *Chilliwack Progress* Archive

dismantled—a historic part of Chilliwack gone forever. The drive-in's former site and the land around it have subsequently been built up with industrial and commercial development. The spot formerly occupied by the theatre's iconic movie screen is now part of an industrial complex at 44955 Yale Road West. There is no evidence or marker to indicate that an important aspect of Chilliwack's entertainment scene and social history once occupied the site.

Even though it has been decades since the last movie played at the Chilliwack Drive-In Theatre, many people still remember heading west on Yale Road with friends and family for fun times at the drive-in on warm summer evenings. When the night's double feature ended (sometimes past midnight), drivers would start up their car, turn on their headlights, and slowly head out the exit, knowing they would soon return. Back in the day, such was the popularity of the Chilliwack Drive-In Theatre that all one had to say was "the drive-in" and people knew what was being referred to. That would come to an end not just in

Chilliwack but throughout the Lower Mainland, which has lost almost all of its drive-in theatres.

THE CULTUS LAKE PAVILION, 1939–1991

Most everyone who has lived in Chilliwack has enjoyed the natural local gem that is Cultus Lake. A deep, jade-green, stream-fed lake nestled among steep forested hillsides on the edge of the Cascade Mountains, Cultus Lake welcomes an estimated two to three million visitors during the summer months. Those of a certain age likely remember the Cultus Lake Pavilion at Main Beach, perhaps even having attended one of the numerous events held there during its time. The pavilion stood for fifty-two years, generally serving as the social hub for the lake community, and many people have special memories of the venue.

By the late 1940s, the Cultus Lake Pavilion had become established as the focus of the lake community. The pavilion was strongly linked with the tourist/fun-and-sun experience of the lake and also served year-round residents. Chilliwack Museum & Archives

Cultus Lake was formally recognized by settlers in 1862, when a Royal Engineer named J. Conroy indicated it on an early map as "Schweltza Lake." This reflected the name "Swehl-tcha," given to the lake by the Stó:lō, whose traditional, unceded territory includes these waters. The name "Cultus," a Chinook jargon word meaning "bad," was adopted by the Geographic Board of Canada in 1914. In the 1870s and 1880s, some citizens of the nascent community of Chilliwack began camping at Cultus Lake, and by the early 1900s the north end of the lake started to gradually develop in response to the obvious recreational potential of the area.

The first permanent buildings were constructed in 1920 in the Main Beach area. In 1924, the federal government transferred Crown lands around Cultus Lake to the city and township "for park purposes and for no other purpose." That same year, a joint committee of city and township officials was struck to govern the lake, and in particular to oversee its commercial and residential growth. This move was followed by the formation of the Cultus Lake Park Board through provincial legislation in 1932. By that time, the lake's summer population numbered in the thousands. It is in this historical context that, seven years later, the park board built the Cultus Lake Pavilion.

This new structure was not the first pavilion at Cultus Lake. Opened on August 13, 1920, the original pavilion was located near the site where its successor would be built nineteen years later. It was primarily a dancing venue, its season stretching from the Victoria Day weekend in May until Labour Day. Many dances, regularly publicized in the *Chilliwack Progress*, were held at the first pavilion. Ultimately it would be taken down when the new pavilion was constructed, as it otherwise would have blocked the "fine sweep of shaded lake shore" afforded by the new venue.

In late 1938, as the Cultus Lake area continued to develop and gain more year-round residents, the park board had plans drawn up for a new, bigger pavilion. On June 21, 1939, the community's second Cultus Lake Pavilion opened, just ninety metres north of the sparkling lakeshore. In addition to providing a modern dance hall, the new pavilion would house a post office, confectionery, dining room, store, library, and beauty salon. It was described as "magnificent" and "an elegant, verandahed building in perfect harmony with its natural surroundings." The pavilion's formal opening was marked by a grand dinner hosted by the park board for local and federal politicians and their spouses, along with others who had contributed to making the vision of a new pavilion a reality. Following the dinner was a dance that was open to the public and attended by four hundred impressed citizens and dancing enthusiasts.

This opening dance marked the first of literally thousands that the pavilion would eventually host. For much of its life, six dance events were scheduled per week; big-band orchestras, in full swing through the 1940s, regularly resulted in a packed house and a full dance floor.

In the 1950s, the various attractions of Cultus Lake—highlighted by dancing at the pavilion—were regularly advertised in the *Chilliwack Progress*. The pavilion had become so synonymous with dancing at the lake that the location of the dance was not mentioned in the ads. *Chilliwack Progress* Archive

With the opening of Canadian Forces Base Chilliwack at nearby Vedder Crossing in 1942, Cultus Lake evolved from a summer resort into a year-round community, and the pavilion consequently took on a more pronounced role in the growing district. For example, a severe war-related housing shortage led to the winterizing of summer cottages near the lake, thus increasing residents' reliance on all that the pavilion offered. And during the Fraser Valley's calamitous flood of May–June 1948, classes for Greendale Elementary School were held in the pavilion.

As well as being a popular dance destination, the Cultus Lake Pavilion hosted numerous concerts during the 1950s and 1960s. Although its capacity for such events was not large (up to five hundred), the venue attracted a number of high-profile acts over the years. One example was Canadian recording artist Bobby Curtola, who captivated concertgoers on the weekend of August 14, 1964, performing two shows in front of one thousand adoring fans.

In 1972, the pavilion underwent a major renovation as a combined restaurant and dance/cabaret facility. Its new look was decidedly upscale by previous pavilion standards, the objective being to appeal to campers from the provincial park, permanent residents of the Cultus Lake community, and weekend gourmets from Chilliwack. However, the pavilion's once-prominent role in the local community began to lessen in the late 1970s. In 1978, the entire structure was up for lease, and in 1984 it became home to a dinner theatre enterprise. By the late 1980s, the pavilion had lost its lustre and was in a growing state of disrepair, making its future uncertain.

In 1987, citizens formed an ad hoc committee to save the pavilion. Some residents felt that the structure had "tremendous potential" as a year-round attraction and should not be demolished in the name of "progress." Nevertheless, the following year both the Cultus Lake Park Board and the Cultus Lake Community Association recommended that the pavilion be taken down. In response, on the occasion of the pavilion's fiftieth anniversary in 1989, there was a move to restore the structure and convert it to the park board's office, a community hall, a visitor reception centre, and the summer office of the local RCMP detachment. A number of studies were undertaken, but in the end the estimated cost of the restoration project was found to be prohibitive, essentially sealing the pavilion's fate.

There would be one last attempt to stave off the inevitable. On April 22, 1990, at a packed meeting held in the Cultus Lake Community

Hall, the large gathering was nearly unanimous in its support for saving the pavilion, and a six-member "Save the Pavilion" committee was formed to identify potential funding sources to preserve the beloved landmark. By that time, the pavilion had also been identified as a possible national historic site, similar to Chilliwack's first city hall (which was so designated in 1984 and is now the Chilliwack Museum). However, nothing ever came of either initiative.

By late 1990, the pavilion had been boarded up and was in an advanced state of disrepair. The restoration estimate had risen to $750,000, which would have significantly increased annual property taxes for Cultus Lake leaseholders. All efforts to secure sufficient funding had been exhausted, and the park board finally decided to demolish the historic structure. In January 1991, tenders went out for the pavilion's demolition and removal. In response, a number of the pavilion's advocates voiced their opinion, to no avail, that the building's destruction would be a tremendous loss for the community, resulting in the whole area becoming one large amusement park. (This concern would prove to be somewhat prophetic, given the nature of subsequent development around the pavilion site.)

The following month, on February 25, 1991, the Cultus Lake Pavilion was demolished by power shovel. During the demolition process, the structure was found to be in worse shape than previously believed, which would have led to an even greater restoration bill than what had been estimated.

Over the course of its full and rich existence, the Cultus Lake Pavilion hosted a wide variety of civic, entertainment, and personal events, along with the countless dances and big-name concerts. Such bookings included Sunday-morning masses, University Women's Club meetings, PTA sessions, Cubs leadership conferences, and Rotary Club meetings. Other events included film screenings, evening sing-alongs, New Year's Eve celebrations, Halloween parties, formal tea parties, bake sales, the annual Cultus Lake Elementary School Christmas concerts, a hootenanny, summer carnivals, hairstyling demonstrations, art

The pavilion was demolished on February 25, 1991, after several unsuccessful attempts to save it. Today nothing marks the site where the vibrant centre of Cultus Lake life used to be—just a vacant patch of lawn. *Chilliwack Progress* Archive

exhibitions, bingo nights, auction sales, Battle of the Bands competitions, country fairs, variety shows, Klondike nights, choir concerts, and flower shows. The pavilion also accommodated yacht regatta banquets, wedding receptions, card parties, Cubs and Scouts father-and-son banquets, christenings, table tennis evenings, operettas, and steakhouse nights.

The Cultus Lake Pavilion has been gone for many years, and at this time nothing marks the site of the structure—just a vacant patch of lawn where the vibrant centre used to be. But for decades this building was the hub of the surrounding community, integrally associated with the fun-and-sun experience of the lake. Besides being a historic anchor in the minds of local residents, the pavilion holds a place in the memories of countless others in Metro Vancouver who travelled from various cities to enjoy what to them was a great dance hall on the shimmering shore of Cultus Lake.

THE PARAMOUNT THEATRE, 1949–2013

Of the numerous entertainment venues that have operated in Chilliwack over time, one arguably stood out from the rest—providing locals with fun, excitement, a relatively inexpensive escape, and lasting memories. The Paramount Theatre, which illuminated the downtown core, was the community's sixth cinema and by far its longest tenured (at over six decades). It was regarded with fondness, and many locals continue to miss what it represented. After its demise, the controversy and emotions surrounding the movie theatre's fate long remained

The Paramount's predecessor, the Strand Theatre, opened on August 25, 1926, at the southwest corner of Main Street and Wellington

This October 15, 1951, image of the two-year-old Paramount Theatre conveys the dominance (physical and cultural) that the striking movie house would have on downtown Chilliwack during much of its life. Chilliwack Museum and Archives

Avenue, with a capacity of 570. By 1940, it was well established as part of the social and entertainment fabric of the community. However, as the decade progressed, the shortcomings of the aging facility resulted in its owner, Famous Players, making plans for a modern new movie house in the city's downtown core. In 1944, Famous Players purchased a lot on the north side of Yale Road East, west of Nowell Street North, with fifty-one feet of frontage. Two years later, the company formally announced plans for its new Paramount Theatre, a bigger, state-of-the-art facility. However, construction did not commence until 1948, and thus the Strand continued to be the only movie house in Chilliwack for virtually all of the 1940s.

The Paramount Theatre's iconic orange blade sign stood as a downtown landmark and beacon for six decades. When it was taken down in 2012, advocates hoped it could be resurrected in the future, but its weakened condition, along with financing issues, made that vision unviable. Today it resides, in pieces, in a city warehouse. Merlin Bunt Collection

The Paramount Theatre promised to be Chilliwack's first "skyscraper," superlative for the times in every respect. Its restrained facade and interior detailing reflected a transitional period of architectural design, when tastes shifted from the fashionable Art Deco and Streamline Moderne styles to the mid-century modern movement. The theatre was reported to have "thoroughly fireproof" construction, and its striking exterior features included a subtly faceted concrete face, terraced roofline, plate-glass windows, and the incorporation of new materials such as fluted aluminum. But its most distinguishing aspect was its huge, orange blade sign, complete with neon-tube lettering and marquee bulbs. At 55 feet high and weighing 5,000 pounds, this instant downtown landmark was the largest neon sign in the Fraser Valley.

Work on the new movie house commenced in September 1948 and continued through the spring of 1949, including erection of the signature neon sign on April 26. Finally, on June 9, the Paramount Theatre opened at 57 Yale Road East as one of the most luxurious and modern cinemas in Canada. Its interior (accommodating 900 seats—608 in the orchestra section and 292 in a balcony) featured a lobby with sweeping staircases and columns, aluminum railings, recessed lighting, extensive bleached mahogany panelling, chromium light fixtures, and "an attractive powder room at milady's disposal . . . off the foyer on the main floor." The auditorium was defined by its streamlined detailing, featuring horizontal banding that extended from the rear along the side walls to the piers that flanked the gracefully curved stage. The balcony, finished in Douglas fir floorboards, featured frosted-glass portholes in fish motifs, and the ceiling slowly undulated from the projectionist's room in the rear to the edge of the balcony. The structure's air-conditioning system was unique to the city at the time, with cooling capacity of twenty tons of ice per day.

To mark the opening of the theatre, Famous Players secured the Canadian premiere of Bob Hope's new movie *Sorrowful Jones*, also starring Lucille Ball. Opening night was a huge event, and a large, well-dressed crowd started lining up for tickets at 5:30 p.m., three hours before showtime. The throng stretched along Yale Road East and then north on Nowell Street up to Victoria Avenue. Usherettes at the theatre's opening were "smartly attired in bolero type double-breasted jackets," and the doorman wore "a smart navy blue double-breasted pea jacket, with light blue trousers." After Mayor T. T. McCammon cut the ceremonial ribbon at 7:30, the floodlit front doors were opened, and at 8:30 the Paramount's long reign as the entertainment centre of the community began. The new theatre's first year of operation was an unqualified success—over 340,000 paying customers for 160 feature films. Given that the combined population of the city and township was less than 19,000 at that time, this level of support was very gratifying to Famous Players.

By the 1970s multi-screen movie theatres had opened in new shopping centres in Abbotsford, and this emerging trend compelled the Paramount Theatre to add a second screen to its facility. On June 9, 1975, it closed for nine weeks to allow the renovation to be completed. The "new" Paramount would have 496 seats in the lower auditorium and 278 seats in the upper level, a net loss of 126 seats. On August 14, the theatre reopened as a twin-cinema venue with the films *Mandingo* and *Young Frankenstein*, both scheduled for one-week runs. At that point, much of the city's movie-going public felt that some of the theatre's classic charm had been permanently lost in the renovation.

During the 1980s, consumers had many new entertainment options, so seeing a movie at the Paramount became less of a priority. The theatre was losing money, and on March 22, 1987, after operating it for thirty-eight years, Famous Players closed its doors. A total of eighty-four patrons attended the final two films shown that Sunday evening. The owner then listed the structure for sale and, after remaining closed for a short period, it was purchased by an unidentified Calgary investor, reopening on July 10. Landmark Cinemas later purchased the theatre, announcing an ambitious expansion vision, but redevelopment never came to pass due to economics. In 1995, Cottonwood 4 Cinemas, the first movie theatre built in the community in forty-six years, suddenly presented direct and serious competition for the Paramount. Located closer to the exploding suburban population south of Highway 1, with free and ample parking, the Cottonwood featured four modern screens. By staggering show times, it presented ten to fifteen different movies in one week. The Paramount, limited by its location, its age, and having only two screens, could not match this flexibility and volume of offerings. Although it continued to operate, its finale seemed inevitable.

In 2009, work commenced on the new Eagle Landing shopping centre in Chilliwack, one of the largest open-air retail complexes in BC. In November 2010, Cineplex Entertainment opened an eight-screen movie theatre as part of the new mall, called Galaxy Cinemas Chilliwack, for a total of twelve modern screens in the area. Combined with the numerous screens located in Abbotsford, this drew the curtain on the aging Paramount—that same month, Landmark Cinemas closed it for good. In 2011, the owner offered the theatre (structure and real estate) to the city as a gift to its citizens for all their years of support. In a move that was subsequently questioned from multiple perspectives, the city accepted Landmark Cinemas' donation, seemingly without examining all the ramifications. Officials later determined that the Paramount needed a new boiler, a new roof, and other repairs totalling in excess of $300,000. This outlay would have been just to reopen the theatre, and was in addition to the cost of necessary upgrades as well as the facility's ongoing operations. The city decided it could not commit to spending taxpayers' money to improve the theatre. This left only the alternative of demolishing the 1949 structure.

At that point, a groundswell of interest in preserving the theatre arose. Several advocacy organizations formed to lobby the city to preserve what they considered an important aspect of Chilliwack's heritage. In March 2012, city council voted to give a group called Save the Chilliwack Paramount Theatre ninety days to develop a new, financially viable plan for saving the aged building. The group later submitted a business proposal to run the building as a repertory theatre. However, on August 21, the city rejected this final restoration idea and in a 6–1 vote decided to proceed with demolition, reiterating that it did not wish to put taxpayer money into the project. Council also accepted an offer from Chilliwack Economic Partners Corporation to demolish the theatre at no cost. News of the decision went national when the Heritage Canada Foundation formally recognized the cultural and community value of the Paramount by including it in its list of the top ten endangered heritage structures for 2012.

With the theatre to be demolished, considerable interest was voiced in at least saving its neon sign, a downtown landmark for several generations. Fans of the large sign were hopeful that when a new development went up on the theatre's site, it might bear the Paramount name and the sign could be incorporated. On November 19, 2012, the distinctive orange blade was carefully brought down and hauled away on a flatbed truck. It was not in good shape after many years weathering the elements, and because of its considerable weight, the sign sustained some damage during the move, buckling slightly in at least two spots (one being just below the letter *P*).

For the next four months, the aging theatre appeared naked without its familiar neon blade sign. Its bland facade was a stark and unsettling sight to those who for years had considered the Paramount, complete with its neon sign, a small but reassuring aspect of their lives. In late February and early March of 2013, machinery and trucks were brought in and the old movie house was finally brought down. After all the debris was hauled away and the site levelled, the property remained vacant until July, when a community garden was planted. The demolition of the historic Paramount Theatre building earned it a spot on the Heritage Canada Foundation's worst losses list for 2013.

For the next five years, the vacant theatre property continued as a community garden, with no clear indication of how and when it might be redeveloped. In August 2018, plans were introduced for the Paramount Project, a new mixed-use development, initially suggesting the original Paramount neon blade sign would be incorporated in the facade of the new structure. This possibility appealed to many as once again the neon sign would be "alive" and a vital part of downtown Chilliwack's profile. Enthusiasts also noted that the new structure would integrate well with the comprehensive District 1881 redevelopment of the downtown core that had been announced several months earlier. However, stakeholders eventually saw that including the Paramount sign was not viable due to its poor condition and the necessary restoration costs. Also, there were now numerous residential

After the failure of intense lobbying to save it, the Paramount Theatre was demolished in March 2013, and locals got an unusual perspective of the balcony area from the building's rear. After the structure was taken down, the site was a community garden for the next nine years. Merlin Bunt Collection

units in the area, and a large neon sign would have detracted from the neighbourhood's livability.

Three more years passed before material progress was made on the city's Paramount property initiative. On February 16, 2022, after the theatre site had sat vacant for nine years, representatives of the federal, provincial, and municipal governments, along with Chilliwack Community Services, announced that construction on an innovative mixed-use development would soon be underway at the high-profile location. At the groundbreaking ceremony that day, the original letter *P* of the Paramount's iconic sign was unveiled, providing an interesting perspective to the ceremony and resulting in speculation as to what the reclusive sign's role in the new project might be.

On March 19, 2024, the six-storey Paramount Building, situated at 46187 Yale Road, opened to rave reviews. In addition to retail and commercial space on the main floor, it provides sixty-six affordable rental housing units for independent seniors and youth. Recognizing the nostalgic value of the theatre's sign in the community, council elected in 2024 to create a three-quarter-size replica of the letter *P* to serve as a wayfinder for the increased parking options in downtown Chilliwack, a respectful reference to the departed theatre. In October 2024, the sign was mounted on a post in the pedestrian breezeway (called Paramount Alley) near the Paramount Building, linking Yale Road with parking lots on Victoria Avenue.

For sixty-four years, the Paramount Theatre shone brightly in downtown Chilliwack. In an era when the community was smaller and had fewer entertainment options, the popular movie house was an important part of life for generations. Although it was ultimately replaced by two larger, more modern venues, its small-town nostalgic charm is still missed. The theatre's orange blade sign of flashing neon served as a reassuring symbol of downtown Chilliwack and a beacon to many—a welcoming and dependable constant promising entertainment, perhaps romance, and occasionally a refuge from inclement weather. For the Paramount and countless similar theatres in North America, the world changed and the last picture show played long ago. Yet it's some consolation that the new Paramount Building keeps the theatre's name and its historic site on Yale Road in the public consciousness.

RADIO STATION CHWK 1270, 1927–1997

Before the advent of television, radio was the main source of news, entertainment, and communication, particularly in smaller towns such as Chilliwack. The thirty-year period leading to the midpoint of the twentieth century was known as the golden age of radio, with AM radio the main platform. Although television became established as the dominant broadcasting medium in North American culture after World War II, radio remained a constant in many people's everyday lives. It continued to be popular partly because early TV channels had little local relevance, since they were provincial or national in scope (and later, after the introduction of cable TV in the mid-1960s, mostly related to the United States).

Radio service in Chilliwack evolved from humble beginnings to ultimately become CHWK Radio 1270, for decades a part of residents' lives and the station many still fondly recall. As the city grew, so too did the power and reach of the station. Over the years, it operated with transmitters of six progressively higher wattages, from four different locations. And the station was not always found at the familiar 1270 position on the AM dial that it occupied for almost a half century. Over time it used three other frequencies (780, 1340, and 1230), the changes generally coinciding with its increased wattage.

At the start of the 1920s, sales of radios were taking off in North America. In 1925 one of Chilliwack's leading hardware stores, Menzies Hardware, moved to new premises known as the Menzies Block, on the south side of Wellington Avenue approximately fifty metres west of Five Corners. The proprietor, Jack Menzies (1884–1960), wanted to sell more radios from his bigger store but felt there wasn't enough local demand. So in 1927, Menzies and Casey Wells (1902–1976), a company salesperson who was also an electronics enthusiast, incorporated Chilliwack Broadcasting Company to get a radio station on the air and ultimately sell more radios.

Wells soon sourced an old transmitter in Mission that had been used on a World War I submarine chaser. Their plan was to set up the new station's operations on the second floor of the Menzies Block, above the hardware store. Such was their limited knowledge of what they were undertaking, they obtained the required licence for their new station only after they started broadcasting. With the basic requisites in

Casey Wells (1902–1976) was with CHWK 1270 for three decades, rising from a one-man show above a hardware store in 1927 to station manager. He sold his shares in Fraser Valley Broadcasters Ltd. in 1955. *Chilliwack Progress* Archive

place, CHWK Radio went live on June 23, 1927. Initially the new station was on the air only one hour per day, from noon to 1:00 p.m. During that time Wells played records, chatted, and offered local news. The station's daily programming soon expanded to two sessions per day, totalling four hours.

Wells was CHWK Radio's sole staffer, alternating between managing the station and being the only voice on the air while continuing to sell radios on Menzies Hardware's main floor. With its modest five watts of power, CHWK Radio was dubbed "the smallest commercial radio station in North America" by an American trade journal. From the start, the new technology was well received in the community, and sales of radios did take off. In 1929, the store advertised for a radio repairperson, and Jack Pilling (1908–1977) landed the job. It was a fortuitous hiring not so much for the hardware outlet as for the new radio station, since Pilling became a pioneer in Chilliwack radio. Before the year was out, he introduced the station's first electric turntable—no longer would records have to be spun by hand. He went on to become an owner and president of Chilliwack Broadcasting Company and one of CHWK Radio's station managers.

By 1930, CHWK Radio's transmitting power had increased to 50 watts, and the demand for new radios in Chilliwack continued to grow. In 1931, the station relocated to the second floor of the Turpin Block, immediately east of the Menzies Block. For the next sixteen years, its tall antenna on the building's roof was a familiar downtown presence. To mark its move to new premises and enhanced broadcasting power of 100 watts, the station started presenting twelve hours of programming per day. In 1932, CHWK Radio gained a greater degree of recognition when it became affiliated with the Dominion Network of the CBC, allowing the station to broadcast higher-calibre programming. During the week of January 21, 1935, Chilliwack's citizens suffered through a major ice storm, awaking to a twisted, crystal-encased nightmare. For a time the community was effectively isolated from the outside world, both physically and electronically. CHWK Radio, "The Voice of the Fraser Valley," as it was known in its formative days, served as the sole means of communication during the disaster. And in 1936, the station started broadcasting baseball live from Athletic Park on Young Road South, near Second Avenue (Chilliwack was then one of the few small towns in North America with a lighted baseball stadium).

A decade on, CHWK Radio announced in 1946 that it would move to the second floor of a building on the south side of Yale Road East, across from the *Chilliwack Progress* building. The year 1947 was significant for the station on several fronts. In light of its growing reach in the region, Pilling and Wells formed Fraser Valley Broadcasters and boosted their station's power to 250 watts. And on June 23, CHWK Radio started broadcasting from its new home at 50 Yale Road East, twenty years to the day after it first went live. The station's new quarters were modern in every sense, its studios said to be among the best in western Canada, including a new curved wall that enabled superior acoustics. The

On its twentieth anniversary, CHWK 1270 moved into new, state-of-the-art premises on the second floor of 50 Yale Road East, across from the Paramount Theatre, *Chilliwack Progress* building, and post office. It remained a staple of downtown Chilliwack for the next thirty years. J.C. Walker

two-page "CHWK Radio section" in the *Progress* applauded the "finest community radio station in Western Canada." When the great flood of June 1948 devastated much of the Fraser Valley, CHWK Radio again played a pivotal role in helping the community weather a natural disaster. The station was on the air twenty-four hours per day for three weeks, serving as the valley's communication centre during the crisis.

At the midpoint of the twentieth century, with post-war Chilliwack and CHWK Radio continuing to grow, the station's reach increased to 1,000 watts on December 10, 1951. Television had yet to establish itself in the community, so this development was considered important, warranting a banner headline in the *Progress*. With the latest increase in wattage, the station's position on the AM dial shifted to 1270, and there it would stay. For marketing and branding purposes, "CHWK 1270" became a popular naming convention for the station, with the word "Radio" somewhat de-emphasized in its logo. On August 14, 1959, CHWK 1270 made a quantum leap in power and reach, moving up to a 10,000-watt transmitter. Of the approximately two hundred private radio stations in Canada at that time, only thirty-one had transmitters with this much power.

CHWK 1270 featured many popular personalities during its operation. One of the community's favourites was Bill Wolfe (1927–2005). In the 1950s, Wolfe hosted a program called *Party Line* that put listeners on the air live to talk about essentially anything that was of interest to them and the many other listeners. This show later became *Let's Talk*, hosted by future station manager Bill Coombes. To support the community and bring its listeners closer to newsmaking stories, CHWK 1270 often broadcast live from local events. Examples included the 1939 and 1951 royal visits, the big Royal Hotel fire in 1958, the opening of Dog n Suds in 1965, and hockey games at the coliseum. In the 1960s the station embraced the continuing ascendancy of rock 'n' roll, and in particular the British Invasion artists, by not only playing the music but also publishing its weekly Top 50 record survey on a single sheet of yellow paper, available primarily at Ronal's on Wellington Avenue (see chapter 8). Appreciating the increasing role of television in society, in 1963 Jack Pilling decided to withdraw from Fraser Valley Broadcasters, and in 1965 he and Bill Wolfe introduced cable TV to Chilliwack by starting Valley Televue.

As the 1970s unfolded, CHWK 1270 outgrew its familiar home on Yale Road East. In 1977 the station moved to its fourth location, on the top floor of Meadowbrook 5 on Hocking Avenue, becoming the first commercial resident of the new Meadowbrook Town Centre. The station operated there for the remainder of its days. In 1997, after almost five decades of having a high-profile identity in the community, CHWK 1270 ceased to be—it was rebranded as Radio MAX 1270. In 1999, Fraser Valley Broadcasters was sold to Rogers Communications and the new owner continued to operate Radio MAX as an AM station. In 2001, Rogers received approval to operate two FM radio stations in Chilliwack but would have to cease operating its AM station. Thus, Radio MAX 1270 left the AM dial, moving to 107.5 FM. For the first time in fifty years, no longer was there a station at 1270 AM.

The home of CHWK 1270 during Chilliwack's post-war boom period has been preserved in the transformation of the city's downtown. Today it is known as the CHWK Building, situated at 46168 Yale Road, which serves as an integral part of the District 1881 development. Merlin Bunt Collection

From its earliest incarnations, CHWK Radio 1270 was successful because of its intimate relationship with the community. It provided a diverse programming mix that appealed to all demographics, including popular music, religious broadcasts, agricultural updates, live sports events and commentary, listener input, and local news. In its heyday, one could walk down a Chilliwack street on a summer's day and hear CHWK 1270 news coming from every car radio as well as from homes and businesses. During weekends and evenings, teens listened to the station on their transistor radios for the latest hits, often phoning in as contestants to win a six-pack of Coke or Paramount Theatre movie tickets. The success of CHWK Radio was also largely attributable to its strong management, with the station having only five managers over the years: Casey Wells, Jack Pilling, Murdo Maclachlan, Dennis Barkman, and Bill Coombes.

Today the building that housed CHWK Radio from 1947 to 1977 is part of the District 1881 renewal development near Five Corners. Now known as 46168 Yale Road, it accommodates the Uptown Grill and Smoking Gun Coffee Roasters. In recognition of the radio station's significant presence at this site for three decades, and its general service to the community, the structure was named the CHWK Building.

Chapter 6
THE DINING-OUT CULTURE

AS CLASSIC-CAR ENTHUSIASTS WILL ATTEST, THE 1950S WERE THE glory years of American automobiles, when sleek, shiny models such as the Chevrolet Bel Air, Ford Thunderbird, and Buick Skylark roared onto the scene. These were "statement" cars designed for the open road, not destined to sit in a garage. With rising levels of disposable income, more free time, and more mobility, people desired to eat outside the home more often and in a casual context. Fast-food chains, including drive-ins, soon established themselves in Chilliwack. This chapter profiles favourite eateries that rose to prominence post-war, among them the Fashion Bakery, Dairy Queen, and the Peaks and Twin Peaks restaurants. But to start, it touches on Chilliwack's popular cruising culture, which connected stylish cars and fast food for more than two decades.

THE CRUISING LOOP AND ITS THREE DRIVE-IN RESTAURANTS, 1961–1988

Similar to the California town in the film *American Graffiti* (set in 1962) and countless other small centres, for over twenty years Chilliwack had an active cruising route. It beckoned the community's young people to gather up their friends for an evening, in their parents' car or better yet their own, and drive a four-mile stretch of the city's main thoroughfare before turning around and repeating the circuit, all with little concern for the gas being consumed. By cruising the loop, you could see and be seen as well as stop for some always-tasty fast food. At the drive-in restaurants, cruisers talked about sports, cars, music, fashion, teachers, girls, boys, parents, food, adult beverages—or perhaps how life in the small town of Chilliwack was just a bit too slow for their liking. Cruising the loop affirmed the freedom young folks felt they had (at least via their automobiles) or provided a welcome diversion from considering the uncertainty that awaited them in adulthood. Many cruisers were known by their car, and on certain evenings (usually Thursday to Saturday), the city's cruising loop was electric with energy, sound, music, and lights.

From the early 1960s until the late 1980s, Chilliwack's cruising loop was defined by three drive-in restaurants—the Dari-Lou, A&W, and Dog n Suds. Starting at the Dari-Lou on Yale Road East, cruisers headed west through downtown, usually turning in for an obligatory lap around Dog n Suds, and then continued on to A&W, where they turned around to retrace the route. The time it took to complete the loop was often extended by proceeding slowly through the parking lot of each of the three drive-ins—again, to see and be seen. And for variety, when heading west and approaching Five Corners, cruisers occasionally veered right onto Wellington Avenue and then left on Main Street, soon rejoining the usual loop. This detour was usually taken to see who was hanging out in front of Eaton's or Ronal's record store, or to check out patrons entering and leaving the Royal Hotel pub.

A functional cruising loop generally required two terminus points, allowing cruisers to turn around and head back, thus completing the circuit. Chilliwack's loop took several years to develop in this regard. The Dari-Lou was the first of the three drive-in eateries, so it was at the local forefront of the burgeoning social trends of fast food and cruising. It opened for business on September 20, 1956, on a lot across from Chilliwack Junior High School that had sat vacant for years; the cruising loop itself only revved up in the early 1960s with the opening of a second fast-food drive-in.

The Dari-Lou, the first of Chilliwack's three cruising-loop drive-ins, operated for six years before its canopy was erected in 1962. After that cars could turn in, drive through, and resume their cruise on the loop. The restaurant closed in 1988, and a new Tim Hortons location opened on the site in 2000. *Chilliwack Progress* Archive

In 1961, Chilliwack's first A&W restaurant opened on Yale Road West, near the cloverleaf at Highway 1. It allowed cars to enter and head back to town, effectively creating the city's cruising loop. However, similar to the Dari-Lou, A&W was not really a drive-in at first, as it had no canopy to protect cars from inclement weather. But by 1962, both the Dari-Lou and A&W had erected canopies, along with commencing carhop service. Soon their parking areas were formalized into a series of stalls where customers waited in their cars to be served by cheerful young women. In 1965 the Dog n Suds drive-in opened about 150 metres south of the CN rail crossing, and the city's cruising loop, now clearly defined by the three drive-in restaurants, became even more popular.

As the 1970s drew to a close, many cruisers no longer had the time to drive the loop because they now had families and jobs, and a fair number of young people regularly left the community upon graduation. The drive-ins and cruising loop carried on, but the 1980s brought a number of further cultural shifts. Social preferences and technology changed, demographic and settlement patterns evolved, and the price of gas and car insurance rose exorbitantly. As a result, cruising had greatly declined from its heyday of the '60s and '70s.

Similar to the Dari-Lou, in 1961 the A&W opened with no canopy and was not truly a drive-in restaurant until the following year. But it immediately became the western terminus of the city's popular cruising loop. After being a staple of city life for almost twenty-five years, it closed in 1987. *Chilliwack Progress* Archive

For A&W in particular, an altered traffic pattern exacerbated its business challenges. To address an increase in traffic associated with the rapid development taking place south of Highway 1, by 1983 the city had extended Vedder Road to Yale Road West, at a point 200 metres north of A&W. This major transportation change resulted in the majority of A&W's former traffic bypassing the restaurant, disrupting the old loop. Inevitably, Dog n Suds shut down in 1984, followed by A&W in 1987 and the Dari-Lou in 1988, and the closures effectively spelled the end of Chilliwack's cruising culture.

When the Dog n Suds opened in 1965, interest in the city's cruising loop greatly increased. Affectionately known as the "Arf 'n' Barf," it closed in 1983—a victim of social, demographic, and transportation changes in Chilliwack. *Chilliwack Progress* Archive

The one-time cruising loop itself underwent a transformative change with construction of the overpass above the CN rail crossing on Yale Road, which officially opened on December 22, 1989.

In 1995, the former Dari-Lou property underwent a rezoning process to pave the way for its redevelopment. Five years later a new Tim Hortons restaurant opened on the site, and is still in operation today. After the A&W closed, its location became home to two similar drive-in operations, BeBop's Diner and Choi's Burgerland, for twelve years. But by 2000, there were no potential buyers for the property, and the building was eventually torn down. The site has since served as a parking lot for industrial vehicles, and currently there is no evidence that this was once a crowded and vital hangout spot for the city's young people.

After the Dog n Suds closure, the property hosted garage sales and bake sales. Then for several years it was home to Charlie Brown's Market, followed by Alendal Farmer's Market. Today, the location of the city's third drive-in on the cruising loop bears no tangible link to the thriving gathering place it once was. The site became integrated into development of the CN–Yale Road rail overpass and is now part of the loop roadway that extends to the south.

The era of the drive-in restaurant has evolved into one that favours drive-through or sit-in establishments, and the city's traffic, demographic, and settlement patterns have all significantly changed for the better, or otherwise. But for many people, happy memories of cruising and frequenting the drive-ins remain fresh, part of that special time when they were young, feeling independent, and relatively carefree.

THE PEAKS RESTAURANT, 1935–1966

Most of downtown Chilliwack's restaurants from the post-war years are now only fading memories linked to some new development, vacant structure, or perhaps an empty lot. One such long-departed eatery is The Peaks restaurant, which operated for over thirty years at a

As Chilliwack's leading restaurant in the post-war boom years, and located on the Trans-Canada Highway until 1960, The Peaks attracted a varied and interesting clientele. One such diner was Hollywood film legend Gary Cooper, who on October 17, 1952, drove his blue Cadillac to the restaurant and enjoyed a salmon steak dinner. BC History

high-profile location—the northeast corner of Yale Road West and Princess Avenue West, only one block from Five Corners. The Peaks was one of the city's most beloved and successful restaurants, serving as the go-to place for many locals to meet and dine, socially or for business. And since Yale Road was the Trans-Canada Highway until 1960, many tourists also stopped for a bite there.

The origins of The Peaks date back to the mid-1930s, at the height of the Great Depression. A man named Harvey Stirling (1892–1988) was struggling with a failing bakery business in Saskatchewan. Forty-three years old and almost broke, he decided with his family to head towards BC in the summer of 1935, looking for a fresh start. At the end of a hot day on their long journey west, as he drove into Chilliwack for the first time, Stirling noticed a vacant, triangular lot in the downtown area that was being used as a hayfield. Here he decided to build a restaurant.

On December 21, 1935, the city's newest eatery opened for business at 26 Yale Road West, with Stirling overseeing all aspects of the diner's operation. It was initially called Aristocratic Hamburgers, as the well-known Vancouver chain had extended financing to Stirling. The structure, costing $2,000, was completely fireproof, with entrances on both Princess Avenue and Yale Road. The property afforded space for parking to the northeast (adjacent to the CIBC building), which facilitated orders being delivered to waiting cars, as well as takeout service.

With good food and service, along with an optimal location, the new diner was soon thriving. In addition to the popular hamburgers, it offered breakfast and lunch specials, and the interior layout was such that the cooking took place in full public view. In 1936, the Aristocratic's prices for a hamburger started at ten cents, and a cup of coffee went for five cents.

In 1937, Stirling was looking for a new trade name for his restaurant that exemplified Chilliwack. He asked his fellow businessman across the street, Earl Brett, for his opinion. They agreed that the most fitting name was The Peaks, and thus an enduring aspect of Chilliwack's downtown culture was established. The new name referenced the tall, snow-covered mountains that made for breathtaking views throughout the city, in particular Mount Cheam and the seven other peaks of the Cheam Range. By June 1938, the transition to the new name was complete.

In 1941, Stirling closed his restaurant for a short time to undertake a $1,500 expansion. The addition extended twenty-four feet east along Princess Avenue West, towards the Empress Hotel. On June 5, the newly enlarged Peaks restaurant reopened, featuring a modern-looking exterior along with increased seating capacity of fifty-three, about double the previous total. The remodelling included mahogany booths and counters and chromium seats with green leather trim, while the walls and ceiling were painted in blended shades of green. At this time,

The Peaks had twelve employees. Its marketing slogan soon became "Where Everybody Goes," which was employed for much of the restaurant's run, and advertising pointed out that it was "in the centre of downtown Chilliwack." The restaurant's logo featured a stylized *A* in the shape of a peak.

In the late 1940s, both Chilliwack and The Peaks were experiencing strong growth due to the post-war economic boom. By 1948, the restaurant's staff of twenty-two was serving six thousand patrons per week and over one thousand cups of coffee per day. In response, Stirling decided to again expand and modernize his diner. By December, the work was complete, doubling the building's area to a size about equal to its footprint today. With soft drinks being a beverage staple of the time, in the 1948 expansion The Peaks installed the Fraser Valley's largest soft drink fountain, a feature Stirling was quite proud of. In 1949, he continued to improve his restaurant, adding new bakery equipment and an electric oven, which allowed The Peaks to turn out its own pies and pastries on the site. He also installed an automatic doughnut machine just inside the Princess Avenue windows; it was said to be the first of its kind in Western Canada, and many pedestrians stopped to gaze at the fresh doughnuts being made.

Circa 1952, The Peaks took down the Palm Dairies sign that stood above the structure and installed a tall, majestic neon sign depicting Mount Cheam and Bridal Veil Falls, a prominent waterfall east of town. The sign's height and size made it visible from much of downtown, clearly marking the restaurant's location. Like the Paramount Theatre's orange blade, erected three years earlier, the new Peaks sign became a local landmark and is evident in many photographs over the years. As a result of Stirling's continuous investment in his establishment, along with his seasoned management and loyal workforce, The Peaks became one of the most modern, successful, and well-equipped restaurants in Canada. Its popularity in Chilliwack was never higher than during the 1950s. By 1957, with a staff of approximately thirty, it was grossing $182,000 per year, the largest volume of trade for any restaurant its size in the country.

The Peaks's large sign on Yale Road depicting Bridal Veil Falls, with Mt. Cheam in the background, became a 1950s downtown landmark, along with the Paramount Theatre sign and the bus depot's vertical marquee. The sign lasted until the mid-1970s, years after the popular restaurant shut down. Chilliwack Museum & Archives and *Chilliwack Progress*

That same year, at the height of its popularity, Stirling sold his successful restaurant. He was sixty-five and wanted to retire, do some travelling, and generally take things easier after many years of struggle and hard work. In 1958, the new owners completed a small expansion of The Peaks that extended northeast of the elevated sign to accommodate the diner's "Rapid Serv" takeout service. Five years later, the lure of restaurant life drew Stirling out of retirement. In 1962, at age seventy, he and a new business partner, Ernie Wintemute, reacquired The Peaks. They immediately shut it down to undertake an upgrading and modernization, followed by a grand reopening. On May 10, they unveiled the "new modernized Peaks." At that time, the Southgate Peaks Restaurant that opened in 1958 (which Stirling had no business interest in) was still in operation, and thus The Peaks restaurant near Five Corners was referred to in marketing material as the "Downtown Peaks."

By the mid-1960s, the fortunes of The Peaks had been gradually declining for several years due to two significant factors: The growing trend of drive-in restaurants was taking away many of its younger patrons, and perhaps more impactful was the effect of the new Highway 1. For a period following its completion on August 1, 1960 (see chapter 2), the new highway was referred to as the Chilliwack Bypass, as this is what it clearly did. After decades of running through the heart of Chilliwack, the highway now bypassed the downtown area by about three kilometres to the south, and many businesses permanently lost patrons. In 1965, Stirling retired from the restaurant business for the final time. He subsequently leased The Peaks to its chef and his wife, but they could not make the diner viable and terminated their lease. The Peaks never operated again, and by early 1966, the building was unoccupied and up for sale. Soon there were reports of vandalism and theft.

After being vacant for two years, the former location of The Peaks took on new life as the Homer Restaurant on February 15, 1968. When it commenced business at its new location (after four years on Yale Road East), Homer's became the only twenty-four-hour eatery in Chilliwack. The new owners subsequently made a number of changes to the building's exterior and interior, including incorporating a Greek theme in 1975, in keeping with the Homer name. For several years they retained the large neon sign depicting Mount Cheam and Bridal Veil Falls, but it ultimately came down in the mid-1970s. In 2022, after over half a century downtown, the Homer Restaurant permanently closed its doors. As of 2025 the building still prominently displayed the Homer's signage but remained vacant, and there were no known plans for its future use.

The Peaks restaurant building, at 46090 Yale Road, remains an integral part of Chilliwack's history, a visual reminder of the restaurant's booming post-war years. Harvey Stirling operated The Peaks from the 1930s to the 1960s, a period of significant change in the urban landscape and social fabric. During these decades, the restaurant was a prime downtown destination, a community-oriented eatery that became a local landmark due to its location, appearance, sign, service, and

After The Peaks closed its doors, Homer Restaurant occupied the historic downtown building for over five decades. Since Homer's closed in 2022, the signage has remained unchanged as the empty building continues to await a new tenant. Merlin Bunt Collection

menu offerings. A short walk from Five Corners, it literally was at the centre of the city, a location ideal for capitalizing on both the tourist trade provided by the Trans-Canada Highway as well as patronage by a loyal local clientele. Stirling will always be remembered as the visionary and driving force behind one of the city's more popular restaurants, always expanding, modernizing, and upgrading the premises.

THE FASHION BAKERY, 1947–1978

The 1950s and 1960s were arguably the high point in the history of downtown Chilliwack, when the economy was strong and people enjoyed dressing up to go shopping and meet their friends. As will be detailed in chapter 8, consumers had a wide range of retail options in the city's commercial core. After shopping, they often stopped in at the Fashion Bakery on Wellington Avenue to rest and recoup, have a coffee or snack, and just catch up on each other's lives. Such was its standing and popularity in the community, it came to be known as simply The Fashion.

The bakery/restaurant greatly benefited from being in the right place at the right time. For its first twenty-plus years on Wellington, high-profile retail concerns thrived in the area, serving as the magnets that drew many shoppers downtown. The most influential retail development downtown in the post-war era was the new Eaton's department store, also on Wellington Avenue, which opened in 1952. Earlier an ultra-modern Safeway grocery store and the city's new liquor store had also opened nearby, along with another large grocery, Super-Valu, near Five Corners. And Woolworth's department store relocated to bigger premises directly beside Eaton's, also in 1952.

When Safeway opened an even bigger and more modern supermarket on Main Street in 1961, more people were heading downtown to

The year that the Fashion Bakery relocated to its high-profile location between Five Corners and Eaton's, 1947, is the same year that CHWK Radio 1270 moved, and thus the landmark antenna atop The Fashion's new home had disappeared. Chilliwack Museum & Archives / Norman Williams, photographer

shop than ever. And the Fashion Bakery, located between Five Corners and Eaton's, was in the middle of all this retail action. Although numerous bakeries have operated in the city over the years, The Fashion stands out as it was considerably more than just a pastry shop in both what it offered and what it meant to locals. For many it served as a social gathering place—the end destination after a busy day of shopping in the heyday of downtown Chilliwack. Whether they were picking up the week's groceries at Safeway or Super-Valu, checking out Eaton's, Woolworth's, Sweet 16, or Ronal's, or visiting some combination of these and other downtown spots, the community's shoppers often ended up at the Fashion Bakery.

The Fashion had its start in the late 1920s, when J. H. Turpin established Turpin's Bakery and Confectionery at 20 Yale Road East, on the south side of the street close to Five Corners. In 1933 he sold his business to Roy Furnell, a long-time city councillor in later years. In 1936, Furnell renamed his pastry shop the Fashion Bakery and Confectionery. In 1946, the structure that housed it was slated for redevelopment, and Furnell needed to relocate The Fashion. He found a prime spot only seventy-five metres to the west, on the main floor of the Turpin Block, a building J. H. Turpin had built in 1925 and which had been home to CHWK Radio on its second floor since 1931.

In January 1947, the Fashion Bakery moved into its new home at 16 Wellington Avenue. That same month, Furnell closed his business for three weeks to extensively renovate the new space. The remodelled confectionery reopened on February 13 to rave reviews. In addition to the usual bakery delights, it now offered lunches and other light fare. All told, Furnell operated the bakery for twenty-two years, selling it to Truman White on September 8, 1955. White ran the Fashion Bakery (as it then became officially known) for nine more years, until March 1, 1964, when Chilliwack native Eileen Eaton purchased the operation. She immediately closed The Fashion for six weeks for another round of extensive renovations, and it reopened in mid-April as the Fashion Bakery and Restaurant.

During the golden age of downtown Chilliwack, the Fashion Bakery was an integral part of the scene. There were many retail stores on Wellington Avenue, including Eaton's a few doors down, and shoppers often ended up at The Fashion. Royal BC Museum and Archives

As the 1970s unfolded, economic, demographic, and retail trends resulted in the gradual deterioration of downtown Chilliwack. Retail activity declined, leading to empty storefronts and an increase in crime. Contributing factors included the opening in 1974 of the city's second shopping mall (after the Southgate Shopping Centre), Cottonwood Corners, which featured the large department stores Zellers and Sears. The new shopping centre was strategically located south of Highway 1, which was becoming the focus of a major population and retail shift. In 1975, the Sevenoaks Shopping Centre opened in Abbotsford with its own new Eaton's, along with a Woodward's store. Eaton's would finally close its Wellington Avenue store on January 22, 1977, and suddenly the viability of a downtown bakery/restaurant operation had become doubtful.

In 1978, with Chilliwack-area residents increasingly doing their shopping south of the highway and in Abbotsford, the Fashion Bakery ceased operations after thirty-one years downtown. Its old home, the

Downtown Chilliwack—including Wellington Avenue, pictured here in 2022—has changed greatly in recent times, and today nothing marks the one-time location of the popular Fashion Bakery. Merlin Bunt Collection

Turpin Block, met its end about two decades later when it was razed in preparation for the courthouse redevelopment project at Five Corners (as was the shell of the burned-out Hart Block). The bakery's old site is now part of a three-storey office building, adjacent to the city's courthouse, that opened in 2002.

The Fashion Bakery was a favourite downtown institution for a number of reasons. To many mothers it represented a reward for having survived shopping with their young and active kids, and for the children themselves for being well-behaved little shoppers. To many youngsters, The Fashion often meant the same great treat—a glass of Coke and a doughnut, either the usual glazed or, on special occasions, jelly. In later years, The Fashion became known for serving good hamburgers and fries, having transitioned from a bakery to more of a restaurant. Patrons sat in wooden booths in the usually crowded and somewhat dimly lit premises, enjoying their coffee and treats while watching busy city life pass by on Wellington Avenue. Although Chilliwack currently has a number of bakeries, coffee houses, and restaurants, none possess quite the charm and prominence the Fashion Bakery held when it was a central part of the urban shopping experience.

THE TWIN PEAKS RESTAURANT, 1944–1985

During Chilliwack's post-war boom period, two popular restaurants on the same street had nearly identical names. The Peaks restaurant stood for three decades at the corner of Yale Road and Princess Avenue, while five blocks to the east was the Twin Peaks restaurant, on the north side of Yale Road East between Williams Street North and Victor Street. The similarity in the two restaurants' names was not a coincidence—the same man, Harvey Stirling, was behind both establishments. The Peaks, opened in 1935, became the city's premier downtown restaurant, and in 1944 Stirling decided to diversify his business interests by opening a second eatery in the city. He took an existing building, at 176 Yale Road East, and completely renovated and modernized it. In addition to installing new kitchen and fountain equipment, he finished it off with a flashy facade that fronted the busy Trans-Canada Highway.

Stirling called his new venture the Twin Peaks for a direct, cross-marketing-inspired connection to his successful diner to the west. On November 15, 1944, the restaurant opened to popular acclaim, with the *Chilliwack Progress* reporting that it was "well patronized throughout the day and evening." Its opening day generated a 500-quart donation to the Kinsmen Club's Kin Milk for Britain fund, evidence of its proprietor's community spirit. The diner sported a black-and-white colour scheme, a horseshoe-shaped fountain, and ten booths, and provided seating capacity for sixty. Advertised features included "charcoal grill" T-bone steaks and "electric fry" chicken dinners. The Twin Peaks also boasted "ample parking" and was open six days a week, closed Mondays.

The facade of Stirling's second restaurant incorporated two peaks, effectively one-upping the single peak that showed on The Peaks's

Although not located in the downtown core, the Twin Peaks was a favoured dining destination due to its proximity to two high schools and (until 1960) the Trans-Canada Highway. The two peaks in its signage highlight its popular steak and chicken dinners. Chilliwack Museum and Archives / Norman Williams, photographer

facade and advertising. A striking, four-colour neon sign, nine by four and a half feet, dominated the new diner's exterior and soon became a recognizable landmark, like its mate. Although it was not as financially successful as the original, the Twin Peaks soon became a popular and well-established dining institution in the community. While The Peaks catered to the downtown crowd, the Twin Peaks, located near Chilliwack's two high schools as well as the traffic-heavy Trans-Canada Highway, was well situated to profit from both tourists and students. During lunch hours and after school, students would deposit dimes in the mini jukeboxes mounted on each booth table, listening to the latest hits as they spent their allowance on tasty treats. Also, Cubs and Boy Scout troops often enjoyed Cokes and french fries there on Thursday nights.

In addition, the Twin Peaks had sizable facilities for banquets and meetings, accommodating up to fifty people. It soon became the regular venue for the weekly and monthly gatherings of various community-based organizations, such as the Christian Businessmen's Association, Club 28, the Chilliwack Area Business and Professional Women's Club, the Canadian Daughters' League, the West Coast Mobile Home Owners Association, the Chilliwack Motorcycle Club, Toastmasters International, and the Mount Cheam Lions Club.

In 1950, Stirling sold the Twin Peaks, the first in a series of ownership changes. On May 7, 1967, a Twin Peaks patron found a white pearl while dining on an oyster burger, and this good-news story made the newswires. In June 1970, the restaurant underwent a major remodelling and renovation, after which it began to cater social events about town, including dances at the Evergreen Hall and the Royal Canadian Legion. On March 25, 1971, the restaurant gained temporary notoriety and national exposure when a man, later determined to be on LSD, shot and killed his girlfriend in one of the Twin Peaks booths. In 1972, the restaurant was offering smorgasbords on Friday, Saturday, and Sunday.

During the late 1970s and into the 1980s, the character of downtown Chilliwack was changing, particularly the area around the Twin Peaks, and its owners were finding it increasingly challenging to stay in business. An early sign of the Twin Peaks's gradual decline occurred in 1977: Due to mounting vandalism, the restaurant's new owners, Gene and Rose Finley, replaced its windows with bricks, citing their inability to continue paying for new windows. When the city and township amalgamated in 1980, the address of the Twin Peaks became 46291 Yale Road. That same year, new ownership took over the diner, and it started specializing in seafood and Chinese food.

On October 1, 1983, the new operators of the remodelled Twin Peaks introduced a Bavarian theme, along with a new menu. However, less than two years later, they gave up and walked away from the whole operation (leaving behind a number of unpaid bills), and a venerable Chilliwack institution closed its doors for good on July 2, 1985. An increasing level of crime, combined with a significant and worsening drop in business, had proven too much.

Following the demise of the Twin Peaks, the owner of the building immediately renovated the structure to accommodate commercial enterprises other than restaurants. Two months later the first new tenant, Country Craft Creations, opened for business. In 1990, a new TV series called *Twin Peaks* premiered, sparking a wave of nostalgia in Chilliwack for its lamented restaurant of the same name. By 1998, Country Craft Creations became Marie's Wool Shop, and in 1999 it converted 500 square feet of its space to a new enterprise called the Chocolate Shoppe. In late 2003, the combined operation became the Yarn Barn, Gifts, and Chocolate Shoppe, and this business lasted until 2004. Afterwards, a small law firm called Kane, Shannon & Weiler occupied a portion of the old Twin Peaks premises.

In 2007, plans were announced for a 228-unit, four-storey condominium complex in the city called New Mark. This comprehensive development comprised almost all of the Orchard Park trailer park property (including the popular corner store) as well as some structures

By early 2007, much of the real estate on the north side of Yale Road between Williams and Victor Streets had been slated for redevelopment. The Twin Peaks building—at that time sporting signage for its final tenant, a law firm—is behind a wire fence, awaiting its demolition. Merlin Bunt Collection

along Yale Road East, including the long-time home of the Twin Peaks. Later that year, all buildings on the development site were razed, and thus went the last physical link to the restaurant. Similar to many other Chilliwack buildings (and businesses) from its golden age, now only memories keep the Twin Peaks alive in people's minds, as locals recall its great food and distinctive facade and signage. It was a welcoming presence on Yale Road in a different era.

CHILLIWACK'S FIRST DAIRY QUEEN, 1955–1971

By 1951, the term "fast food" was recognized to the extent that it was included in dictionaries. The first major fast-food chain to open its doors in Canada was Dairy Queen (DQ), established in 1953 in Melville, Saskatchewan. Other high-profile fast-food purveyors subsequently opened their doors, including A&W (1956), Dog n Suds (1959), Tim Hortons (1964), McDonald's (1967), Burger King (1969), and Wendy's (1975). About 1953, a couple from Alberta named Joe and Kay Tufteland visited the flourishing community of Chilliwack and liked it so much that they decided to relocate and make their home and lives there. Specifically, they planned to open a Dairy Queen, the city's first fast-food outlet, at the northwest corner of Yale Road West and Hodgins Avenue. This new DQ would be the first in the province outside of Vancouver.

During the week of June 7, 1955, construction commenced on Canada's most modern DQ. When extensive vegetation was being cleared as part of site preparation, the Tuftelands ensured that one large, fully mature tree was retained to provide shade and a pastoral setting for their new venture. The location of the project was advantageous, as that same year a developer acquired the three-acre parcel of land directly northwest of the restaurant to build Southgate Shopping Centre. Thus, not only would the DQ soon be next to the community's first (and, for sixteen years, only) shopping mall, it was strategically situated on Chilliwack's main artery, Yale Road West, which until 1960 was also the Trans-Canada Highway.

On August 9, 1955, the new $18,000 Dairy Queen, at 419 Yale Road West, opened its two front service windows for business. Its first customer was a six-year-old boy who rode up on his bicycle and ordered a banana split. On August 13, the Tuftelands staged an opening special, offering a two-for-one sale on everything the DQ sold. Along with good weather, the promotion made the grand opening a hit, and the response from the community was far greater than they'd expected. From 11:00 a.m. to 11:30 p.m. that Saturday, Dairy Queen served 5,000 customers. A further 1,500 people gave up their turn in the long queues as they were not prepared to wait forty minutes in a fifty-person lineup to be served. Nine employees worked feverishly all day to meet the demand, which included the sale of 2,000 banana splits (using 700 pounds of bananas).

On September 20, 1956, the first real competitor to Dairy Queen opened on the other side of town, east of Five Corners—the Dari-Lou, discussed earlier in this chapter, which staged its own successful two-for-one sale as an opening special. On October 16, 1958, Southgate Shopping Centre opened adjacent to the DQ, three years after the latter's arrival. The DQ was not officially part of Southgate at the time, but because of its proximity, it greatly benefited from the increased traffic and ample parking. In 1960, the Tuftelands sold their Dairy Queen to local businessman and Chilliwack native Dave Boyd (1921–1989). For twenty-nine years the Boyd family (primarily Dave, and later his son, Ron) would own and operate the original DQ, as well as a second and more modern outlet.

Dairy Queen's annual sundae and banana split sales soon became a ritual of spring in the community. Long lineups along Yale Road West and Hodgins Avenue became a familiar sight in the 1950s and '60s as people waited to enjoy a tasty ice cream bargain. In keeping with an older, small-town vibe, some DQ patrons enjoyed their cool refreshments at a pine picnic table several metres south of the structure, below the large tree the Tuftelands had saved for that purpose. Relaxing in the tree's shade on a hot day, they savoured their ice cream while watching the world go by.

By the late 1960s, most of Canada's new Dairy Queens were being built with the capacity to serve the company's "Brazier" menu, which featured hot food such as hamburgers, hot dogs and fries. The Boyd family wanted to introduce the Brazier concept to fans of the local Dairy Queen, so in 1970 Dave Boyd applied to the city to expand the DQ at Southgate to "permit 'walk-in' trade to purchase a greater variety of refreshments." Council approved the proposed addition on December 28, but the Boyds never proceeded with the expansion; instead they made plans to build a new Dairy Queen across the street, sixty metres southeast of the original outlet. In September 1971, the Boyds received a permit to build their new state-of-the-art Dairy Queen, equipped to serve Brazier products in a sit-down restaurant environment. On a cold evening in late October, Chilliwack's first DQ closed for good after sixteen years of operation. The small and aging structure was simply not viable for the expansion the Boyds envisioned.

Dairy Queen was Chilliwack's first fast-food outlet and made a big splash when it opened in 1955. Its first customer was six-year-old Gerald Janicki, who rode up on his bike and ordered a banana split (and got his picture in the *Chilliwack Progress*). Later that week, DQ would hold an opening two-for-one sale that served over 20 percent of the community's population. *Chilliwack Progress* Archive

During the second week of April 1972, the new Dairy Queen opened its new red-roofed, two-storey venue at 45858 Yale Road West, as part of Kamar Plaza. The original Dairy Queen structure still stands, although

The original DQ structure was expanded in later years and the roadways around it were transformed, but the restaurant's two serving windows from the early days still exist. However, there is no recognition of what the structure once was. Merlin Bunt Collection

it looks nothing like it did from 1955 to 1971. After the fast-food restaurant departed, the small building was eventually occupied by Martens Agencies, which operated there until the early 1990s. The structure was then expanded to approximately twice its original size. Later it was occupied on a long-term basis by HUB International Insurance Brokers.

Over the years, the city redesigned the road system associated with the intersection of Yale Road and Hodgins Avenue. Both streets were widened, which eliminated the former customer area in front of the first Dairy Queen, where thousands of locals once stood salivating in line. The redesign also removed most of the paved area fronting Hodgins Avenue, where DQ's picnic table had sat below the tall heritage tree. Southgate Shopping Centre has since planted several other trees close to the old DQ site, but they lack the charm of the original tree—the last remnant of times when the site was occupied first by the original

Chilliwack Central School, and later by the Chilliwack Auto Court. Even though it has been decades since the city's first DQ closed its doors, many who drive by the original structure are transported back to the simpler era of the '50s and '60s, when this was the only Dairy Queen in town, the cruising culture flourished, and there was always time to stop in for a quick ice cream treat.

Chapter 7
NOTABLE COMMUNITY EVENTS

AS CHILLIWACK GREW IN THE POST-WAR YEARS, THERE WERE MANY noteworthy events in the community—some planned, some unexpected and calamitous, and many immensely enjoyable and historic. This chapter highlights several of these events and their lasting impact on residents.

The flood of 1951 is less well known than the flood of '48, but it caused considerable damage and inconvenience. In July 1953, Hollywood star Marilyn Monroe made a quick visit that left a lasting "impression" on one lucky high school grad. Weather played a part in the Royal Hotel fire of summer 1958, when residents stepped up to prevent an even worse outcome. The community also came together for the successful royal visit of 1959, and a youthful crowd were lucky to experience Roy Orbison's 1963 concert at the old Ag Hall. The chapter concludes with a brief history of an enduring local favourite, the annual Fall Fair.

THE FLOOD OF 1951

Chilliwack has had two major, well-publicized floods in its recorded history—the first in 1894, and the devastating flood of 1948. However, there was a lesser-known flood in 1951 that greatly affected the urban portion of the city as well as much of the township. The underlying causes were unprecedented levels of rainfall coupled with aged and inadequate drainage infrastructure. The community was (and still is) often associated with rainy weather, but January 24, 1951, was historic—the heaviest twenty-four-hour rainfall in the district's history (since records started being kept in 1892) fell that day, resulting in 88 millimetres of precipitation in the Chilliwack Valley. The total from January 23 to 25 was a staggering 136 millimetres, resulting in some flooded fields and basements.

In late January, council acknowledged the need for urgent drainage work, for the city's infrastructure could not handle the large quantities of standing water following the recent rains. In particular, the area of Portage Avenue and Williams Street North was identified as in dire need of a drainage system. Officials announced plans for a 1,420-foot, 18-inch drainage pipe to be installed in the summer of 1951 over a 4-foot decline from Central School north to the Hope Slough. However, this future upgrade did not address the serious situation in January, which worsened the following month.

The first part of February saw further deluges, with 287 millimetres of rain falling in the seventy-two hours leading up to February 11,

School was definitely out the week of February 5, 1951, as the schoolyard and streets around Central School were submerged in flood waters. The askew sign to the lower right of the photo reads, "Please Go Slow—We Love Our Children." Chilliwack Museum & Archives

wreaking havoc with transportation and communication lines. The twenty-four-hour rainfall record set less than three weeks earlier was broken on February 10, when 116 millimetres of rain came down. The downpour damaged local bridges and roads, and most basements were flooded as pumps could not keep up. Many people were without heat for several days in near-freezing weather as their basement furnaces malfunctioned. Surface water runoff was slow, and much of the urban part of the city was underwater. Most schools in the district were closed due to lack of heat and defective plumbing. The Trans-Canada Highway between Chilliwack and Hope was also closed after a number of landslides in the Bridal Falls area. The Elk Creek water supply experienced an increase in bacterial contamination after the February rains and floods, forcing the city to increase the rate of chlorination. Rowboats were at a premium for getting around one's property and street, and fortunate homeowners had one tied to their front stoop. Sewage disposal was also a major problem—cesspools were inoperative and toilets did not work, resulting in some sewage backing up into people's homes.

The 1951 flood waters were somewhat higher in the Victoria Avenue East area than on College Street. Nevertheless, boys being boys, many tried to ride through the water on their bicycles, some having more success than others. Chilliwack Museum & Archives

By February 10, parts of East Chilliwack and Greendale resembled a huge lake, with wind whipping up whitecaps. Cultus Lake rose by more than a metre, its water covering every wharf and lapping at the front door of many cottages. In Chilliwack's downtown core, eleven homes on Henderson Avenue and College Street, adjacent to Central School, had to be evacuated. Also, two CNR passenger trains became stranded in Hope due to high water and slides, with a full mile of track east of Chilliwack eventually needing replacement. On February 11, the onset of snow and colder weather finally ended the most violent period of rainstorms the city had ever experienced. However, freezing temperatures soon left the entire community a giant skating rink. Several days later, on February 14, district schools gradually started to reopen. Also on that day, one lane of the Trans-Canada Highway between Chilliwack and Hope was reopened after the landslides in the Bridal Falls area were cleared.

On February 19 a two-man township delegation visited Victoria to seek financial aid for Chilliwhack's flood victims and damaged infrastructure, with the government ultimately offering less than what was sought. By February 21, travel on the city's thoroughfares began to

In early February 1951, temperatures fell below zero, resulting in ice and snow on some of Chilliwack's downtown streets (in addition to much water). By February 21, the city had started the long process of gradually returning to normal. Chilliwack Museum & Archives

gradually return to normal. But in late February, electricians were still working eighteen-hour days to drain basements and restore furnace function and electrical wiring. The city of Chilliwack, along with the rural communities of Yarrow, East Chilliwack, and Greendale, took the brunt of the flooding, while Fairfield Island remained essentially dry. Consensus among locals was that the extent of land underwater in 1951 was greater than during the 1948 flood, but the flood water was much deeper during the earlier calamity, and thus more damaging and costly.

Even with the atmospheric rivers that plagued the Fraser Valley in 2021, what happened in the community seven decades earlier would be unfathomable by later standards, but at that time the hardships were real. Schools, highways, railways, local roads, and some utilities were all shut down for a time. However, people were resilient and they coped, and just eight months later Chilliwack was all spruced up to host a royal visit from Princess Elizabeth and Prince Philip. The 1951 flood represents the last significant event of that nature in urban Chilliwack, since both diking and drainage infrastructure were subsequently improved. The graphic images from that time better illustrate the harsh realities than does the written word.

THE DAY MARILYN MONROE VISITED, 1953

In the middle of the twentieth century, Chilliwack was not known as a place where one might see Hollywood movie stars. However, celebrities sometimes passed through the city on the CN line (trains were the main means of travelling long distances at that time), thrilling locals and giving the community an exciting "brush with greatness." Film luminaries often stopped on their way to Banff or Jasper for vacation or film work, or to Harrison Hot Springs and the interior of BC for some relaxation, hunting, and fishing.

One of the most notable visits occurred in the early 1950s. After making her way up the west coast, on Friday evening, July 24, 1953,

Hollywood star and future cultural icon Marilyn Monroe (1926–1962) boarded a CN train in Vancouver that was headed towards Jasper—and would pass through Chilliwack en route.

By this time, Monroe had emerged as a major sex symbol and one of Hollywood's most bankable actors, starring in three movies released in 1953 alone. One month prior to her Chilliwack encounter, on June 26, she had applied her signature, hand, and footprints to wet concrete at Hollywood's famous Grauman's Chinese Theatre, footage of which quickly made its way around the globe. While in Alberta that summer of 1953, she spent six weeks filming *River of No Return*, the twenty-fifth of thirty-three films she would ultimately make. Much of it was filmed in Banff and Jasper National Parks and at Lake Louise, taking advantage of the natural beauty of the Canadian Rockies (and of Monroe herself).

Before heading for Alberta, Monroe had caused quite a stir in Vancouver. Her plane arrived around noon, and for the next eight hours she enjoyed a whirlwind tour of the city while it in turn revelled in her presence. At approximately 8 p.m. she and her travelling party made it to Vancouver's CN rail terminal, forty-five minutes before her scheduled departure, but the special train was held up for about twenty minutes while Monroe battled her way through a mob of autograph seekers and the curious who flooded the station's entrance. News that her train would likely be stopping at the local station had earlier circulated around Chilliwack, hinting at some sort of visual contact, perhaps even a walkabout. Monroe's movie studio likely let information leak as to what might happen, and when, to build more publicity for her upcoming film. Around 10 p.m. a largely young male audience started gathering at the city's train station, at the south foot of Nowell Street at Railway Avenue, in hopes of getting a glimpse of film royalty.

One of the young men in the waiting crowd was a recent Chilliwack Senior High School graduate named Bob Blessin, who came in from Sardis with a few of his buddies, hoping to see a real Hollywood movie star in person. Finally, at 10:30, the train carrying Marilyn Monroe pulled into the station. Much excitement, rubbernecking, and confusion ensued as to where the optimal vantage point might be. Consensus was that Monroe's car was nearer the front of the train, and thus the crowd gradually gravitated east, slightly beyond the train station building. Blessin was carried along to the front of the pack in all the commotion, and to escape the crush, he deliberately moved westward, to the rear of the crowd. When he was away from the throng, he suddenly caught a glimpse of Monroe's blonde hair in one of the cars farther back in the still-moving train, as she was heading down the aisle. Separated from his friends, and telling no one what he had seen, Blessin quickly moved towards where he expected Monroe's coach to end up. When the train finally came to a stop, he confidently and excitedly climbed the car's steps and waited for her.

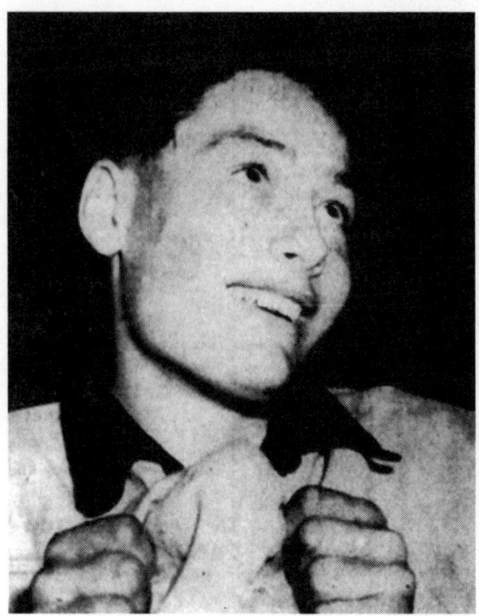

Eighteen-year-old Bob Blessin, from Sardis, became the first man that Marilyn Monroe kissed in Canada, benefiting from a failed attempt to get an autograph. After being kissed Blessin said, "I landed somewhere in Rosedale, I think." *Chilliwack Progress* Archive

When she opened the coach door, there stood Blessin. However, he had not come properly prepared to meet a big movie star that evening, for he had neglected to bring a pen and paper to obtain her autograph. After initial hellos, he asked her if she had paper and a pen. She said she did not, but not wanting to disappoint the first man she met in Chilliwack, she immediately kissed Blessin on his right cheek and asked him if that was okay. He was, of course, more than pleased. After giving him the distinction of being the first man she kissed in Canada,

By thinking contrarily to the excited throng of young males, Bob Blessin was the first to spot Marilyn Monroe and was rewarded with a memory and bragging rights that lasted a lifetime. Rick Horne Collection

Monroe, surprised by the large turnout of local fans, then spent several minutes at her car's entrance waving and blowing kisses to the crowd.

Soon she was back in her coach, and just as quickly as they had arrived, she and the train were gone—she had been in Chilliwack for only ten minutes. Given how small the community was in 1953—the combined city and township population was about 21,000—the news of a big Hollywood star stopping in town and actually kissing a local was a major story. Accordingly, the *Chilliwack Progress* asked Blessin to pose for a clichéd shot showing his now-famous right cheek kissed by none other than Marilyn Monroe. The newspaper also published a story headlined, "Marilyn Monroe 'Wows' Huge Male Audience Here." Reflecting cultural and journalistic standards of the day, the *Progress* saw fit to detail Monroe's measurements as well as refer to her as "voluptuous" and as "the famous ash-blonde beauty."

At the time Monroe bussed him, Blessin had a summer job working at long-time city business George Coombes Appliances & Heating, on Yale Road East near the Paramount Theatre. The next day at work, his employer said he was "still floating on a pink cloud." Popular local folklore was that he did not wash his right cheek for several weeks after Monroe kissed it. He also reportedly kept the *Progress* newspaper clipping close by for a long time to prove to disbelievers that he was actually kissed by Monroe. Meanwhile *River of No Return* was released in April 1954 and was an immediate box-office sensation. From January 19 to 22, 1955, the film played at the Paramount Theatre, only 850 metres north of where Monroe had made her quick visit eighteen months earlier. It is likely that many of the youthful males who saw her at the CN train station in July 1953 took in her movie when it came to town.

Bob Blessin had a strong interest in aviation, and in the fall of 1953 he joined the Royal Canadian Air Force. He served for nine years, becoming a flying officer and spending much time overseas. In the early 1960s, he started a thirty-one-year career with United Airlines, piloting aircraft such as the Douglas DC-6, Boeing 727, and DC-10.

Chilliwack's iconic and beloved train station, opened in 1915 and the site of many goodbye kisses in addition to Monroe's famous hello kiss, was badly damaged in a suspicious 1984 fire and later demolished, never to be replaced (see chapter 3).

Tragically, Monroe died at age thirty-six in 1962. Only nine years earlier, on a warm summer evening, she had caused much excitement in town, in particular making a local's fantasy a reality and providing a memory that lasted a lifetime. When she made her one and only visit to the city, she had just turned twenty-seven, approaching her professional prime. Her time in Chilliwack was fleeting, and there are no known photographs of that remarkable event decades ago. It was a brief, small-town moment from a different era.

THE ROYAL HOTEL FIRE, 1958

The summer of 1958 was a busy one for Chilliwack. As elsewhere in the province, the community was celebrating the centennial of BC's becoming a Crown colony. The various events and mementos included parades, pancake breakfasts, centennial mascots, silver dollars, special licence plates, and a high-profile, ceremonial Centennial Stagecoach Run that thundered through parts of the city on May 14. There was also a touch of royalty when Princess Margaret arrived on July 24 for a two-hour visit and tour. The always popular Chilliwack Fall Fair was set to start on August 13. And two major infrastructure projects were nearing completion—Chilliwack General Hospital was undergoing a major expansion that was substantially finished in the fall, and the community's first mall, the Southgate Shopping Centre, opened its doors on October 16. However, for many who experienced it, the summer of 1958 was defined by a major fire in the city's downtown core, and the manner in which the community responded.

The Royal Hotel, which occupies the southeast corner of Wellington Avenue and Main Street, was completed in 1909 and expanded in 1950. It is one of the oldest buildings in downtown Chilliwack and one of its few remaining wood-frame commercial structures. During its first century, the hotel endured several fires—none more dramatic than what transpired in July of 1958. The community had experienced an unprecedented hot and dry summer, with no rain since late May. Temperatures in some areas of the valley had hit over 100° Fahrenheit, the highest since 1892. Farmers were getting desperate, for their parched crops would soon be beyond harvesting. Locals were wondering how long this could go on and when they would next see rain. Tuesday, July 29, dawned warm but somewhat overcast. As the morning wore on, the sky gradually darkened, and at 10:20 a.m. a thunderstorm struck, accompanied by driving rain and hail. Citizens, particularly farmers, were grateful for the long-awaited change in the weather.

However, the thunderstorm was a volatile one, and ten minutes after it commenced, a bolt of lightning struck an antenna on the roof of the Royal Hotel. The shock of the formidable strike was felt blocks away, with witnesses on the street describing the sound as a "big snap." The manager of the hotel's pub likened the bolt's effect to a World War II

All cars were removed from the Wellington Avenue portion of the Royal Hotel fire in 1958, thanks to the work of fire officials. The fifty-nine-year-old IOOF Hall to the left sustained no damage, partly because of a slight westerly wind. Chilliwack Museum & Archives

bomb detonating. The entire hotel structure shook, and the jukebox in the pub exploded. Lights in the Eaton's store several doors to the east were blown out. But the most serious impact of the lightning strike was that it immediately started a fire on the roof of the hotel. The blaze took hold and quickly spread, with flames and smoke clearly visible.

After a fire alarm sounded, the Chilliwack Fire Department soon arrived, its station being just two blocks from the hotel. A crowd of 2,500 spectators gathered to observe the battle between the fire department and the flames, as the rain continued to fall. Of significance, relative to other fires of similar magnitude in the city's future, the sizable crowd in no way hindered firefighters' efforts.

The Royal Hotel was built with a false attic on top of its third floor, sloping down from a height of six feet on the Wellington Avenue side to two feet facing the alley to the rear. This part of the building was most affected by the blaze, with fire damage to the hotel rooms being minimal. But it was water, more than the fire, that represented the bigger risk for damage to the hotel. The tremendous amount of water applied

The "Mens Entrance" sign for the Royal Hotel's beer parlour remains unharmed while volunteers form a human chain to remove furnishings from the pub during the 1958 fire. Years later, after the Royal Hotel Pub closed, the sign found its way inside the hotel, having been placed directly above the door to the men's washroom at the southeast corner of the "64" meeting space. Chilliwack Museum and Archives

by firefighters made its way down to the hotel's lower rooms, lobby, and pub. The water was a foot deep in the lobby, and Wellington was described as having turned into a river. A call went out for community-minded, able-bodied citizens to assist in removing the hotel's furnishings to the street to minimize further damage. Many in the crowd stepped up, forming human chains on both Wellington Avenue and Main Street to methodically remove all the furnishings and other chattels from the lobby, the restaurant, the pub, and in some cases the rooms. Meanwhile, radio station CHWK 1270 was broadcasting live updates from the scene for the benefit of those not in attendance, such was the magnitude of the event.

Fifteen firefighters from the township's fire department were called in (along with one pumper truck) to assist the city's twenty members. Although two firefighters were overcome by smoke, otherwise no injuries were reported, and apparently there was no panic. All told, the fire departments took two hours to complete their work, but only a half hour to bring the fire under control once they started pumping water into the hotel. Amazingly (and perhaps a statement on timeless priorities), that very evening the Royal Hotel's pub reopened for business. The next day, the air around the hotel bore the telltale odour of the fire's aftermath, and many locals made the trip downtown to view the scene. The damage from the blaze was initially estimated at $60,000, a figure later reduced to $40,000. Not all of the replacement cost was covered by insurance, but owner Buck Berry nevertheless soon rebuilt his Royal Hotel—this time without a false attic on its roof.

On August 9, 1974, the Royal Hotel suffered a more costly fire, but its impact on the citizens of Chilliwack was not close to that of the one sixteen years earlier. As the city was smaller then, and times and culture were different, a more tightly knit community had pitched in to help deal with the blaze. Perhaps indicative of changed local and societal standards, reports on the 1974 fire suggested spectators obstructed the firefighters and that patrons were still in the pub finishing their beer as smoke wafted throughout.

The large crowd watching the Royal Hotel fire is kept back behind Main Street to the west and towards Five Corners to the east, as radio station CHWK 1270 broadcasts live updates from the scene. The 1958 centennial decorations adorning light standards are obscured by the smoke from the blaze. The timing of the fire could have been worse—Princess Margaret had made a royal visit just five days earlier. Chilliwack Museum and Archives

The Royal Hotel lobby currently displays photos of the big 1958 fire as part of a collection paying tribute to its long and colourful history in Chilliwack. Fortunately, an effective firefighter response in 1958, coupled with citizen involvement, prevented what could have been a disaster. And the fire did little to affect the hotel's longevity and spirit, as the iconic structure continues to thrive, now well into its second century.

THE ROYAL VISIT OF 1959

For most of the twentieth century, the British monarchy was of much interest to people around the world, in particular member nations of the British Empire. Every appearance, move, comment, opinion, relationship, scandal, and fashion choice involving members of the royal family was examined, judged, and occasionally emulated, for there was a much higher degree of reverence for the monarchy than exists today. To foster Commonwealth and diplomatic relations, every few years members of the royal family embarked on a tour of Canada, initially by rail and later by air. These tours included official visits to Canada's bigger cities, but the royals also made a number of unofficial short stops in smaller towns. These brief events were important to such communities, putting them on the national or global map and boosting local civic pride. Infrastructure was often spruced up in advance, if not newly built, and the visits gave citizens a chance to directly affirm their allegiance to the British monarchy.

Canada's longest-serving monarch, Elizabeth II, visited Canada twenty-two times as Queen, but only once was a stop in Chilliwack on the itinerary. Late in 1958, Buckingham Palace announced a major royal tour of Canada for the following year, the most ambitious ever to that point. The 24,000-kilometre, forty-five-day journey would take the Queen and Prince Philip through every province and territory (as well as parts of the United States) between June 18 and August 1. At that time, Elizabeth was thirty-three years old and six years into her reign. Organizers were adamant that the trip be dubbed a royal tour, not a royal visit, to reinforce the idea that the Queen was not only a visiting dignitary but also the Queen of Canada. Unbeknownst to those coordinating the trip, Elizabeth was pregnant with her third child at the time—Prince Andrew was born seven months later.

In January 1959, royal officials confirmed that Chilliwack was a scheduled stop on the upcoming tour, with Tuesday, July 14, set for the big event. An organizing committee was immediately struck to plan and oversee the Queen's visit (within the framework of what Buckingham Palace envisioned). Taking into account that the Queen had earlier expressed interest in viewing the local agricultural scene, the committee decided that a six-car motorcade would include a representative sample of Fairfield Island's farming operations, preceded by a walkabout and welcoming ceremony at the city's CN train station. Due to the complicated logistics of the lengthy national tour, along with the popularity of the Queen, the monarch's time in the community was tightly planned and choreographed, down to the minute. The royal train was scheduled to arrive in Chilliwack around 9 p.m., perilously close to nighttime darkness. Nevertheless, a sixty-five-minute program was intricately planned: fifteen minutes devoted to a walkabout and welcoming ceremonies, forty-five minutes for the motorcar tour, and a five-minute send-off.

At 9:18 p.m. on July 14, 1959, a limousine carrying Queen Elizabeth II and Prince Philip turns onto Yale Road East at the start of the royal couple's forty-five-minute tour of the community. The Queen's visit took place in a different and simpler era in terms of security standards—an international figure parading in a wide-open car with minimal visible security, before a large turnout in a small town, is a scenario that would not occur today. *Chilliwack Progress* Archive

THE QUEEN'S VISIT
TO
CHILLIWACK

THE QUEEN'S ROUTE THROUGH CHILLIWACK JULY 14 WILL BE AS FOLLOWS:

. . . STARTING AT THE CNR STATION THE ROYAL PARTY WILL PROCEED NORTH ON NOWELL ST. TO YALE ROAD, WEST ON YALE ROAD TO FIVE CORNERS, NORTH ON YOUNG ST. TO THE HOPE RIVER ROAD, EAST ALONG THE HOPE RIVER TO McCONNEL ROAD, WEST ON McCONNEL, THEN SOUTH ON McCONNEL AND GILLANDERS TO THE TRANS-CANADA HIGHWAY, THEN WEST ON THE TRANS-CANADA HIGHWAY TO NOWELL, AND SOUTH ON NOWELL TO THE CNR STATION.

THE SLOWEST PART OF THE ABOVE TOUR WILL BE:

- From the CNR Station Through Five Corners to the Corner of Young St. North to Young Road Bridge.
- From the Corner of Yale Road East and Woodbine Back to the CNR Station — End of the Tour.

The organizing committee for the 1959 royal visit ensured every detail was addressed, including numerous communications with the public regarding the parade route, how to decorate homes along the way, how to act, and so on. *Chilliwack Progress* Archive

Large crowds were expected to line the parade route, and to give them a chance to be relatively close to the Queen, the organizing committee made two decisions. First, no parking would be permitted along Nowell Street up to the Young Road Bridge from 5 p.m., with any violators being immediately towed. Second, it designated two speed zones for the cavalcade—5 to 8 miles per hour from the CN station to the Young Road Bridge, 20 to 30 miles per hour for the rural portion of the drive, and then resuming the slower speed at Woodbine Street until the royals returned to the train station.

Finally, the big day arrived and weather conditions were ideal—clear with a high of 75° Fahrenheit. As early as 6 p.m., a large crowd started to form at the CN station, and by 7:30, people were lining the parade route from Nowell Street up to the Young Road Bridge. The train station was appropriately decorated with flags and bunting, and five hundred daisies surrounded the reception stage. The royal train had earlier left an official stop in Kamloops, with subsequent ten-minute stops in Boston Bar and Hope. As 9 p.m. approached, the train's light and horn could be detected in the distance to the east.

With the energy of the crowd surging, right on schedule the sixteen-car train, powered by three diesels, pulled into the station with the royal couple in the final coach. Mounties jumped from several cars, along with royal tour officials, journalists, and photographers, and a band on hand struck up a lively march. As soon as the train came to a full stop, the royal couple appeared on its rear deck to thunderous cheering, at which point the band played "God Save the Queen." Elizabeth descended from the deck, and with Prince Philip slightly behind her, she completed a short walkabout along the station's platform, close to literally thousands of adoring fans. In the first row of the crowd, many young children had been sitting in little chairs their parents had brought to help them cope with the long wait to get a close look at the royal couple.

After completing their brief walkabout, Elizabeth and Philip stepped across the red velvet carpet that had been laid for the event and ascended to the raised reception stage, where the Queen was presented with a bouquet of flowers. At that point, eighteen dignitaries, mostly Fraser Valley mayors or reeves and their wives, were presented to the royal couple. After the formal introductions and a few brief speeches, the royals signed the city's and township's guest books. After formalities concluded on the stage at precisely 9:15, the motorcade headed north on Nowell Street in the advancing twilight, with Elizabeth and Philip in a shiny black, open, and brightly lit limousine. The royal vehicle was preceded by an RCMP pilot car for the entire route. Also, the Queen's security detail, sensing a degree of informality, allowed crowds at the train station and along the motorcade route to press as close to the couple as possible.

What was described at the time as the biggest-ever crowd to assemble in the downtown area was five deep on most of the slower parts of the route. Street corners were packed, and many royal enthusiasts were stationed atop office buildings. The downtown crowd included seventy RCMP members in their scarlet tunics, along with four hundred soldiers from CFB Chilliwack, who saluted the royal car as it passed by. As the cavalcade headed north on Young Road, it passed Central School, where a sizable contingent of Brownies, Cubs, Boy Scouts, Girl Guides, and Canadian Girls in Training members cheered and waved Union Jack flags. Homes along the route were decorated with flags, bunting, and signs of welcome, as requested by the event's organizers. On the Fairfield Island portion of the route, the royal car repeatedly slowed down for large groups of fans who had waited for a chance to see the royal couple. It was a perfect evening for a starlit motorcade tour, although towards the end of the ride the air became somewhat chilly.

The Queen had arrived in Chilliwack wearing a mink stole, and although she removed it for the onstage festivities, she wore it for the rest of the evening once the cavalcade started. The royals arrived back at the train station after their nineteen-kilometre trip at 10 p.m., with stars sparkling in the otherwise dark sky and the Queen still holding the bouquet of flowers she had received earlier. Officials thanked Elizabeth and Philip, giving them an appropriate farewell as they stood on the rear deck of the royal coach. As the train slowly pulled out at 10:05, they remained on the deck waving to the remaining crowd until the coach disappeared out of sight to the west. The royal train then headed to New Westminster, where it remained for the evening.

The Queen and Prince Philip's visit to Chilliwack, just over an hour long, was judged a success by all who were associated with it. Thousands saw the royal couple up close and were impressed by their charm, wit, and warmth. The next day's edition of the *Chilliwack Progress* was full of positive stories and photographs. That this royal visit came off so well was attributed largely to the detailed planning of the organizing committee, which communicated early and often with the community about where they should be to view the monarch, how they should act, how they should decorate their homes, and so on. The visit took place in a different and simpler era in terms of interest in the monarchy, cultural values, entertainment options, and security standards. Organizers estimated that 25,000 people enjoyed the 1959 royal visit to Chilliwack (5,000 at the CN station and 20,000 on the cavalcade route), a crowd equivalent to the community's entire population at that time.

Royal train tours and stops are now a relic of a bygone era. But for one brief moment at the end of the 1950s, Chilliwack experienced all of the pageantry, excitement, pride, and attention that went with a visit

At 10:03 p.m., Queen Elizabeth and Prince Philip stand on the rear deck of the royal train, about to depart the CN station for New Westminster after a successful visit to Chilliwack. By share of the local population, the estimated 25,000 people who turned out for the spectacle is equivalent to 100,000 attending an event in the city today. Chilliwack Museum & Archives

from royalty. Many who were there that evening still fondly recall the aura of the event, which provided what for most was a once-in-a-lifetime experience.

ROY ORBISON LIVE AT THE AG HALL, 1963

The great Roy Orbison (1936–1988), a member of the Rock and Roll Hall of Fame, once performed in Chilliwack. An artist of his calibre appearing in the city is interesting enough, but the timing of his show is even more noteworthy and, in retrospect, improbable. Orbison's performance took place only five months after he completed a tour in England with the Beatles in which he was the co-headliner. It was also less than ten months before he had the number-one record in the world.

Orbison's concert was a fateful stroke of scheduling luck for the community's music fans, a "calm between the storms."

That he so quickly went from headlining with the Beatles in major centres in England to performing in smaller communities in BC was largely attributable to his relationship with Red Robinson, the rock 'n' roll broadcasting and promotion legend. The first radio personality to air rock 'n' roll music in Vancouver, Robinson later staged shows around the province featuring established or up-and-coming performers that he brought in.

America's No. 1 Song Stylist
ROY ORBISON
plus BOB LUMAN
CHILLIWACK AGRICULTURAL HALL
SATURDAY, NOVEMBER 9th
SHOW 7 - 9 p.m. ★ DANCE 9 - 12 p.m.
Advance Tickets available at McAlpine's

Publicity for Roy Orbison's upcoming appearance in Chilliwack was minimal and there was no report on the show afterwards. An editing oversight in the only advertisement suggested that the dance portion of the evening would go on for fifteen hours, ending at noon the next day. Somewhat surprisingly, McAlpine's is listed as the only place where advance tickets can be obtained, not Ronal's. *Chilliwack Progress* Archive

Being just one year apart in age and having hit it off from the start, Robinson booked Orbison for several performances in 1962. His first show, at Vancouver's PNE Garden Auditorium, was the first time he had ever performed outside of the US. Later in 1962, Robinson and his fellow promoter Les Vogt brought Orbison back to BC for more shows. After another successful performance, this one in Port Alberni, they gave Orbison a bonus of $1,000 to express their appreciation for him touring Vancouver Island. This was the first and only time in his career that promoters ever gave him more than the performance contract called for, and he never forgot the gesture. For the rest of his career, whenever Orbison toured Canada, he insisted that Robinson promote any of his shows near the West Coast.

In late spring 1963, Orbison's popularity in England was soaring, much more than in the US and Canada. He was asked to join a UK concert tour featuring the rapidly rising Beatles and Gerry and the Pacemakers. On the first night, Orbison went on just before the Beatles and ended up performing fourteen encores before they could get onstage. On a flight in England during this tour, a seemingly innocuous incident led to Orbison developing a performing trademark. Inadvertently leaving his regular glasses on an airplane and due to go onstage shortly, but unable to see without corrective lenses, he was forced to wear his only other pair of glasses—his dark prescription Wayfarer sunglasses. Since he was shy and subject to severe stage fright, he found that wearing sunglasses helped him in this regard. He ended up wearing the dark glasses for the rest of the tour and ultimately for the rest of his career, with the look becoming an integral aspect of his persona. The sunglasses, along with his black clothes and song lyrics dealing with mystery and introversion, all contributed to eventually making Orbison a global star.

The month following his show in Chilliwack, Roy Orbison concluded his busy year by performing in Port Alberni, this time in a sold-out New Year's Eve show. The next morning, January 1, 1964, Red Robinson drove his good friend Orbison and Bobby Goldsboro to the Nanaimo ferry in his 1962 Grand Parisienne convertible, and black ice on the road almost put them in Cameron Lake a few times, much to Orbison's uneasiness. CBC/Red Robinson Collection

Buoyed by the success of the Beatles tour and his summer 1963 release of two more hits, Orbison toured Britain again in September–October. This time there were no Beatles to contend with and he was the undisputed headliner. After his sold-out British tour, Orbison was scheduled for some Canadian dates, including several in BC—again as a favour to Robinson.

A show was scheduled for Chilliwack on Saturday evening, November 9. Similar to the format of his other smaller-town engagements at that time, it was a "Show & Dance" event, with the artists performing between 7 and 9 p.m., followed by a dance ending at midnight. The concert/dance was booked for the aging Agricultural Hall at Chilliwack's fairgrounds. Two acts were to precede Orbison: The opening artist was The Newbeats, a group from Texas best known for their 1964 hit "Bread and Butter," and following The Newbeats was Bob Luman, a country and rockabilly singer also from Orbison's home state of Texas. Orbison's regular touring band was called the Candymen, named after his 1961 hit "Candy Man." One member of the group who enjoyed future international success was Bobby Goldsboro, an accomplished guitar player who stayed with the Candymen until 1964, when he embarked on a solo career that resulted in sixteen Top 40 hits.

Advance publicity for one of the most significant shows in Chilliwack's history was minimal. There was just one advertisement for the event, appearing in the *Chilliwack Progress* on the three Wednesdays preceding the concert. The simple text-only ad referred to the twenty-six-year-old Orbison as "America's No. 1 Song Stylist." While the advertisement said Bob Luman was also performing, it made no mention of the other supporting act, the Newbeats.

By all accounts, Orbison, backed by the Candymen, delivered a great performance that evening. Comments from attendees suggest that the Ag Hall's acoustics were satisfactory and Orbison had no problem hitting the high notes in hits such as "Only the Lonely" and "Leah." Others at the show were initially puzzled as to why Orbison just stood in one spot in front of the microphone with minimal movement while he sang his songs, but they soon realized that was how he expressed the heartfelt emotions inherent in his lyrics, and nothing else in terms of stage presence was needed. Many felt privileged to have seen such an artist in their hometown.

The rickety, aging Ag Hall hosted numerous dances and concerts over the years, few more popular than Roy Orbison in 1963. Four years later, it would be converted to Evergreen Hall.

Chilliwack Museum & Archives

In addition to Orbison, another celebrity was in the Ag Hall that November evening. After Orbison finished the concert, backstage was buzzing as preparations for the dance segment of the event were being finalized. A rather large man appeared and asked if he could see Orbison. It was Johnny Cash, who was in Vancouver to do a show of his own and had driven out to Chilliwack to see his good friend.

In 1964, Orbison was again on the road, doing another tour in the UK as well as a tour of Australia with the Rolling Stones at the end of the year. That summer he and his new writing partner, Bill Dees, wrote a song called "Pretty Woman," which was released as a single in August and soared to No. 1 around the world, selling an estimated seven million copies in 1964. And yet just eleven months earlier, Orbison had played Chilliwack's rickety Agricultural Hall. The success of "Pretty Woman" resulted in Orbison's one and only appearance on *The Ed Sullivan Show*, on October 11. In his trademark black suit and dark sunglasses, Orbison sang his biggest hit live on the same stage where his friends the Beatles had made their North American breakthrough eight months earlier.

The world lost Roy Orbison long before his time. Two days after playing a concert in Ohio, he died of a heart attack on December 6, 1988, at age fifty-two. He was at home, preparing to head off for another tour of England. At the time of his performance at the local Ag Hall, nobody foresaw how big he would soon become. But for a brief moment, between his career-boosting Beatles tour and having the number-one record in the world, the small community of Chilliwack played host to a future musical legend with one of the greatest voices many have ever heard.

(To put the era into historical context, on November 9, 1963, President Kennedy was still in the White House, just thirteen days from his assassination. Three weeks later, the BC Lions played in their first Grey Cup game in Vancouver's Empire Stadium. And three months after Orbison played in Chilliwack, the Beatles made their transformational North American debut on national TV before record viewership.)

Surprisingly, there are no known photographs or written accounts of Orbison's performance in Chilliwack. The *Chilliwack Progress* never reviewed or referred to the show in subsequent editions, almost as if it never took place. However, for the large crowd of young people who attended the event, it was a wonderful evening of entertainment, headlined by a future Rock and Roll Hall of Fame inductee, followed by three hours of energetic dancing. Though Orbison's time in Chilliwack was fleeting, he left an indelible mark on his local fans that special evening.

CHILLIWACK'S LONG-RUNNING FALL FAIR

The Chilliwack Fall Fair is BC's third-oldest community fair, behind those of Cowichan and Saanich. For multiple generations, this annual three-day event has been (and still is) anticipated by locals with much pride and excitement. The fair has a broad appeal, offering midway rides, exhibitions of agricultural produce and livestock, tasty junk food, concerts, races of various types, games of chance, and opportunities to socialize. Its origins date back to when Chilliwack was an agricultural-based economy and society. To showcase their production, early settlers staged the first Chilliwack Agricultural Exhibition in September 1872 on Jonathan Reece's farm, with his great barn serving as the focal point. Given the success of the inaugural exhibition and the continued emergence of the valley's agricultural sector, prominent local farmers formed the Chilliwack Agricultural Society on May 7, 1873, with Reece appointed its first president. From that point onwards, the feature event on the society's annual agenda was the Agricultural Exhibition, eventually to be known as the Fall Fair.

For its first twelve years, the exhibition was held primarily on either Reece's farm or Isaac Kipp's. It was also held twice at Henry Kipp's farm, as well as that of Mrs. Charles Evans. From 1884 until 1909,

From the start, Chilliwack's annual Fall Fair was focused on the community's agricultural sector and culture. This image from about 1947 captures local agricultural enthusiasts parading their prized livestock in front of judges, with a large, well-dressed crowd enjoying the event. The Ag Hall is partially visible to the right. Chilliwack Board of Trade

the event took place at the community's first dedicated fairgrounds, comprising the four and a half acres bounded by what later became Wellington Avenue, Mary Street, Princess Avenue, and Edward Street. At the turn of the century, the Fall Fair and the Sunday School picnic were considered annual holidays in Chilliwack—often the only ones that residents took off from work. In 1909, the location of the fairgrounds shifted to the twenty-three acres bounded by Hodgins Avenue, Corbould Street, Spadina Avenue, and Ashwell Road. It is this second fairgrounds that many locals fondly remember, as the Fall Fair was based there for the next ninety-two years. The 1910 event, held September 20 to 22, was an unqualified success, described as "the three-day exhibition that will go on record as the most successful display of the products of the rich Chilliwack Valley." The large turnout was partly attributable to the drawing power of horse racing events on the grounds' newly completed racetrack.

In 1935, the fairgrounds expanded when the city sold a group of lots farther south on Corbould Street to the agricultural society. In 1936, the new Agricultural Hall was completed on the fairgrounds, and it hosted many fair events and displays in the coming years. Despite poor weather, approximately 10,000 admissions were recorded at the 1941 fair, at a time when the combined population of the city and township was only 11,400. In 1944, a rumour circulated in fair circles within BC that Chilliwack's annual fair would not take place due to the ongoing effects of World War II and related financial challenges, but the event did proceed. The fair of 1950, its seventy-eighth edition, was plagued by high labour costs, low attendance numbers, and "poor community spirit" in terms of volunteerism.

Fair organizers responded by making a fundamental and lasting change. Up to this time, the exhibition had regularly occurred in the early fall. But officials were aware that the continued growth of the two-week Pacific National Exhibition in Vancouver, starting mid-August, along with Chilliwack's fair taking place after the start of school, had resulted in declining attendance. Thus, after 1950's poor showing, the next Fall Fair was scheduled to start on August 15, 1951, a month earlier than previously. This start date, slightly ahead of the PNE's, immediately resulted in higher visitor numbers. And with the Chilliwack Coliseum finally completed in 1958 (see chapter 1), the scope of the event was greatly enhanced. For the next forty-two fairs, this sizable venue played a significant role, hosting a wide variety of agricultural exhibits as well as other attractions and displays.

By the 1950s the Fall Fair was being marketed as a family event, with less emphasis on agriculture. Newspaper advertisements portrayed the fair's crowded midway, side shows with carney barkers, games of chance such as pellet-rifle shooting, fireworks, a Ferris wheel, and a family happily enjoying the fair. *Chilliwack Progress* Archive

Many view the 1950s and '60s as the Fall Fair's golden era, when the event had a bigger midway, bigger crowds, more live shows, and more rides, vendors, and exhibits. The fair's official opening was a well-publicized event with a dignitary making a speech, media presence, ribbon-cutting, and so on. Favourite midway rides among the younger set included the Tilt-a-Whirl (a.k.a. the Whip), the Octopus, the Rocket (a.k.a. the Salt and Pepper Shaker), and the Ferris wheel. Some fairgoers considered themselves lucky when their seat on the Ferris wheel stopped at the top of its arc, affording them a bird's-eye view of Chilliwack. On the last day of school in late June, students received a ticket to the upcoming fair stapled to their final report card (sometimes along with a PNE ticket). Some students wanted to get in a second time without paying and snuck into the fairgrounds through a hole in the

During the 1950s and '60s, the Fall Fair's midway was always crowded—even inclement weather didn't keep the crowds away. Two years after this 1965 shot was taken, the Ag Hall was transformed to Evergreen Hall, further expanding the fair's ability to stage various presentations. Chilliwack Museum & Archives and *Chilliwack Progress*

property's fence near Jackson Street (west of the racetrack). Eventually this security breach was plugged. Also in the 1960s, a large pool in front of the coliseum was stocked with hungry trout where youngsters could try their luck (guaranteed to be good). They paid per inch for their catch, after which it was put in a plastic bag to take home to show friends and family and then be cooked.

In 1962, for the first time in its history, the Fall Fair—known officially as the Chilliwack Exhibition—was set to host a circus. The three-ring Carson & Barnes Circus would be held under a big top to be erected on the fairgrounds. The production was to arrive in forty-six trucks, bearing "a menagerie of jungle animals." However, less than two weeks before the event started, the circus company cancelled its performance, leaving a major "void in entertainment."

Over the years, despite the August timing but perhaps consistent with Chilliwack's reputation, the fair was sometimes plagued by bad weather. For example, in 1963, gale-force winds ripped down tents set up on the fairgrounds. And on August 18, 1964, a torrential downpour sent fairgoers scurrying for cover, resulting in cancellation of children's races and forcing 4-H judging to move indoors. During the mid-1960s, Battle of the Bands contests were a popular event, fuelled by the unprecedented and global impact of the Beatles and the British Invasion. The Fall Fair accordingly hosted a number of well-received rock 'n' roll concerts. With favourable weather in 1966, approximately 20,000 patrons passed through the fair's gates (when the community's population was 28,750). Attendance then increased to 23,000 by 1969.

In 1970, as it approached its centennial, the Chilliwack Exhibition was acknowledged as the top B-class fair in BC (and some believed it was top in Canada as well). In 1971, a major fire at the fairgrounds destroyed four barns, leaving only one livestock building standing. As a result, for the first time in its history, the fair was held over four days the following year to allow all scheduled events to be completed in the single remaining livestock facility. And in 1981, city council staged a Fall Fair parade through the streets of the city.

The official name of the fair has changed over the years. In the 1950s, it was the Chilliwack Regional Exhibition; in 1985, it became the Chilliwack Rainbow Fair, the result of a renaming contest in which the majority of entries included the word "rainbow." However, this new name lasted only two years, and by 1988 it reverted to the long-time standard Chilliwack Fall Fair. By the turn of the twenty-first century, the event was again officially known as the Chilliwack Exhibition, and in recent times it has been called the Chilliwack Fair.

The last Fall Fair to be held on the community's second fairgrounds, on Corbould Street, took place in August 2000. After almost a century at this location, in 2001 the fairgrounds (and the fair) moved to their present location at Chilliwack Heritage Park, on Luckakuck Way at Lickman Road. Comprising sixty-five acres, this complex is home to a 150,000-square-foot multi-use exhibition building, a racetrack, a rodeo arena, and a seven-acre field for concerts, festivals, and camping—all close to both Highway 1 and the growing population base south of the highway. The facility also offers greater space (indoors and outdoors) and a more functional layout to facilitate future expansion. Since the fair's change in location, attendance has increased significantly.

First and foremost, the Fall Fair has always been an agricultural showcase event, given the community's farming roots. Over time, fair activities grew to include other aspects of society's ever-changing culture. For young people in earlier times, the fair represented much of what was good about summer in Chilliwack. It was a big event when it hit town, often viewed as the community's own mini-PNE, and was usually well attended. The Chilliwack Fall Fair has touched thousands of people's lives over the years and will undoubtably continue to be an integral feature of the community's cultural and historical landscape, always evolving with the times, with its two long-time constants continuing to be agriculture and fun for all.

Chapter 8

THE SHOPPING EXPERIENCE

MANY RETAIL OPERATIONS AROSE IN CHILLIWACK TO MEET INCREASED consumer demands after World War II, ranging from the Eaton's department store near Five Corners to numerous specialty shops. This chapter looks at a representative cross-section of the city's shopping destinations in the 1950s and 1960s, all of which—except one—are gone today. The busy downtown Eaton's store was a major economic and social hub, swinging into the '60s with a "sophisticated" remodelling in 1965. Close by, the smaller F. W. Woolworth Company department store, established in 1928, had a significant presence. For groceries, locals could shop at the new downtown Safeway that opened in 1950, replaced a decade later by a mid-century modern Safeway in the "Marina" style, also in the urban core. The city's first mall, Southgate Shopping Centre, opened in 1958, and a history of the retail scene would not be complete without mention of Ronal's, the centre of Chilliwack's exploding music scene in the 1960s.

EATON'S, 1948–1977

Eaton's department store was Chilliwack's commercial anchor for three decades—the biggest retail concern in the city and the one that drew people downtown. Eventually the department store left the city, and ultimately the corporation ceased to exist. Decades previous, several other department stores had occupied Eaton's high-profile downtown location, going back to the late nineteenth century. In 1887 George Ashwell relocated his general store operation from Chilliwack Landing to near Five Corners on the south side of Wellington Avenue, the site that accommodated Eaton's years later. In 1923, the established Alberta retail chain Pride, Nash and Company approached the Ashwell family with a proposal to purchase their long-time local business, and the family agreed to sell.

Effective November 1, 1923, after operating in Chilliwack for over fifty years, suddenly the familiar Ashwell store was gone from the city's retail landscape. Pride, Nash and Company operated its new department store for less than three years; in November 1925 the business was purchased by David Spencer Limited, commonly known as Spencer's. After significant alterations Chilliwack's new department store officially opened on March 19, 1926, with a big sale. For the next twenty-three years, Spencer's served as the local shopping scene's anchor. However, much like the previous occupants, the Spencer's chain itself would be acquired (and eliminated) by a bigger department store entity.

As of December 1, 1948, all Spencer's stores in BC were purchased by the T. Eaton Company, the prominent national retailer renowned for its mail-order catalogues. This corporate takeover was a well-guarded secret, and the sixty staff members of Spencer's had no warning. Most were stunned when at the end of their workday on November 30, they were read the announcement of Eaton's acquisition of their long-time employer. After Chilliwack got used to having a new department store downtown (the dominant retailer in Canada, no less), locals speculated that with its considerable financial means, Eaton's would soon renovate the aging Spencer's premises, effectively upgrading that portion of the city's business district.

But for the next three years, Eaton's operated out of the existing space. In 1951, with the department store based in four adjoining and outdated buildings, construction of a new store on the prime downtown site appeared imminent. Finally, on July 9, Eaton's took out a building permit for a $400,000, two-storey building. The structure would be built of reinforced concrete and have 172 feet of frontage on Wellington Avenue and a depth of 106 feet. Counting mezzanine space, the new store covered 42,000 square feet. While the building had no windows on the second floor, the impressive facade was solid-face precast terrazzo, "in line with modern department store architecture." The street-level main floor had two sizable entrances and featured a series of large and small display windows. A six-foot rain canopy protected shoppers along the store's entire frontage. And Eaton's planned to pave the rear parking lot as well as the lane between the store and the parking lot.

Demolition of two of Eaton's old structures commenced the day after the building permit was obtained. The plan was to build the

As the 1951–52 construction of the new Eaton's store progressed, the *Chilliwack Progress* published a rendering of how the finished project was expected to look. The store itself, along with the first block of Wellington Avenue in general, was made to appear grander and larger than they were, such was the accepted importance of the new Eaton's to the city's economy. *Chilliwack Progress* Archive

new store in two phases, allowing operations to continue while construction was underway. The first construction phase encompassed the eastern 100 feet of frontage and was finished on December 6, 1951. Work on the remaining 72 feet of frontage then began, and it was completed on April 24, 1952. There was no visual evidence of the two sections having been built separately (except when viewed from the air). City officials credited the new building with "having a profound effect on restoring property values on the whole of Wellington Avenue." At the time, an Eaton's spokesperson described the new store as "the most modern, from every standpoint, in Canada," and its opening at 48 Wellington Avenue marked the start of the golden age of shopping in downtown Chilliwack. Two years earlier, a liquor store and the city's modern Safeway (on Victoria Avenue West and Mill Street, respectively) had opened, and for the rest of the 1950s and much of the '60s, these three key retail outlets thrived, drawing many shoppers downtown.

The 1958 opening of the city's first mall, Southgate Shopping Centre, appeared to have minimal impact on the downtown retail scene—in fact, some observed that the two shopping areas now complemented each other. When Safeway opened an even bigger and more modern store on Main Street in 1961, still more people were heading to downtown Chilliwack. But the Eaton's store was the main draw, after which shoppers headed to other establishments nearby. In 1962, the Five Corners Super-Valu store embarked on a major expansion, nearly doubling its size. Eaton's gladly allowed Super-Valu customers to use its parking lot, as this meant more shoppers for both establishments.

During this era, shopping downtown on a Friday night was an exciting experience. The city's core was alive with lights and sounds, Wellington Avenue was crowded, people were dressed up, and you always ran into someone you knew. And, invariably, the focus was Eaton's. Those who shopped at the store as children have numerous fond memories of the establishment, including patiently spending time with their parents in the store and then heading a few doors down to

As the 1960s unfolded, Eaton's continued to be the downtown retail anchor. The fabulous street-level display windows recognize special times of the year, in particular the colourful annual Christmas celebration. Over the years, placement of the store's signage varied between perpendicular to the facade and flush to it. Dean Roosevelt Collection

the Fashion Bakery (see chapter 6) for a Coke and glazed doughnut. On the way, they'd respectfully decline the overtures of the conservatively dressed and always smiling individuals who held up religious pamphlets for hours near the store's east entrance. Each August, kids would shop for must-have school apparel at the first-floor boys' and girls' clothing departments. And on the shortened first day of school (the first Tuesday after Labour Day), they would head for the main floor of Eaton's to buy school supplies.

Locals recall parking in the vast lot behind the store after obtaining a ticket from the good-natured attendant in the small wood-frame booth by the Princess Avenue West entrance. Fabulous window displays on Wellington Avenue recognized special times of the year, including Christmas. Teens would browse the LP albums on the second floor (but never actually buy any, since they were always cheaper at the Ronal's store directly across the street). Young people would also hang out with friends in front of the store on Friday nights and Saturday afternoons.

By 1965, the combined population of the city and township had grown to approximately 28,300, a 40 percent increase since the new Eaton's building was completed in 1952. The company felt its store needed updating, and that summer it announced plans for a $125,000 "remodelling" that would make it the chain's first non-metropolitan location in BC to be "swept into the mood of the Sixties." When asked why its Chilliwack branch was the first to undergo this type of modernization, a company spokesperson said that not only had its management long had faith in the local market, but its research indicated that residents of the township had incomes and levels of sophistication essentially equal to those of the city.

Features of the upgraded department store included recessed lighting, glowing wall colours, and carpeted floors in the apparel sections. Almost the entire main floor was devoted to clothing and accessories for men, women, and young people. Women's fashions were given the greatest prominence. The store opened with a splash on November 25, 1965, with women shoppers receiving a red rose, and pink lemonade being enjoyed by all. A headline in the *Chilliwack Progress* read, "Sophisticated Mood of the Sixties is Keynoted in Eaton's New Look." That same year, the new Canadian flag replaced the Union Jack on the store roof, a downtown constant for decades.

By the 1970s, however, the retail fabric of downtown Chilliwack was gradually changing for the worse. Eaton's management believed that the community was no longer a viable market and that its store's expansive retail space, viewed as so modern and optimal twenty-five years earlier, was now considered "a poor design for modern department store merchandising." Thus, in shocking but perhaps inevitable news that reverberated in the community for years to come, on November 4, 1976, Eaton's announced its permanent closure effective January 22, 1977, resulting in the laying off or transferring of its eighty employees. Two circumstances were cited for the venerable chain's demise in Chilliwack. One was the July 1974 opening of Cottonwood Corners, the city's first new shopping mall in over fifteen years, which featured a Zellers and

The Eaton's building was the dominant downtown structure for decades and still stands, though its appearance and use have changed greatly since its heyday. In 1981 Chilliwack's new bowling centre, Chillibowl Lanes, officially opened at the location. Merlin Bunt Collection

a Sears. Of significance, this mall was located south of Highway 1, which was becoming the focus of a large population and retail shift. The second catalyst behind Eaton's departure was the new Sevenoaks Shopping Centre in Abbotsford, which opened in 1975 with its own new Eaton's, along with a Woodward's store.

For many Chilliwack residents, the unthinkable had happened—Eaton's had shut down and left town. Either Eaton's or an earlier department store had occupied the same site on Wellington Avenue for ninety years, and local retailers were understandably concerned about the effect of the anchor store's departure. Some felt it would accelerate the outflow of shopping dollars to the Sevenoaks mall, while others speculated that another department store, perhaps the Hudson's Bay Company, would set up shop in the vacated space. But in the end there were no takers, and the Eaton's structure remained vacant for the next four years. In early 1981, the owners of the city's two existing bowling alleys, Park Lanes and Chilliwack Bowling Centre, joined forces to create one large recreational complex located in the old Eaton's building, the focal point of which was a consolidated "super bowling centre." On September 4, 1981, Chillibowl Lanes officially opened (see chapter 10).

The bowling centre, at 45916 Wellington Avenue, has carried on for years as the city's only downtown bowling alley. But the view facing west along Wellington from Five Corners has changed dramatically since the heyday of Eaton's and Spencer's. The street is now a one-way, one-lane thoroughfare between Five Corners and Main Street, with angle parking, and city-planted trees make it difficult to see what once was. Eaton's, gone now for almost fifty years, left an indelible mark on the community's rich retail and social past. The store's central location, its broad range of merchandise, the era in which it operated, and the smaller-town culture all combine to make it an unforgettable element of downtown Chilliwack's history.

SOUTHGATE SHOPPING CENTRE, 1958

One of the biggest developments in Chilliwack's retail history was the opening of Southgate Shopping Centre in 1958. Not only was the new mall the community's first, it was also just the second one in BC. The name Southgate was chosen partially in recognition of the new plaza's proximity to the ceremonial gates to the city, which stood fifty metres south of Hodgins Avenue between 1933 and 1954. The Southgate property has a long and interesting history. In 1882, Isaac Kipp donated land near the northwest corner of the future Hodgins Avenue and Yale Road West for construction of a much-needed public school. A school occupied the site until 1929, when the new Central School opened on Young Road North. The City of Chilliwack, which owned the aging school structure and its surrounding three acres of land, sold the property in 1931 for $2,500. The school was dismantled and the lumber used to build a house and cabins for the new, eighteen-unit Chilliwack Auto Camp (later known as the Chilliwack Auto Court), which opened on the site in 1932.

By the early 1950s, Chilliwack was viewed as one of the most growth-oriented and viable communities in BC. In 1956, the Chilliwack Auto Court property was acquired by developers planning to build Southgate Shopping Centre. In 1957, architects released a rendering of the $1.5 million, L-shaped project, with four stores making up the north wing and a two-storey office section to the south. Incorporated in the new plaza's design was the first pedestrian mall in BC, located in the southwest area of the complex, where shoppers were away from automobile traffic and there was minimal distance between the stores. A further innovation was multiple parking lots, enabling shoppers to park conveniently near their destination. Finally, there were "lovely planted areas" that caught the eye instantly, providing "an air of leisure and relaxation."

The opening of Southgate Shopping Centre in 1958 was a big deal for Chilliwack. It was the community's first shopping centre and the first retail or commercial development situated away from the urban core, portending the city's future expansion to the south. On October 15, 1958, the *Chilliwack Progress* ran a splashy announcement/advertisement in large type about Southgate's official opening the following day. *Chilliwack Progress* Archive

In late 1957, construction commenced on Southgate. This was a big event in town, and interest grew stronger as the shopping centre took shape. Along Yale Road West (the Trans-Canada Highway at that time), there was no shortage of traffic to view the project's progress.

Amidst all the optimism over this development, existing city retailers were concerned that the new shopping centre might take away business from the established commercial core of Five Corners. But the mall's developers believed that with the community's continued rapid growth, as evidenced by a steadily high rate of building permits being issued (both residential and commercial), Southgate and the downtown shopping area would complement each other, ultimately drawing more shoppers downtown. An editorial in the *Chilliwack Progress* in August 1958 ended with the view that "the breakaway from the Five Corners business area is a natural development that had to come and both areas will benefit."

On October 16, 1958, after most of the new mall's tenants were up and operating, the developers staged a well-attended opening ceremony. Mayor T. T. McCammon officially opened Southgate Shopping Centre, with twenty-three retail outlets and twelve commercial offices. The mall's anchor tenant, Super-Valu, had floor space of 11,000 square feet, making it one of the largest supermarkets in BC. Approximately 20,000 people visited Southgate during its first three days, a huge turnout for a community with a population of about 24,400. Retail outlets in the new complex reported serving customers from Agassiz, Hope, Abbotsford, and Langley. The *Progress* described Southgate as "British Columbia's finest and most convenient shopping centre." On November 28, Stedman's opened to much fanfare as one of the final new Southgate stores, employing a workforce of twenty. As door-crasher deals, the Canadian-owned variety store chain advertised baby pants, four pairs for 88 cents, and ladies' rayon briefs for 29 cents per pair.

Sixteen years later, in the early morning hours of June 25, 1974, a major fire destroyed the north wing of Southgate. The four stores that made up the wing (Stedman's, Southgate Footwear, Sherwin Williams Paint, and BC Tel) were all gutted before the flames were slowed. More than fifty firefighters attended the blaze, but their efforts were hampered by a delay of more than one hour as they waited for BC Hydro to arrive to disconnect the power lines. An initial estimate of the damage

For its one-year anniversary, Southgate Shopping Centre staged a three-day celebration, including floodlit square dancing in the parking lot, pony rides for children, free gifts, special sales, and remote coverage from CHWK Radio 1270. This image from September 13, 1959, captures the classic mid-century sign just north of the Dairy Queen, and the mall's north wing, which burned to the ground in 1974. Chilliwack Museum & Archives

was over $585,000, characterized as "the most expensive fire in the history of the city." Authorities believed the blaze was the result of an arson attack that was started in the office area of Stedman's. Adding to Southgate's challenges, just two months later Cottonwood Mall opened, becoming the first new shopping mall in Chilliwack since Southgate itself in 1958. Cottonwood was newer, was bigger, had more parking, and most importantly, featured major anchor tenants. Its opening marked the start of the urban area's southward sprawl across Highway 1 and the consequent decline of the downtown retail centre. It also marked the de-emphasis of Southgate Shopping Centre as a destination mall. The opening of Cottonwood Mall had a much worse effect on Southgate's fortunes than did Southgate on the city's central business district when it opened in 1958.

After the fire, Southgate's ownership rethought how the mall could look. Instead of restoring the L-shaped design, rebuilding plans called for a straight, block-long, north–south configuration running from

Pictured in 2025, Southgate Shopping Centre continues to operate, albeit with a lower profile than in its heyday. The large space that Super-Valu occupied for thirty years is now home to Shoppers Drug Mart, and the area of the old north wing now provides access to Ontario Avenue. Merlin Bunt Collection

Hodgins Avenue to Ontario Avenue. The burned-out north wing of Southgate was not rebuilt, its location ultimately becoming an entry/exit point between the mall and Ontario Avenue. The mall's parking lot at the corner of School Street and Ontario Avenue was used for rebuilt or new retail space, part of a net addition of 4,000 square feet to the mall. On April 1, 1975, ten months after the blaze that destroyed its north wing, construction began on the redesigned mall property. In July the work was completed and tenants were in Southgate's new space. It took a while for locals to get used to the new Southgate configuration, but they welcomed other improvements to the mall, such as covered walkways, a stylish brick facade, and improved parking.

Undoubtedly, some retail spending had shifted south to Cottonwood Mall, but Southgate retained a critical portion of its loyal clientele that appreciated the new look and ease of movement, and it carried on more or less as before. However, on February 23, 1988, Super-Valu closed its doors and went into receivership, ending its thirty-year run as the dependable anchor of the shopping centre. The mall continued to operate, albeit with a lower profile than in its heyday and with a different mix and calibre of tenants. The large Super-Valu space later became home to a Shoppers Drug Mart store.

Southgate Shopping Centre was a prominent aspect of the Chilliwack retail/commercial scene until that pivotal year of 1974, when a major fire led to a permanent change in the look and dynamic of the mall, soon followed by unprecedented competition from south of the highway. However, in some respects the unfortunate blaze laid the foundation for the evolution of Southgate, which continues to be a viable shopping presence in Chilliwack.

TWO NEW WOOLWORTH'S STORES, 1952 AND 1969

For most of the twentieth century, a popular shopping outlet in many cities and towns was the F. W. Woolworth Company store. Generally referred to as Woolworth's, or occasionally the five-and-ten-cent store, this smallish department store operated for over sixty years in three different buildings in Chilliwack's downtown core. With this history it well represents the community's period of growth and prosperity during the '50s and '60s. Despite ongoing competition from other stores, its solid customer base resulted in the city at one time having the largest Woolworth's outlet in the province. By the late 1920s, ten Woolworth's stores were operating in BC, and Chilliwack was about to become home to the eleventh. On April 26, 1928, the *Chilliwack Progress* announced that a new Woolworth's would soon be located near Five Corners, on the south side of Yale Road East across from the post office. On September 28, the new Woolworth's officially opened at 40 Yale Road East, welcomed by an orchestra, company officials, and local politicians.

With its prime fifty-two feet of frontage, Woolworth's was a popular retail destination at this location for the next two dozen years. The store's signage, displaying the chain's red-and-gold corporate logo, became a familiar landmark. In the years after World War II,

The Yale Road East location of the original Woolworth's in Chilliwack is today an integral component of the new District 1881 development. The refurbished heritage structure is home to a craft brewery on the ground floor, while the upper floor accommodates the Woolworth Flats residences. Chilliwack Museum & Archives

Chilliwack's overall population was growing greatly—by the 1950s it had more than doubled since the store first opened—and the company's 3,000 square feet of space was no longer sufficient, so it decided to move to larger premises. In April 1951, F. W. Woolworth Company purchased two adjoining properties at 30 and 32 Wellington Avenue, immediately to the east of Eaton's. One had been home to Brunswick Billiard Parlour since 1911, while the other was being used by Eaton's for its meat department. Woolworth's undertook a $100,000 renovation prior to moving to its new location. The resulting store had double the space of its former premises, allowing it to carry a wider range of merchandise and capture a higher proportion of the community's increasing retail spending.

On September 11, 1952, Woolworth's opened its new store on Wellington Avenue. The revamped operation had a staff of twenty-six, twice the number of employees at the previous location. Three aisles ran the length of the layout and three ran the width, separating the various sales counters into individual departments. The renovated structure's second floor served as the stockroom. The timing and location of Woolworth's move was prescient. With a strong local economy and low unemployment, people enjoyed dressing up to go downtown to shop and meet their friends, and they also had an increasingly wide range of consumer options and more money in their pockets. The opening of the new Eaton's store, also in 1952, had a big impact on the burgeoning shopping scene, drawing many shoppers downtown. Woolworth's directly benefited from the ongoing wave of urban expansion, as well as its proximity to Eaton's, and the Wellington Avenue location remained popular until the late 1960s. By 1967, the community's population had increased by another 45 percent, and once again the store had space and operational limitations.

Woolworth's second home in Chilliwack was on Wellington Avenue from 1952 to 1969, a central location in the city's prime shopping district. It benefited greatly from being next to Eaton's during the post-war boom years. Chilliwack Museum & Archives and *Chilliwack Progress*

Mindful of a looming relocation, F. W. Woolworth Company was strategically acquiring options on eight contiguous properties partially bounded by Main Street and Princess Avenue West, with plans to build a large department store in excess of 40,000 square feet. In September 1968, demolition commenced on buildings within that block. Two of the more noteworthy structures taken down were the Texaco service station at the corner of Main and Princess, which had opened in 1950, and adjacent to it the Elks Lodge, located at the site since 1946. Construction of the department store started in December, and on October 9, 1969, with Mayor A. B. Holder cutting the ribbon, the community's new mega-Woolworth's opened at the northwest corner of Main and Princess. The day prior, the *Chilliwack Progress* carried an eighteen-page Woolworth's supplement—part information, part advertisement/catalogue. Situated at 21 Main Street, the structure had 126 feet of frontage on Main and extended 330 feet along Princess. When it opened, it was the largest single-floor Woolworth's in BC, providing a sevenfold increase in retail space.

On Friday, October 16, 1970, the department store held a "Pyjama Party" event as part of its one-year-anniversary celebration. Over one thousand people showed up after midnight to take advantage of a 10 percent discount on all items in the store—20 percent if the shopper was actually wearing pyjamas. Due to the large crowd attending the promotion, the store's doors were locked at 1:15 a.m.

For the next two decades, Woolworth's was a dominant downtown concern at its new location, particularly after Eaton's shut its doors in 1977. On February 1, 1990, however, the outlet was converted to a Woolco department store. Woolworth's, as owner of the Woolco chain, was implementing what it referred to as a "marketing change," with twenty-six Woolworth's stores across Canada converted to Woolco outlets to "maximize the strengths of the company by reorganizing into more cohesive units of like-sized physical plants."

Woolco operated for the next four years in its parent's former premises before closing in May 1994. Later that year, the building became

The building that housed Woolworth's on Wellington Avenue for 17 years today serves as the home of the long-time Chilliwack retail business Payton & Buckle Fine Footwear, next to Chillibowl Lanes (originally the Eaton's building). Merlin Bunt Collection

home to Liquidation World, which occupied it for most of the next two decades. In 2010, Promontory Community Church purchased the property, whose building had grown to 57,000 square feet by then. In 2014 this and another downtown Chilliwack church came together under one roof at the ever-expanding location, 9325 Main Street, forming Main Street Church, the structure's current occupant.

Today the building that housed the original Woolworth's in Chilliwack, at 46140 Yale Road, has been reborn as an integral component of District 1881, the redevelopment/renaissance of the downtown core. The refurbished heritage structure became home to a craft brewery / restaurant on the ground floor, while the upper floor accommodates the Woolworth Flats residences. The location of the second Woolworth's store in Chilliwack, now identified as 45930 Wellington Avenue, went on to serve as the home of long-time Chilliwack retail business Payton & Buckle Fine Footwear.

The F. W. Woolworth Company no longer exists, as the venerable business ceased all operations in 1997. But for over six decades serving multiple generations of loyal shoppers, Woolworth's was part of everyday Chilliwack life—a popular retail destination operating from prominent locations.

TWO MODERN NEW SAFEWAY STORES, 1950 AND 1961

For most of the twentieth century, Chilliwack residents generally associated grocery shopping with a trip to Safeway in the city's vibrant downtown. Until the 1980s, Safeway dominated the city's supermarket shopping scene, even when there were two Super-Valu stores. Over the years, the Safeway chain has operated from six different locations. Two of these structures (one gone, one still standing) were built in the boom times following World War II, representative of the community's newfound optimism and rising level of affluence. They also greatly contributed to the social dynamic of downtown Chilliwack.

The Safeway chain was established in the city in 1928, taking over an existing 960-square-foot unit in the two-year-old Gilbert Block (a.k.a. the Auld Phillips Building) at the northwest corner of Yale Road East and Nowell Street North. After operating for seven years in this limited space, the supermarket—still the only one in town—moved to bigger, more central premises. On May 10, 1935, it opened in a space of around 3,900 square feet at 35 Wellington Avenue, immediately to the west of the Davies and Logan Hardware Building, across from Spencer's. As the city continued to grow during the 1940s, Canada Safeway's head office recognized that its Chilliwack operation had long outgrown its cramped quarters, and plans for a bigger and more modern store were set in motion.

In March 1947, Safeway purchased a lot at the corner of Mill Street and Victoria Avenue West, just under half an acre in size, and announced plans to build its new supermarket there. The new location was just eighty metres north of its current store. A call for tenders for construction of the $165,000 project went out in August 1949. Plans called for a structure 75 by 106 feet, twice the size of the existing outlet. The contract for the project was let in April 1950, a building permit issued later that month, and construction commenced the week of May 15. To provide sufficient customer parking, Safeway purchased a strategically located lot from the city. Situated on Young Road North, between Langley Greenhouses and the new fire hall, this acquisition extended the supermarket's parking lot from Mill Street through to Young Road, accommodating about fifty cars. Finally, on Thursday morning, November 9, 1950, after fifteen years at its previous location, the city's new brick-and-glass Safeway store was officially opened at 20 Mill Street. Not only was it much bigger than its predecessor, it was state-of-the-art in all supermarket aspects. Thousands of shoppers flocked to the new store during its first two days of operation. Newspapers in the valley headlined it as "British Columbia's Most Modern Food Store."

Reflecting the rapidly evolving nature of modern supermarkets and the community's robust growth, Canada Safeway deemed its once industry-leading store inadequate after only a decade of operation. Planning ahead, in early 1960 the chain acquired options on ten lots making up a large parcel of land on the west side of Main Street between Princess Avenue West and Kipp Avenue. Here it intended to build a large and ultra-modern supermarket that would be a leader in both contemporary design and functionality. In April 1961, construction began on the city's fourth Safeway since 1928, and throughout the rest of the year residents watched with excitement as the futuristically designed supermarket structure gradually took shape. On October 25 the new store officially opened its doors for business at 115 Main Street, featuring ample free parking and a wide selection of grocery products.

The impressive-looking structure was a concrete-block building with a distinctive gull-wing roof form that employed arching,

When Chilliwack's new, modern Safeway store opened the morning of November 9, 1950, a large crowd of waiting shoppers lined up on Mill Street, mostly women and some with baby carriages. Thousands attended the store's two-day opening, attracted by the promise of bargains, small prize draws, and a grand prize of a purebred Holstein heifer worth $400. *Chilliwack Progress* Archive

glue-laminated timber beams and an area of extensive glazing on its facade. This Marina-style design, which originated in San Francisco, would appear in communities across North America in the 1960s, accompanied by the store's red-and-white *S* logo atop a tall sign. The new store's spacious parking lot accommodated over 135 cars. At the time it was the second-largest Safeway store in all of BC, and it was an instant hit, drawing shoppers from beyond the city's boundaries. In addition to all the new technological and architectural features, it had a twenty-seat cafeteria immediately left of the south entrance, where shoppers could enjoy a Coke, sandwich, or doughnut. Chilliwack's economy in the 1960s remained relatively strong, with Eaton's and Safeway continuing to draw shoppers downtown. On December 1, 1965, the community's new (and bigger) liquor store opened next to Safeway, which further increased consumer traffic.

By the early 1980s, two factors contributed to the ultimate end of Safeway's reign as the dominant downtown supermarket. First, the population south of Highway 1 was starting to boom, due to both organic growth and population migration from north of the highway, and one consequence of this demographic shift was the development of two new shopping malls—the second of which included the fifth Safeway in Chilliwack's history. Second, the city began consolidating land in the downtown core with plans to create an urban development called Salish Place. This project included a shopping mall called Salish Plaza that was anchored by a supermarket and a new liquor store, and it was located a mere two blocks southeast of the Main Street Safeway. The supermarket was Save-On-Foods, offering ample parking and complemented by various other proximate businesses. Save-On-Foods opened to much fanfare on February 15, 1988, drawing 11,000 shoppers in its first two days. Canada Safeway still wanted to maintain a presence in the downtown core and, despite increased competition and dwindling sales, it continued to operate its Main Street store for almost two decades.

In 2004, developers announced plans to expand and improve the City Gate Shopping Centre, located near the intersection of Yale Road and Cheam Avenue. This expansion included Canada Safeway building a bigger, industry-leading store as the mall's anchor tenant. On July 13, 2006, the city's sixth Safeway store opened for business. Not coincidentally, the next day the chain's once grand store on Main Street closed its doors for good after operating there for forty-five years. A discount grocery store then leased the old space and tried to make a go of things. Eventually the presence of strong, more modern competition nearby precluded any future grocery store tenants in the old Main Street structure. After sitting vacant a while, the aging building housed a liquidation entity for a time, but that business also failed and no more new tenants could be attracted. The forgotten building at 9299 Main Street was then boarded up.

For the next decade, the Safeway structure on Main Street was increasingly referred to as an eyesore. Its facade was covered with plywood and there were broken windows, peeling paint, numerous graffiti tags, and unkempt vegetation growing on the lot. Numerous incidents of vandalism and mischief were reported. Finally, on November 9, 2015, the structure was demolished. Sobeys, which had earlier purchased the Safeway company, then put the four-acre Main Street site up for sale for $3.2 million. In 2016, the land was purchased by the Mann Group, but nothing happened with the property for two years. By late 2018 the city was attempting to expropriate the land, with the Mann Group going to court to try to stop it. Eventually the issues were resolved, and in 2022 a groundbreaking ceremony was held at the site for phase 1 of a comprehensive development, which includes 193 apartment units in two six-storey buildings served by underground parking. A subsequent phase of this project features development of two commercial buildings fronting Main Street.

For about ten years, the vacant Main Street Safeway structure was often referred to as an eyesore—its storefront was boarded up and it had broken windows, peeling paint, numerous graffiti tags, and unkempt vegetation growing on the lot. The aging building was finally demolished in 2015, and in 2025 a comprehensive development was underway that will see construction of 193 apartment units on the site. Merlin Bunt Collection

In 2007, what at one time was Chilliwack's showcase supermarket was vacant, boarded up, and neglected. But the building would soon undergo a major renovation, with part of the structure subdivided into several small commercial/retail units facing the old parking lot, while the main portion was reborn as Chilliwack's new Home Hardware store. Merlin Bunt Collection

The structure that Safeway built in 1950 on Mill Street was still sound and functional at the time the chain relocated in 1961, and thus a buyer for the property was actively sought, but it remained unoccupied for eighteen months. In January 1963, Overwaitea purchased the property, and on April 2 the rival grocery chain opened its new store to large crowds. In the ensuing years the aging brick structure became unviable for a large-scale grocery store, and ultimately it was boarded up and remained vacant for a considerable time. After 2006 the building underwent a major renovation, with part of the structure subdivided into several small commercial/retail units facing the old parking lot, while the main portion was reborn with much fanfare as the city's new Home Hardware store. The hardware outlet eventually closed and until the end of 2024, the city's old Safeway building, at 9360 Mill Street, was anchored by Flashback Brewing Company.

Safeway is now just one of several major supermarkets operating in Chilliwack, but in the post-war era, Safeway dominated the local shopping scene while also serving as a retail stimulus. In those days, downtown Chilliwack was the place to be, and shopping at Safeway was a regular part of the retail experience.

RONAL'S RECORD STORE, 1963–1976

Musically speaking, the 1950s ended with Elvis Presley still in the army and the recent death of Buddy Holly. The youth-oriented music scene then entered a period of relative stagnation. However, as the 1960s unfolded, the worlds of popular music and young people changed dramatically, fuelled by the arrival of the Beatles and the emergence of many other English artists in the "British Invasion." At that time, long before Spotify or even eight-track tapes, popular music was enjoyed via phonograph records—45s for singles and LPs for albums. Record sales took off in North America starting in early 1964, and the place to be in Chilliwack for everything music and all the accompanying excitement was Ronal's on Wellington Avenue. By the mid-1960s, the popular record store had become something of a club and was always packed, especially on Friday evenings and Saturday afternoons. One could spend hours at the store listening to and talking about music, browsing through records, and often running into like-minded friends.

Officially known as Ronal TV-Electric, although seldom called that, the business was started by two brothers, Ron and Al Hiebert. Ron and Al (hence the name Ronal) were primarily electronics technicians, and they were eventually joined by a third brother, Jack, who oversaw the business end of the operation. Ronal's opened its doors in 1958, later moving to the city's first mall, Southgate Shopping Centre. In 1963, the Hieberts seized the opportunity to relocate to the heart of downtown Chilliwack and moved Ronal's into premises at 25 Wellington Avenue, directly across from Eaton's. Around the same time a transformation was underway in the global music business. Near the end of 1963, several Beatles singles entered the North American record charts. The group's hit "I Want to Hold Your Hand" quickly sold a million copies, becoming the number-one record in the US by mid-January 1964. Beatlemania was underway, opening the door for many other pop groups and creating an energy that lasted the rest of the decade. The impact of the Beatles on the prominence of Ronal's as Chilliwack's record centre—and its role in the lives of the community's youth—cannot be overstated.

Ronal's opened its doors in 1958 on Yale Road West, later moving to the Southgate Shopping Centre. It was initially an appliance and radio/TV repair service, but in the early 1960s, as the popularity of rock 'n' roll and demand for records continued to increase, the business expanded its services to include selling vinyl—45s and LPs. *Chilliwack Progress* Archive

The Beatles were slated to make their North American TV debut on *The Ed Sullivan Show* on February 9, 1964, amidst a growing hysteria caused by their singles now flooding the airwaves. Similar to their counterparts across the country, most young people in Chilliwack (and their parents) were very aware of the Beatles and their upcoming TV appearance. That Sunday evening many families gathered around their black-and-white TV sets at 8:00 p.m., turned on KVOS Channel 12, and watched the Beatles blow away the viewing universe—or at least its record-buying youth segment. This program was the most-watched show in TV history to that point, with 73 million viewers in the States and comparably high ratings in Canada. The next day the only thing that students at Chilliwack's schools were talking about was the Beatles' TV performance. After seeing the group performing the songs they were enjoying on radio station

CHWK 1270 (see chapter 5), many kids headed to Ronal's after school to buy Beatles records. In particular, students from Central School, located only a few blocks from Ronal's, flooded the store on February 10 to buy Beatles 45s and LPs; the shop was a madhouse, quickly running out of some 45s.

Soon after the Beatles emerged, many more British groups appeared on the scene, each one producing a new single every few months. Ed Sullivan would have one of these new groups on his show every Sunday, which often resulted in young music fans flocking to Ronal's the following day. Local radio stations such as CHWK 1270 (along with CKLG 73 and CFUN 1410 in Vancouver) played the 45s, record stores like Ronal's sold them, and young people everywhere bought them.

During this time the only competition to Ronal's for record sales in Chilliwack was McAlpine's, an electronics/music store at 121 Yale Road West, but it had a more limited selection. It was also quieter and darker than Ronal's, with none of the cool, energetic vibe of the store on Wellington Avenue. Eaton's had a record department on its second floor, but it mostly sold pricier LPs. The usual place to obtain a copy of CHWK 1270's weekly Top 50 record survey was also Ronal's. Invariably, a tall stack of these yellow, typewriter-produced, mimeographed charts sat on the front counter of the store, and they were quickly snapped up.

Ronal's capitalized on music fans' passionate following of the Top 50 songs of the week by directly linking its merchandising to the CHWK 1270 survey. On the west wall of the store were fifty pegs, numbered 1 to 50, each holding a supply of the 45 corresponding to that week's list. The familiar orange-and-yellow Capitol record label dominated much of the left side of the upper row of these singles, denoting the numerous Beatles records often in the Top 10. Another popular feature of Ronal's was that one could listen to a 45 by simply taking it down from a peg, placing it on one of several turntables, and putting on a set of headphones. At times, there were likely more free listens at Ronal's than records purchased. The store also had rows and rows of LPs in alphabetical order, each at that time costing $4.20, relatively expensive for a young person. However, 45s sold for 99 cents, and kids soon acquired sizable collections. The two faces of Ronal's record department for much of the 1960s and '70s were Dave Dickinson and Lynda Walker. Both were knowledgeable about contemporary music, plus they were patient and accommodating with all customers, many of whom were students. Chilliwack's younger music fans generally considered these two staff members as friends and peers.

By the late 1960s, Ronal's was advertising that it had the "largest record stock in the Upper Valley." Eventually the business expanded to Abbotsford, and in 1974 it opened a third outlet in the new Cottonwood Mall, south of Highway 1. However, changing times and consumer

In 1963, just prior to the British Invasion, Ronal's moved to a prime retail location on Wellington Avenue and became Chilliwack's leading music retailer. In 1976 the business ceased operations, and today its old premises are more sedately occupied by The Book Man, at 45939 Wellington. Merlin Bunt Collection

tastes along with increased competition conspired to spell the end of Ronal's. On August 20, 1976, a receiver was appointed for all the property and assets of Ronal Television, and soon the business was no more. In later times, with Ronal's and Eaton's both long gone, the first block of Wellington Avenue had nowhere near the buzz that existed there in the 1960s when the music scene was exploding and Ronal's was the epicentre for records. The musical energy of the '60s, driven by the Beatles and the subsequent British Invasion, was well captured and personified by Ronal's. Its old location, at 45939 Wellington Avenue, was later more sedately occupied by a new-and-used bookstore, The Book Man.

Chapter 9
SCHOOL DAYS

SCHOOLS IN CHILLIWACK, AS ELSEWHERE, WERE ALL-IMPORTANT SOCIAL institutions where students formed lasting relationships, absorbed fundamental values, and gained life directions. But in the post-war boom period, the local school district scrambled to catch up with capacity demands. This chapter profiles two of the city's main secondary schools, starting with Chilliwack Junior Secondary, which occupied a school building dating from 1913. It became a junior high school with the opening early in 1950 of the new, larger Chilliwack Senior High School nearby. Also profiled is a school built to accommodate the baby boom, Little Mountain Elementary. Opened in 1954, this popular school on the eastern edge of town was frequently expanded to accommodate increased enrolment. The chapter concludes by profiling a well-known educator, J. Y. Halcrow, one of the many teachers, administrators, and others who contributed to the city's educational landscape in the 1950s and 1960s.

CHILLIWACK JUNIOR SECONDARY SCHOOL, 1950–1996

In 1945, at the onset of the baby boomer generation, Chilliwack had only one high school. Situated on the south side of Yale Road East, between Charles Street and Williams Street South, the school's campus comprised three connected buildings. The oldest and most familiar opened on May 21, 1913, as the community's second Chilliwack High School

(CHS), enrolment sixty-three. To commemorate the event, a procession of students marched ten blocks from the existing high school on Young Road North to the new, classically designed institution. The new school was much too big for the community's senior educational needs at the time, but it was built with a view to the future that was spawned by the district's burgeoning growth.

Described at the time as "the pride of the province," it was a distinguished building of grey and pink brick, with a trapezoidal roof made of genuine Welsh slate that sloped at the edges to a high, flat top. At the centre of the roof over the north-facing main entrance was a raised, bell-shaped motif of deeper pink. This same decorative accent also appeared at the east, south, and west ends of the roof. A grove of cherry trees to the east supplied shade to students during breaks, and a stable at the southeast corner of the soccer field behind the building accommodated students who rode their horses to school. The two-storey structure had a full basement, eight classrooms, a principal's office, and separate staff rooms for men and women. At the back of the classrooms were full-length cloakrooms, with hooks for coats along with shelves for lunches and extra books. Since the school had no gymnasium for its first sixteen years, the halls were used for club meetings and social activities. To the west of the building, on the site of a large future expansion, were two grass tennis courts, while a ten-foot-wide, semicircular drive/sidewalk led to the front steps. And at the front was a seventy-three-foot flagpole flying the ever-present Union Jack, topped by a weathercock showing the direction of the prevailing wind.

As World War I drew to a close, the need for an assembly hall / gymnasium at CHS was growing. Its student body was continuing to expand, reaching 130 students in 1921 and 261 by 1928, but finances were tight after the war and it took a thirteen-year fundraising campaign to cover the cost of a new gym. In 1928, construction commenced on the long-awaited addition, a one-storey frame structure, and on March 21, 1929, the new auditorium was opened in an impressive ceremony attended by local and provincial officials. The gym was built to the east of the

From 1939 to 1997, this was the view of Chilliwack High School/Chilliwack Junior High School/Chilliwack Junior Secondary School. However, in 1950 the original structure's trapezoidal roof, made of genuine Welsh slate, was removed due to accumulated wear and tear, along with a desire to give the three buildings an integrated and even appearance. Chilliwack Museum & Archives

original brick structure, adjacent to Charles Street, and a covered walkway connected it to the main building.

By 1933, the original CHS building was overflowing with students, with some being taught at Central School on Young Road North. In 1938, 393 students were jammed into the 1913 structure, which was originally designed to accommodate 200. After much delay and lobbying for government funding, the school board announced plans for a major addition to CHS. On April 17, 1939, a new stucco-framed, seventeen-room structure opened that was connected to the original building. The addition was known as the junior high school, while the existing building was referred to as the senior high. A ramp with a fire door connected the two facilities. Also, to the west of the new structure was a shop addition, where students learned woodwork, metalwork, leatherwork, rope work, tool sharpening, harness repair, farm plumbing, glazing, window repair, and farm machinery repair.

The new premises now gave CHS its three distinct component buildings. In July 1941, work began on expansion of the gymnasium, and later that year the bigger and remodelled two-tier auditorium opened. The "upper gym" and "lower gym" were eventually shared by boys' and girls' gym classes. On March 23, 1944, an arsonist set fire to CHS in six different locations, all within the five-year-old junior high school building. The damage was considerable, estimated at $30,000. While the Grade 11 and 12 students in the original 1913 building returned to school on March 27, students in Grades 8 to 10 were off for two weeks while the damage was repaired.

Despite the expansions, with Chilliwack's growing post-war population, there would once again be capacity issues at CHS. The eventual solution was a new high school constructed across the street, which opened in early 1950 as Chilliwack Senior High School (CSHS). The existing CHS was renamed Chilliwack Junior High School (CJHS). The new senior high accommodated Grades 10 to 13, while the junior high had Grades 7 to 9. (This grade allocation eventually shifted, with Grade 7 returning to elementary and Grade 10 to the junior high.) Also in 1950, the slate roof of the 1913 structure was failing in spots, and the school board decided it was more economical to replace it with a flat tar-and-gravel roof. This change would give the new CJHS an integrated appearance, with its four raised, pink, bell-shaped accents and sloping trapezoidal roof all removed.

In June, the contract was let, and by September the new look was in place. Consequently, the gym, the 1913 building, and the 1939 addition were essentially all the same height, which is how most CJHS grads recall the school's general look. Back on September 3, 1912, a cornerstone had been set in the original structure at the front west corner, near the basement windows. It had eroded over the years, and by the early 1960s the inscription was obliterated. However, it is believed the stone read, "Chilliwack High School, 1912, Placed by Hon. Richard McBride." In the summer of 1962, CHS's original cornerstone was replaced with a bronze plaque. That same year, the names CSSS (Chilliwack Senior Secondary School) and CJSS (Chilliwack Junior Secondary School) were adopted.

In the 1990s, CJSS was aging and deemed not viable for current and future students' educational needs. The school board decided to demolish the three component buildings and replace them with a new institution known as Chilliwack Middle School (CMS). By 1996, plans

When demolition of the original 1913 Chilliwack High School commenced in April 1996, workers came across a long-forgotten time capsule in a heavy box made of lead that had been sealed on September 3, 1912. It was opened on May 2 in the gymnasium in front of a special assembly of students and found to include the August 28, 1912, edition of the *Chilliwack Progress*, a copy of the long-defunct *Chilliwack Free Press*, and four coins from back in the day. Chilliwack Museum & Archives

and contracts were finalized. CJSS was torn down in April of that year, and by September the new CMS opened on what had been the location of CHS, CJHS, and CJSS for over eight decades. In March 1996, just prior to demolition of the 1913 brick building, a grand reunion was held to say goodbye to CJSS and, in particular, the venerable original structure. Approximately 1,500 staff, students, and others associated with the school over the years came out to celebrate and pay their respects to what was a big part of their lives and of Chilliwack's history. A highlight of the weekend was recreating the original procession from the old CHS to the succeeding one. A parade of vintage cars and students, some in costume, accompanied by a 100-piece marching band, made its way from the location of Central School's gymnasium (roughly the site of the first high school) to CJSS. An enthusiastic pep rally then followed.

Today, CMS occupies the site of CHS and what eventually became CJSS, but the actual location of the original 1913 brick building is now

Chilliwack Middle School is now over a quarter century old and bears no resemblance to its predecessor, Chilliwack Junior Secondary School. One stark difference is the security fencing around the perimeter of the school property, a sign of changing times. Merlin Bunt Collection

a parking lot. For over a century, there has been a school on Yale Road at Charles Street. Although the structures have changed, memories live on for the forty-thousand-plus students who attended school at this location.

LITTLE MOUNTAIN ELEMENTARY SCHOOL, 1954

One of Chilliwack's higher-profile schools is Little Mountain Elementary, situated two kilometres east of Five Corners at the northern foot of Carleton Street in the city's northeast sector. Construction of the school and its frequent expansions in later years were largely in response to the community's growth after the end of World War II. At the start of the 1950s, there was no elementary school to accommodate the growing number of school-aged kids in this area of town. Most elementary students were then travelling to Central School, with some later attending Cheam Elementary. Exacerbating matters, the new Menzies Subdivision (see chapter 4) was developing as an important residential neighbourhood, home to many young families with baby boomer children. Although Chilliwack Senior High School opened in 1950, somewhat easing the pressure on overall classroom supply, it was still not enough to address the school overcrowding issue, the effects of which ultimately trickled down to the elementary grades.

On October 29, 1952, A. D. Rundle, chair of the Chilliwack school board, announced that to meet enrolment growth, four new school classrooms were required in the district per year for at least the next six years. As an early step in addressing the anticipated demand, in 1953 the school board acquired a four-acre parcel of vacant land adjacent to both Portage Avenue and Carleton Street for a new elementary school. In early 1954, plans were unveiled for a three-room school, with provision for expansion to six rooms in the coming years, as enrolment needs dictated. In July, the land was graded, and construction of the new school commenced shortly thereafter. The name chosen for the new institution was Little Mountain Elementary School (LME), in recognition of Little Mountain, the prominent Chilliwack landmark only 225 metres to the east. Completion of the new school was targeted for the start of the 1954–55 school year. Although it was designed to be an elementary school, two of LME's three rooms were occupied by Grade 9 students when it first opened, such was the overcrowding at the high school level.

The opening of Little Mountain Elementary resulted in many young people congregating on busy Yale Road East on their way to school. Part of the attraction was Little Mountain Market, built in 1947 at the northeast corner of Yale and Carleton. It was immediately embraced by students, given its proximity to the school. To improve their safety, in November 1954 the speed limit between Prest Road and what later became Windsor Street was reduced to thirty miles per hour (still considerably above the limit in today's school zones). For the two decades following the opening of LME, its students continued to frequent Little Mountain Market before and after school, as well as at lunch hour, and school administrators were challenged to prevent them from spending too much time in and around it.

The significant overcrowding of schools in Chilliwack continued into the mid-1950s, and in December 1954, Chilliwack taxpayers approved a comprehensive, five-year school capital plan. This enabled LME to expand by three classrooms for a total of six. Plans for the $25,680 addition were finalized in April 1955, tenders were called in May, and the three new rooms opened on September 11. The school's total enrolment was now dominated by 150 Grade 9 students. While this and other incremental expansions of elementary schools somewhat eased the district's space crunch, it was the opening of the new 525-student, 24-room Sardis Junior High School on September 10, 1956, that largely reduced overcrowding in the community's schools. This quantum increase in classroom supply ultimately allowed the Grade 9 students attending LME to return to Chilliwack Junior High School, which in turn allowed LME to finally be a true elementary school.

On May 10, 1956, Chilliwack's School District 33 appointed Bill Bunt Sr. (1929–2008) as the first full-time principal of Little Mountain Elementary. Bunt had served as principal of Rosedale Elementary School for the previous three years and was principal of Atchelitz Elementary School for two years prior to that. For his first year at Little Mountain, enrolment was 214 students. As Chilliwack's strong growth continued through the 1950s, so did the need for elementary classrooms, particularly in the school's catchment area. Accordingly, a further three classrooms would be added to Little Mountain Elementary, bringing its total to nine. Tenders for the project were called in October 1958; one new classroom opened in January 1959 and the other two in September. Also in 1958, a future third access road to the school was added—in addition to Carleton Street and Portage Avenue, students were eventually able to travel along Macken Avenue. In February 1960, with a view to adding still more classrooms in the near future, an adjacent acre of land was purchased. And in 1961, the school's campus was further augmented by acquisition of a two-acre site to expand its playground. However, new classroom construction did not occur when anticipated, and overcrowding at the school mounted. For the 1961–62 school year, the school board reached an agreement with the nearby Broadway Mennonite Brethren Church, renting its basement for $125 per month to serve as an overflow classroom to accommodate some of Little Mountain's 355 students.

In late 1961, school board officials approved further expansion of LME, including three new classrooms, a new gymnasium (also referred to as an "activity room" at the time), and expansion and landscaping of the school grounds. Tenders were called in February 1962, and work commenced the following month. The three new classrooms were completed in time for the start of the 1962–63 school year, bringing the school's capacity to twelve. As part of the project, a four-acre section of school land was cleared and graded for a larger kids' playground. While the area was being landscaped, a significant archaeological discovery occurred. In what was described as a "major historical find," over

Students play in front of Little Mountain Elementary School's western doors in 1961. A new gymnasium would be added in this spot the following year, part of expansions that saw the school double its classroom capacity in just a few years, growing to nine rooms and then twelve. Chilliwack Museum & Archives

one hundred Indigenous artifacts and implements were uncovered on the school's grounds. The unearthed artifacts included scrapers, pipe bowls, grinding pestles, and tools for cleaning and working hides. On May 1, members of UBC's Archaeology Department visited the site to assess the find. Ultimately, the discoveries were presented to the Chilliwack Museum and Historical Society for display.

Until the 1960s, Central School's eighteen classrooms were expected to handle all overflow placement needs for elementary students in the district. However, by September 1962 this pressure had eased, since there were now twenty-seven other elementary classrooms in the district, including LME's twelve. By 1963, the school was an

L-shaped structure, and with its student body numbering in excess of 450, still further expansion loomed. At the start of the 1966–67 school year, another two classrooms were in place, bringing the school's total to fourteen—a far cry from the small, three-room school built twelve years earlier. An additional classroom was added in 1968, and in June 1970, approval was received for construction of two more rooms.

Bill Bunt oversaw much of the change at LME over the years, including expansion of its physical structure, its school grounds, and the size of its student body. He became the school's longest-serving principal, leaving in 1973 after seventeen years of service. In his time, he positively influenced many of the hundreds of students who walked the halls of Little Mountain during his time there as a teacher and chief administrator.

Today, while Little Mountain Elementary is considerably larger than in earlier times, its south-facing facade remains essentially the same, notwithstanding the addition of two overlapping arched canopies in 2015. The inspiration for the school's name, Little Mountain, is always present, less than 250 metres away. Merlin Bunt Collection

On the occasion of its fiftieth anniversary, on May 14, 2004, LME held an open house celebration ("a gala Mardi Gras Carnival"), inviting numerous alumni and teachers to the event. Long-time principal Bill Bunt was a guest of honour, reminiscing with many of his previous students and teachers.

There are currently over twenty elementary schools in Chilliwack, with Little Mountain Elementary, at 9900 Carleton Street, being the second-largest in the district. As it grew over time, its physical footprint evolved from I-shaped to L-shaped to U-shaped, and its school grounds now extend north to Portage Avenue and east to Quarry Road. In 2015, two overlapping free-standing arched canopies were added in front of the school's main entrance, intended to introduce some architectural flair and a fun element, and to a lesser extent provide shelter from rain.

Thousands have walked the school's halls and played on its sports fields over the decades, and many students retain fond memories of their formative years at this venerable school in the shadow of its namesake Little Mountain.

CHILLIWACK SENIOR SECONDARY SCHOOL, 1950–2013

During the twentieth century, smaller communities generally had only one senior high school, and this civic institution affected almost everyone in town in some manner. Students, especially, formed many lasting relationships, values, and life directions while attending high school. Such was the case with Chilliwack and its dominant Chilliwack Senior Secondary School. Tens of thousands of students attended this school, and the experiences they had there, for better or worse, largely remain with its grads to this day.

The genesis of CSSS dates back to the early 1940s. Chilliwack High School, located on Yale Road East, was experiencing overcrowding issues despite a large expansion in 1939. By 1944, projected increases in student numbers and community growth prompted plans to develop a separate new senior high school, with the existing CHS to become a junior high. The school board acquired options to purchase a twenty-two-acre site just north of Yale Road East at Charles Street, essentially across from CHS. Five acres of the site were already being cultivated by CHS's agricultural students, while the remainder would be devoted to the new high school campus.

At that time, all municipal borrowing for capital expenditures required 60 percent approval in a bylaw vote put to city and township taxpayers. To the frustration of many, two bylaw votes for the new school were both defeated in 1944, with the ongoing World War II felt to have been a factor in voters' minds. The school board decided to withdraw its initiative and instead focus on making do with its current facilities. But over the next three years, as the community's population continued to grow, overcrowding problems in Chilliwack's schools worsened.

By early 1947, some of the high school's 1,150 students were forced to attend classes in ten temporary classrooms elsewhere in the city. Well aware of the mounting pressures, school district trustees prepared to present another bylaw proposition to the community's voters for development of a new senior high school. This time the initiative was bigger and more ambitious, augmented by increased government support. The new school was described as a "low sprawling example of modern design," and tentative plans called for a structure with twenty-two rooms. The seventeen-acre site was divided into areas for the school structures, parking lot, playing fields, and additional cultivated plots for use by agricultural students. (At the time, agriculture played an important role in Chilliwack's economy, and it was given commensurate weight in the curriculum.)

Ongoing refinement of the plans revealed a 60-foot-wide vehicle access off Yale Road East as well as a 440-foot walkway from the street to the school's front entrance. The proposal was put to a taxpayer vote on February 7, 1948. On that stormy day, voter turnout was relatively low, but the bylaw was finally approved with a solid majority of

75 percent. Final details were addressed, and after the two municipal councils gave their joint approval in July to proceed, construction was set to commence later that year. It was postponed, however, because by October it was evident that the overall cost of the project was going to exceed the taxpayer-approved amount. After exploring options, in January 1949 officials confirmed that the school's gymnasium would be delayed until the necessary funding became available.

Construction of the community's new high school finally started in February 1949, and by March the foundation was laid and framing underway. The project, described as "a harmony of glass, wood, and concrete," was 80 percent finished in October, and by the end of the year it was essentially complete and ready to accept students. On January 9, 1950, despite a major snowstorm, the new institution opened its doors to its first student body. Chilliwack High School principal G. W. Graham led a ceremonial trek of 875 students north across the Trans-Canada Highway to the new Chilliwack Senior High School (it would take the name Chilliwack Senior Secondary School in 1962). One popular feature of the new school was a 350-seat cafeteria, with all cooking done in "specially designed kitchens." Students were also impressed with the school's windows and all the light that streamed into their classrooms (though during the warmer months, there were complaints that they allowed in too much heat). A public open house took place on March 9, and the consensus was that students were "a very lucky modern generation" and that the new school was a magnificent addition to Chilliwack. At the conclusion of their tour, upwards of 1,500 district residents were treated to refreshments in the new cafeteria.

The need for a gymnasium was definitely not forgotten, and in August tenders were opened for construction of the postponed structure. The district received four bids, each significantly higher than budget. As a result, on September 27 the school board abruptly announced that it was yet again cancelling plans to build a gymnasium. But trustees did note they would continue efforts to produce a plan for a suitable gymnasium with an acceptable budget.

Pictured in the spring of 1950, the new Chilliwack Senior High School had opened just a few months earlier. The campus grounds north of the buildings were undeveloped, and it would not be until 1959 that the cinder track was in place. Similarly, the future location of the school's gymnasium accommodated only trees and a couple of sheds at this time. Both of these school infrastructure components were delayed due to funding issues. Merlin Bunt Collection

On April 9, 1951, city and township councils approved a funding allocation for a scaled-down gymnasium at CSHS. With plans back on track, work on the new structure was underway by May. However, due to a series of unanticipated delays, it was not substantially completed until February 1952. The first event in the new facility occurred on Friday evening, February 8, when the school's eight hundred students and teachers participated in a costumed indoor track meet.

On May 16, the school's gleaming new gymnasium was officially opened at a well-attended ceremony. Speakers noted that it was considered to be one of the finest in BC. The *Chilliwack Progress* reported that "a sparkling new era in physical education is coming up." The new gym had a number of unusual and desirable features, including the latest in air-conditioning systems. The floor was made of springy eastern maple, and the basketball backboards, normally composed of wood or Bakelite, were made of glass—the gym was one of only three venues in BC at the time with this innovative feature. The auditorium's entrance hall, connecting it to the main school structure, featured a glass trophy showcase that remained until the school was taken down in 2013.

CSSS has long featured strong sports teams, but when the school was completed in 1950, the ten-acre athletic field at the rear of the structure (fronting Portage Avenue) remained largely undeveloped. Tentative plans called for a 440-yard track, two full-size soccer fields, and two baseball diamonds. By the spring of 1951, permanent pole vault, high jump, and broad jump pits were already in place, as were the two baseball diamonds, complete with backstops. Officials hoped that the cinder track would be operational by the spring of 1952, but it was stalled for

Students study on a lush lawn below large shade trees in an idyllic image taken in front of Chilliwack Senior High School in the 1950s. The school had replaced the old Chilliwack High School to ease overcrowding. Royal BC Museum and Archives

the next three years due to funding and supply issues. In October 1956, officials announced that work on the long-awaited track would start in the spring of 1957; ultimately, it was not completed until late 1958, eight years after CSHS opened. Eventually, in 2004, CSSS's long-standing team names of Frontiersmen for boys and Tillicums for girls were phased out, to be replaced by Storm. The new Storm theme was displayed prominently in the gymnasium, with storm graphics adorning all four walls.

But as the twenty-first century dawned, the imminent end of CSSS's functional life was evident. Rather than invest in required seismic and energy efficiency upgrades for the fifty-year-old structure, school trustees planned for a new school. In 2008, the provincial government approved construction of a new CSSS. Three years later, after much dialogue and focused planning, the vision for the new secondary school was publicly unveiled. The new facility was double the size of the existing one, and the main playing field had an all-weather surface. The

The final event at the J. Y. Halcrow Gymnasium took place on June 10–11, 2013, and on the morning of July 29, demolition of the aging gymnasium began. Phase 1 of the new Chilliwack Secondary School project had commenced in May 2011 with demolition of part of the north wing, along with the music building, and construction of the school structure began two months later. *Chilliwack Progress* Archive

professional-sized gymnasium was expected to attract athletic students to the school, which also had a second, smaller gym.

The challenge of constructing a new school on the same site as the existing one, with classes in session as usual, was met by building it in two phases. Phase 1 commenced in May 2011 with demolition of part of the north wing, along with the music building. Phase 2, construction of the school structure, started in September north of the existing building and closely abutting the original cinder running track. The new 224,000-square-foot Chilliwack Secondary School would finally open its doors to students on September 3, 2013 (though construction was not fully completed until early 2014).

Earlier in 2013, with the approaching demise of the remaining portion of CSSS, a large and well-attended community celebration was organized. The tribute was called Chilliwack Senior Secondary School—Hello, Goodbye Reunion 1950–2013. Held March 1–3, it included a series of events at various venues that chronicled and paid respect to the high school's history. Approximately five thousand former students, staff, and teachers attended the celebration over the weekend. All the socials and parties were sold out, and the sentimentally reminiscing crowds travelled down a number of literal and figurative memory lanes within the old CSSS building on the Saturday.

For over six decades, CSHS/CSSS accommodated thousands of Chilliwack students, in some ways serving as their second home. Many who graduated prior to 2013 have a difficult time visualizing where their old high school was located, such was the complete transformation of the campus and its structures. Nevertheless, countless cherished memories of high school life in the community remain intact, including favourite teachers and the formation of lifelong friendships. For Chilliwack alumni, photographs, yearbooks, and regular grad reunions help to keep those memories fresh.

J. Y. HALCROW, PRINCIPAL OF CHILLIWACK SENIOR SECONDARY, 1955–1977

Over the years, a number of Chilliwack citizens have distinguished themselves by leaving a positive and lasting mark on the community. One such individual was J. Y. Halcrow. For those of a certain age, he was their senior high school principal during their final years of public schooling. Halcrow bridged a number of cultural eras in the twentieth century, touching the lives of thousands of local teenagers. For twenty-two years, he ran a tight operation at Chilliwack Senior Secondary School, overseeing students from the button-down Elvis/Eisenhower era of the '50s, through the Beatles and turbulent counterculture '60s, and concluding with the funky disco and garish fashion era of the '70s. With a passion for teaching, he strived to ensure that all his students received a balanced education so that when they graduated from CSSS, they were ready to adapt to an ever-changing world as adults.

Long-time Chilliwack Senior Secondary principal Jim "J. Y." Halcrow, pictured in 1967. A former RCAF pilot, Halcrow was considered an authoritarian figure in some circles, yet was unfailingly charming in person. CSSS 1967 Annual

Born in 1915 in Winnipeg, James Ypres Halcrow relocated to BC with his family at an early age. Upon graduation from high school, he wanted to study architecture, but his father suggested that teaching would be a better career choice. Halcrow decided to give it a shot, doing well in the training phase and, to his admitted surprise, quite enjoying it. He chose an accelerated path to teaching that involved studying for a year at the Provincial Normal School in Vancouver, from which he graduated at age eighteen. He was then issued an interim licence to teach, with the proviso that he make specified progress towards attaining his university degree within a given timeline. The following year Halcrow received his first teaching assignment, at a one-room schoolhouse in Yahk, BC, a tiny community near Creston. After teaching there for one year, he moved on to Canal Flats, a CPR company town northeast of Kimberley, where he became principal of a four-room school for four years. In 1939, at age twenty-four, Halcrow became principal of a much larger school in Penticton, covering Grades 1 to 10. He took a break from teaching a year later and enrolled at UBC to complete the requirements for his Bachelor of Arts degree. While at university, Halcrow became active in the UBC Players Club, and he first visited Chilliwack on a theatrical tour of BC on April 29, 1940, performing in two presentations of *Pride and Prejudice* in the gymnasium of Chilliwack High School before full houses.

With World War II soon in full swing, Halcrow took a leave of absence from teaching and joined the Royal Canadian Air Force. He was based in eastern Canada and served as a pilot and navigator, as well as teaching these disciplines. While stationed in Prince Edward Island, he married Billie Freeman in 1944. He returned to the Okanagan after the war ended and was appointed vice-principal of the 1,300-student Penticton High School. Here he also became one of BC's first high school counsellors. In 1948, he was offered the role of superintendent of schools but declined, preferring to teach and have continuing close contact with students.

In 1955, the Halcrows were on their way to Mexico for a family vacation. While stopped in Seattle, Jim Halcrow was reading the *Vancouver Sun* and saw an advertisement for the role of principal of Chilliwack Senior High. The Halcrows immediately postponed their vacation and drove to Chilliwack so that he could investigate the opportunity, spending three days at the Rainbow Motor Inn on Yale Road West. He was ready for a change, and he and Billie were impressed by the Chilliwack area after spending some time there several years earlier. The newness of the five-year-old high school was also an appealing factor.

He ultimately got the job and in September 1955, at age forty, Halcrow began his career as principal of CSHS. At the time it was the only high school in the Chilliwack area, with an increasingly unwieldy enrolment of 1,148 students, from Grades 9 to 13. For the first ten years of Halcrow's tenure, virtually every senior high school student in the entire Chilliwack area passed through his halls. (Having earlier relieved some of CSHS's capacity pressures, Sardis Junior High became Sardis Junior-Senior High in 1964, splitting the area's senior student population.)

Given the nature of high school students, they had a number of nicknames for Halcrow (seldom, if ever, uttered directly to his face). Probably the most common one was simply J. Y. If some students were hanging around doing nothing or perhaps up to no good and Halcrow was spotted approaching, they muttered "Yipes," which was code for "Look out, J. Y.'s coming," and any inappropriate behaviour immediately ceased. The nickname "Yipes" was also a play on Halcrow's middle name, Ypres, after the significant 1914 World War I battle staged in Belgium just before his birth.

To students new to Chilliwack Senior High, it was evident early on that Halcrow ran the school. Whatever the situation, he was on top of it, and he made things happen as he envisioned they should. He was considered somewhat of an authoritarian figure in some circles, yet was unfailingly charming in person. Although it was an entrenched policy during most of his era, Halcrow did not believe in corporal punishment (that is, using the strap), explaining that he could never strike another person's child. One enduring memory of Halcrow was his deep, resonant voice (perhaps honed through his drama training) on the PA system in the morning announcements, although not all of the students were totally onside with the content or length of his messages. And, as evidenced by his carefully considered pieces in the school annuals over the years, he was somewhat of a philosopher.

J. Y. Halcrow took an active interest in all student affairs and activities. In this 1957 image, he is attending a Chilliwack Senior High School student council meeting. CSSS 1957 Annual

Performing in live theatre, as he had done at UBC years earlier, became a passion for much of Halcrow's adult life. As a member of the Chilliwack Players Guild, he performed in numerous local productions, including *Caligula*. In 1961, he also directed a Mexican comedy called *Sunday Costs Five Pesos*. Halcrow was known as a stylish dresser, at least for a school principal. No matter what the era or fashion, he seemed to keep current. And he always turned out to support school events, often with Mrs. Halcrow, and in costume if circumstances warranted. Under his watch, CSSS became the first high school in BC to adopt a semester system. He was also a founding member of the British Columbia Principals' and Vice Principals' Association, the predecessor to the BC Teachers' Federation.

In 1977, after more than two decades as principal of CSSS, Halcrow announced his retirement at age sixty-two. On June 28, in his last official duty, he shook the hands of the 330 students from that year's graduation class as they walked across the stage of the school's gym.

His final speech drew a standing ovation from the 1,200 in attendance. The *Chilliwack Progress* noted that Halcrow's retirement marked the passing of an era. Over the years, he gained students' respect, treating them like adults and teaching them to think accordingly. When he announced his retirement, he said he hoped to do some travelling and pursue other neglected interests. He did just that for the next several years, occasionally coming back to his beloved school as a speaker or guest at some function. However, by the early part of 1984, he became critically ill. On June 21, at a well-attended gathering, school officials announced that CSSS's auditorium was being officially named the J. Y. Halcrow Gymnasium in his honour. Halcrow was too ill to attend and hear this announcement in person, and less than a month later, on July 18, he passed away at St. Paul's Hospital in Vancouver.

About thirty years later, the final event at the J. Y. Halcrow Gymnasium took place—basketball tryouts for the CSSS girls' team for the upcoming season. On the morning of July 29, 2013, demolition of the aging gymnasium started. It took two large excavators only a matter of hours to reduce the storied structure to a heap of bricks, wood and twisted metal. By contrast, J. Y. Halcrow's time in Chilliwack as an educator was lengthy and his legacy within the community substantial. He was a man of substance, style, principle, and empathy, and even decades on, his positive impact on students is indelible. The memory of his persona, achievements, and life lives on in the consciousness of thousands of grads who consider him an integral part of their high school years.

Chapter 10

THE SPORTING SCENE

THE ONSET OF WORLD WAR II CURTAILED A NUMBER OF SPORTING AND recreational pursuits in Chilliwack, for many athletes were deployed overseas and local resources were scarce. After the war there was a groundswell of renewed interest in various sports. Events and facilities discussed in this chapter include Monarch Park, the city's first complete hardball and softball diamonds. Local interest in baseball was so intense that park improvements were ongoing, and the city eventually developed additional fields. Bowling was another popular pastime, with two long-time bowling alleys serving the local demand. The history of Meadowlands Golf & Country Club has as many ups and downs as the course itself. And hockey pros and amateurs both show up in this chapter, in accounts of a Toronto Maple Leafs exhibition game played before a packed Chilliwack Coliseum in September 1962 and a legendary Chilliwack Peewee hockey championship in December 1965.

MONARCH PARK, 1947–2001

Until the 1950s, the three biggest sports in North America generally were baseball, boxing, and horse racing. The first in particular had a broad appeal, since both genders and most ages could play, and the sport did not require much equipment. Earlier in the twentieth century, most smaller towns throughout Canada had a dedicated baseball park with at least one local team that residents supported. Chilliwack was no different.

The community's first baseball facility, Athletic Park, opened in 1934 at a fifteen-acre property bounded by Young Road, Second Avenue, Fifth Avenue, and almost to Nowell Street to the east. During World War II, interest in baseball waned, as did finances available to maintain the park, and it gradually fell out of favour. City council decided to put roads through the site, opening up the land for forty-six residential lots. (In 1946, returning veterans were given right of first refusal for the lots at discounted prices.) The demise of Athletic Park set the stage for what later became Chilliwack's second major baseball venue, Monarch Park, which more than carried on the legacy of its predecessor. For over half a century, it played a key role in the community's social fabric and sporting history.

In early 1945, as the war was winding down, there was much interest in Chilliwack developing its own community centre. At a council meeting on November 5, the city ended months of spirited debate by officially designating the fairgrounds as the location for the new development. Plans called for a new baseball park, arena, and grandstand to join the existing Agricultural Hall (built in 1936—see chapter 3), a few barns, and a large horse-racing track surrounding the grassed oval. For the 1946 baseball season—the first after the end of the war, with many local men back home looking to resume playing the sport—both a hardball and a softball diamond were set up within the large fairgrounds oval. However, many felt the transition from Athletic Park to the new venue was unsatisfactory. Locals voiced much dissatisfaction with the new layout, which lacked outfield fences, proper backstops and dugouts, and adequate spectator seating. As a result, discussions commenced in October on creation of two new baseball diamonds (one for hardball, one for softball), to be located at the northwest corner of Corbould Street and Hodgins Avenue.

In early 1947, with the new baseball season rapidly approaching, local players were complaining that they could not join a baseball league because they had no viable park to play in. In response, the city levelled some of the land at the proposed baseball site in April, and on May 20, on an unseeded "field" of dirt and gravel, teams played the first softball game at the future Monarch Park. This historic contest took place on what was ultimately the smaller softball field, directly north of what became the larger hardball diamond. A temporary makeshift backstop and mobile bleachers borrowed from the Ag Hall were employed for this game, far from optimal conditions but nevertheless an encouraging start for the community's baseball enthusiasts.

Baseball and softball were highly popular in Chilliwack after the war, with multiple leagues and more players than available venues. A baseball game at Monarch Park was a social event, and upcoming games were usually advertised in the *Chilliwack Progress*. This ad, from the June 19, 1957, edition of the paper, refers to the Monarch's Ball Grounds, to be renamed Monarch Park in 1960. *Chilliwack Progress* Archive

By the spring of 1948, the fairgrounds hummed with activity. In addition to work starting on the arena project, Chilliwack was to field a baseball team in the eight-team Dewdney League starting in April. Grass was planted on both the hardball and softball diamonds, and $400 was granted for extending the backstop, erecting bleachers, building a board fence to enclose the outfield, and installing a public address system. The fairgrounds' two baseball diamonds were completed in time for the 1948 season, although they were still rudimentary. They also did not have a formal name at this point and were often simply referred to as "the ballparks at the fairgrounds."

In 1950, a new baseball team called the Chilliwack Monarchs

was formed, playing in the Fraser Valley Baseball League. Several years later, the team's name served as the basis for naming what became a popular destination on the local social and sports scene for the next five decades. The terms "Monarchs' Ball Park" and "Monarchs' Ball Grounds" were first mentioned in 1954, referring to both the hardball and softball diamonds, and they were known as such for the duration of the 1950s. In 1960, the name was shortened to Monarch Park, which endured for the rest of the twentieth century. While the Connie Mack and Babe Ruth Leagues used the larger field, hardball Little League games were often played on the smaller softball diamond.

Circa 1960, the larger hardball field also served as home to the Chilliwack Mustangs of the Fraser Valley Football League, with an understandably adverse effect on the outfield grass. By 1961, both baseball diamonds were described as "teetering on their last legs due to neglect." This sparked a campaign of donations and volunteerism, along with grants from the city and township, to make repairs and upgrades: Bumps in the fields were levelled, backstops repaired, decayed fencing along Corbould Avenue ripped out, and rotten stands and dugouts replaced. On May 31, 1970, a record crowd of over 1,000 turned out at Monarch Park for a five-team Connie Mack hardball tournament.

In 1974, numerous complaints were raised about the number of August baseball games being called on account of darkness, since Monarch Park had no lights for nighttime action. Typical of the slow pace of improvements to the community's main baseball facility, not until 1976 were lights added, along with new brick dugouts and a new scoreboard. In 1980, Monarch Park was described as "poorly drained and overused." Exacerbating the situation, more leagues and teams were competing for time at the city's limited number of baseball venues.

To address the dearth and quality of facilities, the city made a major investment in Monarch Park later in 1980. It spent $60,000 on redesigning and upgrading the old hardball diamond adjacent to Hodgins Avenue, turning it into a smaller softball diamond with the same dimensions as the existing one directly to its north. This new field also had a

This 1974 image captures the pastoral splendour of the Monarch Park fastball diamond. The facility would later be converted to two softball venues in 1980 before being demolished in 2001. The site would be redeveloped as the home of the Chilliwack Landing Leisure Centre in 2002. Merlin Bunt Collection

new name—Fraser Park. It was an immediate hit, in play every day of the week. More than five leagues and thirty teams used the field, which also hosted weekend tournaments. The city also invested $30,000 in improvements to the existing softball park, directly south of the coliseum, which continued to be known as Monarch Park. The fairgrounds' two "new" softball diamonds—side by side, significantly upgraded, with lights enabling night baseball, and with distinct names—brought a new level of efficiency and harmony to Chilliwack's burgeoning softball scene. But with still more leagues and teams, by the mid-1980s there was again a call for more baseball facilities.

In response, in early 1985 the city took steps to acquire the Townsend property, a forty-acre parcel of undeveloped land at the southwest corner of Ashwell Road and Wolfe Road (475 metres west of Fraser Park). The intention was to turn this land into an expansion of the existing Chilliwack Exhibition Park, as the fairgrounds were then called. By July 1985, before any work had started, the land was being referred to as Townsend Park. The city envisioned that the project would be undertaken in multi-year phases. First, an all-weather soccer field that would be used extensively by both soccer and touch-football leagues was completed in 1988. Phase 3, finished in May 1991, featured four dedicated softball diamonds and two larger diamonds that could be used for hardball. At this time, Monarch Park and Fraser Park were still in high use, as there were over thirty teams in the Chilliwack Softball Association, including men's, women's, and church leagues. In 1992, the two venues received electronic scoreboards (at $8,000 per board), as did two of Townsend Park's softball diamonds. Also that year, the Chilliwack Softball Association further improved Monarch and Fraser Parks with new sprinkler systems that provided full irrigation of the infield and outfield, in addition to new outfield fencing, a storage hut, and new foul poles.

As the turn of the twenty-first century approached, plans were afoot for Chilliwack's fairgrounds to relocate, after almost a century at its familiar location, to Chilliwack Heritage Park, on Luckakuck Way at Lickman Road (see chapter 7). In anticipation of this big change, in June 1999, the city introduced a proposal to build an aquatic centre along with a new arena on the current exhibition grounds. Planners envisioned that the aquatic centre would be located on the site of the two baseball diamonds, Monarch Park and Fraser Park. Eventually the first Chilliwack Coliseum was also taken down and replaced by an arts and performance venue, the Chilliwack Cultural Centre. On February 22, 2001, both the Monarch and Fraser baseball diamonds were dug up to allow work to start on the future Chilliwack Landing Leisure Centre. The topsoil from the two fields was removed and trucked over to Townsend Park to be used there. Some locals, including long-time fans and players, watched the dismantling of these two baseball parks with a shared sadness, as a significant aspect of local sports history was now gone.

The official groundbreaking ceremony for the new recreational facility took place two months later, on April 28, 2001, and it officially opened on August 24, 2002. Some found it ironic that two baseball diamonds that were plagued by poor drainage over the years, with sometimes water-filled trenches, were replaced by a swimming pool. And others who were particularly upset to see the end of the ballparks voiced sentiments along the lines of "they paved paradise and put up a leisure centre," resulting in baseball players and fans going elsewhere. However, the majority recognized the evolution of the old Monarch Park site as progress, with Chilliwack baseball clearly coming out a winner. But long before these changes, back when the games were played on real grass in the sunshine, baseball dreams were very much alive on the two diamonds at the old fairgrounds.

TWO POPULAR BOWLING ALLEYS, 1946 AND 1958

In an era of limited entertainment options, bowling was a popular post-war recreational and social activity. It made its first appearance in Chilliwack in the early 1920s when Richards' Bowling Alley opened a three-lane facility on Wellington Avenue, across from what became the Royal Hotel Pub. But not until the 1940s did bowling really take hold in the city. On August 23, 1941, Chilliwack Bowling Alley, a seven-lane establishment, opened its doors to the public at 124 Young Road South, near Five Corners and directly across from the site of the future bus depot. The building had been constructed in 1938 as a roller-skating rink, but that venture failed after three years. Advertisements for Chilliwack Bowling Alley marketed bowling as a healthy sport, suggesting people should bowl to keep "trim" and that it was "healthy and fun," and the new alley was an instant success. City council conducted two investigations into the "moral, mental, and physical aspects of bowling alleys" and determined that unlike the reputation of pool halls, bowling venues were not the cause of juvenile delinquency or public nuisance. So on October 6 council voted to allow the city's two bowling facilities to extend their closing time from 11 p.m. to midnight each weekday, and to lower the legal age for bowling from eighteen to fourteen.

In 1946, W. D. "Doug" Hartley (1909–1975) purchased Chilliwack Bowling Alley and immediately changed its name to Chilliwack Recreations. He also soon discontinued ten-pin bowling due to "lack of enthusiasm for the sport," offering only the five-pin version. With Richards' Bowling Alley having permanently closed the previous year, Hartley's business was now the only bowling venue in town. By 1947, the largest bowling league ever organized in Chilliwack had 450 bowlers (also known as "keglers" and "trundlers" in newspapers of that era) vying for time on the city's limited number of lanes, essentially doubling participation from the previous year. To accommodate the rising demand, in September Hartley installed an eighth lane in his establishment, along with semicircular benches at the head of each alley to improve seating. He also remodelled the building's facade.

Demand for bowling time continued to grow, so in 1949 Hartley undertook an ambitious expansion. At a cost of $25,000, he added a second storey to his building to accommodate eight new lanes. He also created more space on the main floor for spectators and amenities by doing away with two of the existing lanes. The new layout had fourteen lanes under one roof, effectively increasing Chilliwack's bowling capacity by 75 percent. The main-floor reconfiguration included the addition of a new, modern coffee bar. The new second-floor lanes were dedicated to bowling leagues, while those on the lower level were for individuals and casual bowling. On Saturday evening, September 24, the improved and expanded Chilliwack Recreations officially opened to a big crowd of bowlers, generating positive reviews. Soon after, its name was changed to the Chilliwack Bowling Centre, as it would be known for the next three decades.

By the late 1950s, over seven hundred adult bowlers were registered in five-pin leagues in Chilliwack, in addition to two hundred students. The growth of television was making the sport even more popular, and entire families were now coming out. Once again the

Park Lanes Recreation opened in 1958 and was enthusiastically welcomed by Chilliwack's bowling community, as it nearly doubled the number of lanes in the city. The venue did not have automatic pin-setting technology, unlike Chilliwack Bowling Centre, so local youths supplemented their allowance by working as "pin boys" at Park Lanes. *Chilliwack Progress* Archive

availability of bowling times and lanes became an issue. Local businessman (and avid bowler) Jim Butchart recognized this market opportunity and proceeded with plans to develop a new ten-lane bowling centre on the second floor of an existing building at 11 Victoria Avenue East, near Young Road North. (It had been built in 1947 as a one-storey structure, adding a second floor in 1955 above its long-time tenant, the Chilliwack Second Hand Store.) On Friday evening, September 5, 1958, Park Lanes Recreation opened to the public. Mayor T. T. McCammon officially opened the venue, which featured a twelve-stool coffee bar serving food and drinks, and everyone present received a free game. Park Lanes also offered a standing $1,000 prize for anyone who bowled a perfect game. And it still employed "pin boys," as opposed to the automatic pin-setting equipment that was gaining popularity across North America.

Over the years, a friendly competition for Chilliwack's bowling dollar developed between Park Lanes and the Chilliwack Bowling Centre, although demand was strong enough to keep both alleys busy. Less than one year after Park Lanes opened, Hartley remodelled his facility, enlarging the downstairs area for both spectators and bowlers. In 1961, he modernized the bowling alley further, the highlight being installation of automatic pin-setting machinery on the six ground-floor lanes. The eight lanes on the upper level remained manually set, so its rates for bowlers were set a bit lower. Also, the entrance to the bowling alley was moved to the south corner of the structure to improve upstairs access. The interior was repainted, and new U-shaped seating was installed around modern scoring stands.

For the twenty-three years following the opening of Park Lanes, Chilliwack's bowlers got by with the two facilities and their total of twenty-four lanes. In 1978, developers announced plans for construction of a third bowling alley in the city, a twenty-lane venue atop the roller-skating rink called Fraser Valley Rollercade, which had opened at the corner of Princess Avenue East and Nowell Street South in 1977. However, this project never proceeded.

In the late twentieth century, Chilliwack's retail landscape was changing. As described earlier, a consumer migration south of Highway 1 exacerbated the decline of the downtown retail scene. At the same time, recreation options were growing with the advent of VCR players, video games, cable TV and more, reducing bowling's popularity. In response the owners of the city's two existing bowling alleys, the Gillespie family (Park Lanes) and the Hartley family (Chilliwack Bowling Centre), joined forces to create one large recreation complex for the community, the focal point of which was a consolidated bowling super-facility. In March 1981, the families announced they had leased the old Eaton's building (vacant since 1977) and were investing $750,000 in the venture. The new recreation centre included twenty-four five-pin bowling lanes on two levels, along with a restaurant, cocktail lounge, video games arcade, billiards lounge, five rental units, meeting rooms, and showcase window areas. Much of the equipment for the new bowling operation came from the former alleys, including the wooden bowling lanes

In 2006, the home of Chilliwack Bowling Centre for over four decades became the long-term location of Room by Room Furniture. In 2024, officials announced that the historic structure would be demolished to accommodate a comprehensive new residential/commercial development. Merlin Bunt Collection

themselves, which were removed by crane and transported by flatbed truck. After much local anticipation and curiosity, Chilliwack's new bowling centre, Chillibowl Lanes, officially opened on Wellington Avenue on September 4.

Chillibowl Lanes, at 45916 Wellington Avenue, is now into its fifth decade and is Chilliwack's only remaining bowling alley. The old Chilliwack Bowling Centre building, at 9232 Young Road, was completely renovated and upgraded (internally and externally) after Hartley vacated it in 1981, and in 2006 it became the long-term home of Room by Room Furniture. The second-floor space in the building that had accommodated the Park Lanes bowling alley, at 46017 Victoria Avenue, was reabsorbed by the Chilliwack Second Hand Store. That business gradually wound down and ultimately the structure became vacant. It

For twenty-three years, Park Lanes operated on the second floor of the Chilliwack Second Hand Store building on Victoria Avenue. This historic Chilliwack structure was demolished in 2022, along with the heritage Ashwell House next door, and in 2024 a paved city parking lot opened on the site. Merlin Bunt Collection

was listed for sale in 2018, but there were no takers. In 2022, the city issued a permit for demolition of the aging building, with the property slated for use as expanded parking, along with the old site of the heritage Ashwell House directly east.

The role of Doug Hartley in the development of bowling in Chilliwack cannot be overstated. Hartley was posthumously inducted into the BC Bowling Hall of Fame on January 29, 1977, for "tremendous contributions to bowling as a sponsor and in the area of promotion." Although the role of bowling in current culture is less than it once was, it is still enjoyed locally by the sport's enthusiasts, and the centenary of the pastime in the community was recently observed. For those of a certain age, bowling at the Chilliwack Bowling Centre and Park Lanes was an important part of their youth.

HOCKEY CAPITAL OF THE WORLD FOR A NIGHT, 1962

In the early 1960s, the National Hockey League had only six teams. It was generally held that the best 125 hockey players in the world played in the NHL (a belief disproven by Russia in 1972). This was long before Major League Baseball and the National Basketball Association made inroads into Canada, and thus hockey was by far the country's pre-eminent sport, with men and boys (and certainly some women and girls) religiously following the NHL. For those living west of Quebec, their favourite team was often the Toronto Maple Leafs, and Chilliwack had many Leafs fans. A much-anticipated ritual in the community—repeated across Canada in different time zones—was the family gathering around their black-and-white television set on Saturday to watch *Hockey Night in Canada*. Starting at 5:30 p.m. on CBC Channel 2, the action was described live by Foster Hewitt in Maple Leaf Gardens or Danny Gallivan in the Montreal Forum. Since there was no instant replay or recording capability, viewers had to hope they would not miss a goal when they had to be away from the living room. Youngsters followed their NHL hockey heroes via the weekly game on TV as well as through hockey cards, magazines, colourful coins found in potato chip packages, and the *Star Weekly*'s full-page, colour hockey posters, which often adorned their bedroom walls.

In this context, Chilliwack got a taste of being the centre of the hockey universe for one evening. In the early 1960s, some NHL teams made a road trip out west to play several exhibition games prior to returning east for the start of the regular season. The main reason for these lengthy pre-season trips was public relations—an opportunity to spread the gospel of the game and the league, as well as increase a team's fan base. For a couple of years Chilliwack was on this West Coast NHL circuit, since it was relatively close to Vancouver and the Chilliwack Coliseum was new and big enough to host NHL-calibre hockey.

In an afternoon game on October 1, 1961, the Detroit Red Wings became the first NHL team to play in Chilliwack, taking on the minor-league San Francisco Seals before a crowd of 2,500 enthusiastic fans. In April 1962, the Toronto Maple Leafs won the Stanley Cup, and five months later they were set to make a brief West Coast trip as the reigning champions, with an exhibition game scheduled for Chilliwack. As was the case the prior year, the NHL team's opposition was the San Francisco Seals, a Western Hockey League team that held its training camp in the city several times in the early 1960s. The big game was set for September 25, 1962, with the opening faceoff at 8:30 p.m. As the Toronto Maple Leafs, viewed by many as "Canada's team," were coming to town, tickets moved quickly, and adults and children alike were excited about the prospect of seeing NHL hockey live.

Although several advertisements for the Toronto Maple Leafs game ran in the *Chilliwack Progress*, they were not necessary. The whole city was aware of the big event, and the game was a sellout. The record crowd on hand at the Chilliwack Coliseum that evening is equivalent to attendance of 12,000 in 2025. *Chilliwack Progress* Archive

The big day finally arrived, and with the event an assured sellout, promoters held back four hundred tickets to go on sale as rush seats a few hours before faceoff, just to increase the hype surrounding the game. It was Tuesday, a school night, and many students were out long beyond their usual bedtimes. As game time approached, there was a loud buzz of energy in the air outside the fairgrounds on Corbould Street, with most every parking spot in the area taken, and many people about on the warm autumn evening. Once fans got inside the coliseum, most received the simple "Souvenir Programme," a yellow, one-sheet, two-sided summary of the teams' lineups. At 8:30 the puck was dropped, and Chilliwack was watching the best hockey team in the world in action.

To many of the young fans in attendance, the Maple Leafs looked big, fast, heroic, and impressive in their blue uniforms. The game set a record to that point for the biggest crowd in the history of the four-year-old coliseum—3,086, considerably above the arena's stated capacity of 2,303. The Seals took an early 1–0 lead in the contest, but ultimately the Maple Leafs cruised to a 6–2 victory, much to everyone's expectation and delight. The unseasonably warm late-September weather made for sluggish ice conditions late in the game, but this bothered no one at the sold-out arena (other than perhaps the players).

In that era, obtaining autographs of their sports heroes was important for kids. And in the case of hockey-obsessed youngsters, nothing was more prized than the autographs of NHL players. It was cleared in advance with many parents that as soon as the game was over, the kids would head down and get a few autographs—which was usually innocuous enough, but many in the big crowd that evening had the same idea. With the coliseum's north–south corridors being relatively narrow, the post-game scene was bedlam. The Maple Leafs were in a locker room on the west side of the rink and their team bus was parked close to the exit door, which in turn was proximate to their dressing-room door. But getting the short distance from the locker room to the bus proved challenging. In the west corridor there were people everywhere, hoping for even a glimpse of an NHL player, let alone an autograph. One could literally not move in the scrum, and some of the bigger boys were crowding out small kids as they clamoured for autographs. Many fathers did manage to manoeuvre their kids into a position where they could see a few players, now showered, dressed in suits, and signing autographs for a long line of young fans. While many wanted to get the autograph of rising Leafs star Dave Keon (who had scored two goals that evening), the one most of the kids coveted was that of Frank Mahovlich.

In 1962, Mahovlich was regarded as one of the three best hockey players in the world, along with Bobby Hull and Gordie Howe. At six-foot-two, he was considered a tall player for his era, and he could skate and score. And in the generally acknowledged hockey capital of the world, Toronto, he was the focus. To give an indication of Mahovlich's stature at that time, just nine days after Mahovlich played in Chilliwack, the owner of the Chicago Blackhawks offered the Toronto Maple Leafs $1 million for the twenty-four-year-old left-winger, a staggering amount that stunned the hockey world. Fans in Toronto were immediately in an uproar, fearing the Leafs would accept the offer, but they turned it down. Meanwhile, back in the Chilliwack Coliseum's crowded west concourse, savvy kids looked for the longest lineup and the tallest player, and there stood Frank Mahovlich, looking splendid in his suit and signing autographs. The Leafs players were getting pressured to conclude the autograph session because their bus was soon leaving, but Mahovlich stayed as long as he could, accommodating most of the requests.

Most kids got home well past 11 p.m. that evening, and the next day they took their prized autographs to school to proudly show their friends who were unable to attend. The Maple Leafs soon returned home to Toronto, as the NHL All-Star game was set for Maple Leaf Gardens on October 6. The team went on to win the Stanley Cup that season and again in 1964, a rare three-peat that many fans viewed as justification for the team declining the big Mahovlich offer. (The Leafs won their

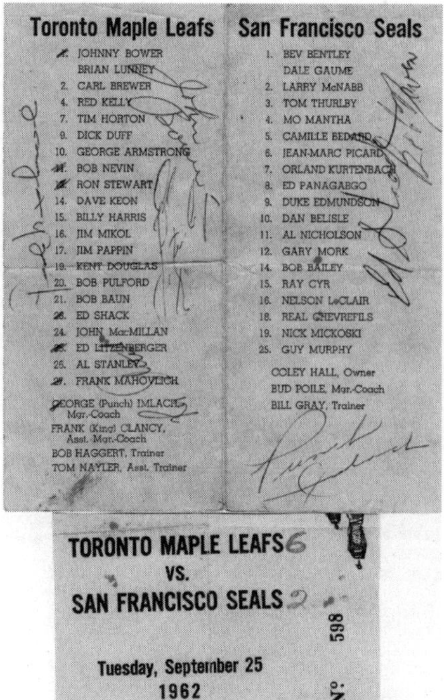

Toronto Maple Leafs

JOHNNY BOWER
BRIAN LUNNEY
2. CARL BREWER
4. RED KELLY
7. TIM HORTON
9. DICK DUFF
10. GEORGE ARMSTRONG
BOB NEVIN
RON STEWART
14. DAVE KEON
15. BILLY HARRIS
16. JIM MIKOL
17. JIM PAPPIN
19. KENT DOUGLAS
20. BOB PULFORD
21. BOB BAUN
ED SHACK
24. JOHN MacMILLAN
ED LITZENBERGER
26. AL STANLEY
FRANK MAHOVLICH

GEORGE (Punch) IMLACH, Mgr.-Coach
FRANK (King) CLANCY, Asst. Mgr.-Coach
BOB HAGGERT, Trainer
TOM NAYLER, Asst. Trainer

San Francisco Seals

1. BEV BENTLEY
DALE GAUME
2. LARRY McNABB
3. TOM THURLBY
4. MO MANTHA
5. CAMILLE BEDARD
6. JEAN-MARC PICARD
7. ORLAND KURTENBACH
8. ED PANAGABGO
9. DUKE EDMUNDSON
10. DAN BELISLE
11. AL NICHOLSON
12. GARY MORK
14. BOB BAILEY
15. RAY CYR
16. NELSON LeCLAIR
18. REAL CHEVREFILS
19. NICK MICKOSKI
25. GUY MURPHY

COLEY HALL, Owner
BUD POILE, Mgr.-Coach
BILL GRAY, Trainer

TORONTO MAPLE LEAFS 6
VS.
SAN FRANCISCO SEALS 2

Tuesday, September 25
1962

No. 598

The free, two-sided programs handed out at the Toronto Maple Leafs game served as an "autograph book" for many young fans, who braved the post-game madhouse outside the Leafs' dressing room in hopes of obtaining autographs of their heroes. On this particular program, one of the seven autographs collected that evening is the prized signature of Frank Mahovlich, to the left. Merlin Bunt Collection

fourth Stanley Cup in six years in 1967 but then endured a lengthy championship drought, leading to much derisive humour over the years.)

In addition to Mahovlich (who later served a fifteen-year term in the Canadian Senate), a number of other hockey icons were on the ice that night in Chilliwack in 1962. Tim Horton, of Tim Hortons coffee and doughnut fame, was an outstanding defenceman. Eddie "The Entertainer" Shack, better known for clowning around and fighting, was the MVP of the 1962 NHL All-Star game. Aging goaltender Johnny Bower was already thirty-eight years old and went on to play to the age of forty-five, not once wearing a mask. Bob Baun scored an overtime goal in the 1964 Stanley Cup playoffs while playing with a broken leg. Defenceman Red Kelly became the first active NHL player to be elected as an MP. And George Armstrong, captain of the Leafs for thirteen years, holds the distinction of scoring the last goal in the old NHL, prior to the league's expansion to twelve teams for the 1967–68 season.

Although the Chilliwack Coliseum eventually became old and obsolete, to be replaced in 2004 and torn down in 2005, many locals still remember when the city was the centre of the hockey world for a moment, and they were watching the Stanley Cup champion Toronto Maple Leafs at the local arena. For one glorious evening, it was *Hockey Night in Canada* live from Chilliwack.

MEADOWLANDS GOLF COURSE, 1933

Along with sports like baseball and bowling, golf became increasingly popular in Chilliwack after the war, aided by the early television era and a 1950s culture that held that aspiring business professionals must be proficient at the sport. The community's second golfing facility, Meadowlands Golf Course (situated on the north side of Yale Road, four kilometres east of Five Corners), became a prominent recreational destination during this era, and its name became synonymous with golfing in a beautiful Fraser Valley setting. Its history is characterized by an eventful series of highs and lows: a seventeen-year golfing monopoly in the city, high-profile owners, being sold numerous times, grandiose but unfulfilled expansion plans, significant financial difficulties, being foreclosed upon, a devastating fire, striving to survive, and eventually achieving a sound operational balance.

Meadowlands was built during the throes of the Great Depression. Robert C. Philipson (1883–1941) and his wife, who arrived in Chilliwack from England in 1919, purchased an existing farm in the area near Shannon Mountain (now called Little Mountain). Here Philipson focused on dairying and breeding Jersey cattle. About 1927, he realized his farming enterprise was no longer providing a fair return on his investment, and he ceased operations and sold his herd. For the next two years, the Philipsons rented out their land while they tried to decide what to do with it. Meantime, at the start of the 1930s, thousands of Canadians were taking up golf, and in Chilliwack there was only one golf course. Opened in 1924 on Fairfield Island, the Chilliwack Golf and Country Club enjoyed a local monopoly with the growing sport.

The Philipsons, recognizing the demand from the district's would-be golfers, decided to convert their farmland into a modern golf course.

For the next two years, the Philipsons painstakingly worked on the transformation, with Robert's hands on the plough turning the sod and his wife assisting him in the field. With some assistance, they removed hundreds of stumps before cultivating acres of golf-course-calibre grass. Philipson did retain a number of old farm structures, incorporating them in the course layout to add character to the whole experience. One barn became the Golf House, with men's and women's dressing rooms and a lounge with a fireplace. They named their course Meadowlands, since it was largely built in the vast meadow on the property.

Although the new Meadowlands Golf Course had only nine holes, Philipson cleverly engineered it to play as a full-size eighteen-hole course. Each of the nine holes had two tee boxes, differing in length to the hole by thirty to forty yards and positioned so that the two approaches to the green were not the same—an entirely different strategy was required on the same fairway, ultimately providing the same variety as larger courses. This approach resulted in Meadowlands essentially having a length of 6,040 yards, with no hole being fully repeated. On July 8, 1933, after over three years of hard work and preparation, Meadowlands Golf Course officially opened. Dignitaries from Vancouver attended, and afternoon tea was served in the Golf House following the games. Golfers who played a round that day opined that "the Philipsons have a course that will make a strong appeal to the expert as well as less-proficient player." The magazine *Canadian Golfer* described it as "the most unique golf course in Canada."

Meadowlands was popular from the start—after nine years, no longer was the Chilliwack Golf and Country Club the only option for the community's golfers. As Meadowlands was newer, larger, and ideally located on what soon became the Trans-Canada Highway, gradually the new course began to win over the earlier club's clientele. By 1934, Meadowlands was partnering with the Empress Hotel to provide golf packages to out-of-town visitors. In 1935, it built a new, rustic clubhouse

Golf became increasingly popular in Chilliwack after the war, as represented in this 1950s image. From 1941 to 1958, Meadowlands was the only course in town and well patronized. It had only nine holes until 1970, but its clever design allowed it to play as a full-size course.
Chilliwack Museum and Archives

with men's and women's change rooms, a dance floor, and a full kitchen. At the same time it introduced a separate practice fairway and putting green. In early 1941, the Philipsons sold Meadowlands to Jim Brodie, and on March 3, the Chilliwack Golf and Country Club closed for good, leaving Meadowlands the only golf course in town—a status it would enjoy for the next seventeen years.

But by 1942, the ongoing viability of Meadowlands was in question due to the impact of World War II. A six-man committee was appointed to devise a viable operating plan to keep the club open for the duration of the war. Through the diligence and care of its members, Meadowlands did survive the war years, although some corners were cut. In 1951, the course was purchased by Vancouver golf pro Dunc Sutherland, who vowed to "make it the best golf course in British Columbia." No purchase price was disclosed, but it was rumoured to have been approximately $50,000. Sutherland brought a wealth of golf experience and prestige to Meadowlands. Locals believed his arrival would elevate the course and the sport to a higher level in Chilliwack. In 1957, Sutherland quietly put Meadowlands up for sale. A group of prominent local golfers attempted to purchase or lease the course, but when a deal was not reached, they decided to build their own course, on the Trans-Canada Highway 400 metres east of Chadsey Road. The new Chilliwack Golf & Country Club (not to be confused with the earlier one on Fairfield Island) opened in 1958 with four hundred members, and it started taking away some long-time Meadowlands patrons. Nevertheless, by the early 1960s "lush and beautiful" Meadowlands was said to have "been manicured to perfection and bathed in atmosphere."

Starting in 1962, housing was being built on a portion of Little Mountain, much of which overlooked Meadowlands. Mount Shannon Estates (Phase 1) was a fifty-three-lot, contoured subdivision on the eastern slope of the mountain between the golf course and the cemetery area. Its official opening was on June 22, 1963, and much of its marketing efforts attempted to tie in its proximity to the pastoral and magnificent setting of Meadowlands. In October 1966, after fifteen years of owning and managing the course, Sutherland sold to two professional golfers: Johnny Johnston of Vancouver and Bill Mawhinney, then of Toronto, with a rumoured asking price of $135,000. At the time of the sale, the new owners announced that Meadowlands would continue as a public course and soon be expanded to eighteen holes. By May 1, 1970, the new nine holes were completed, and Meadowlands was officially an eighteen-hole, par-70 golf course, measuring 5,750 yards and fully utilizing its ninety-two acres. As the 1970s unfolded, the Sportsman Motor Hotel, located only 350 metres southeast of the course, started courting out-of-town golfers by offering package deals, similar to Meadowlands' arrangement with the Empress Hotel thirty-five years earlier.

In 1979, after owning Meadowlands for thirteen years and overseeing its expansion, Bill Mawhinney sold the course. The new owner soon announced plans to build a $700,000 clubhouse. The ambitious 20,000-square-foot project included a restaurant, racquetball courts, squash courts, sauna, whirlpool, and gym facilities. Work on the complex was to start in September, with its opening anticipated for January 1980. This development meant the end for Meadowlands' quaint original clubhouse, which was taken down on November 6. Due to bad weather and other factors, the vaunted new clubhouse was not even half finished by April 1980. To add to the uncertainty, later that year Meadowlands was again sold. There were delays with redevelopment plans, and the course itself was described as being in "serious condition" after four years of relative neglect.

In February 1981, the owners announced that the restaurant tenant in the new clubhouse would be Harvesters IV, which had operated for a number of years on Nowell Street downtown. After numerous delays, the new clubhouse complex was finally completed in November, the restaurant having opened the previous month. By spring 1982, in a worsening economic downturn with historically high interest rates, the ownership group of Meadowlands could not meet its financial obligations. The entire operation was placed in receivership while new capital was sought. Nevertheless, the golf course and its clubhouse continued to operate as usual.

Despite the grim economic picture, the club's owners announced expansion plans to turn Meadowlands into a major resort and convention destination, including a fifty-room hotel. City council supported this expanded vision, advocating for removal of two hectares at the southern tip of the property from the Agricultural Land Reserve. By summer 1984, despite the ongoing financial issues, work was expected to start soon on the expansion project, whose ambitious plans now included a 250-seat theatre in addition to the hotel. However, financial pressures persisted, and on October 1, 1985, First National Properties (Meadowlands' mortgage holder) foreclosed and became owner of the golf course, pledging to "provide the very best recreational and social facilities to the residents of the Chilliwack area." First National cancelled the hotel and theatre expansion ideas and then said it did not want to be in the golf course business, immediately putting Meadowlands up for sale, but there were no takers for the next three years.

A fire that destroyed most of the Meadowlands clubhouse on February 25, 1987, led to confusing messages about whether it would be rebuilt, and if so, to what scale. A smaller one was built in 1988, followed by a larger clubhouse in 1993 that overlooked the eighteenth green. *Chilliwack Progress* Archive

To add to Meadowlands' myriad challenges in the 1980s, on February 25, 1987, a devastating early-morning fire totally destroyed the top floor of the clubhouse, which housed the Harvesters IV restaurant, as well as much of the main floor. A burglar alarm sounded a few hours before the flames took hold, leading investigators to suspect arson, although this was never confirmed. Nevertheless, the golfing season at Meadowlands started as usual the following month. In April, temporary trailers were moved in to serve as a lounge and kitchen facility for the club's golfers. The mortgage holder, First National, initially announced it would rebuild the burned clubhouse but likely not include a restaurant component. Then, in December, the company announced it was not rebuilding the clubhouse. At that point, the property had been for sale for two years. In 1988, council unilaterally changed the zoning of the Meadowlands property, despite First National's objection. This change ensured the property remained a golf course, which was council's long-term vision, as opposed to being developed with other commercial ventures that might facilitate a sale.

In May 1988 Meadowlands was finally sold, to Jim Bryce, owner of a golf course in Fort Langley. He pledged to rebuild the clubhouse, upgrade the greens, install a new irrigation system, improve maintenance equipment, and spread flower gardens throughout the course. The rebuilt clubhouse, smaller and with fewer features than the previous version, was completed in August. South Sea Trading Corporation later bought Meadowlands from Bryce, and in 1993 it built a new clubhouse with banquet facilities that overlooked the eighteenth green.

Most of the old farm structures that were retained when Meadowlands opened in 1933 are gone today. But the course features numerous full-growth trees that contribute to its beautiful setting and layout, which helped it survive a long series of financial challenges. Merlin Bunt Collection

Notwithstanding all of its dramatic highs and lows over the years, Meadowlands remains a favourite with Chilliwack golfers, due in part to its beautiful setting and convenient location. Bordered by the Hope River on the east, the hills of Mount Shannon Estates to the southwest, a farm on the north, and Yale Road on the south, with abundant mature trees and surrounded by snow-capped mountains, Chilliwack's oldest surviving golf course has withstood numerous challenges yet always provides its members and guests with a memorable golfing experience.

THE CHILLIWACK PEEWEE HOCKEY JAMBOREE, 1959

Chilliwack has a long history of supporting junior hockey. However, the local hockey scene for youngsters did not seriously start until 1958, when the Chilliwack Coliseum was finally completed after ten years of delays and obstacles. With this welcomed facility finally in place, scores of kids could now learn and play hockey in an actual arena. The community's minor hockey movement soon became organized and quickly grew, supported by parents and volunteers. Various leagues and divisions were formed based on age and ability, including Pups, Peewees (for boys aged ten to twelve), Bantams and Midgets. From the outset, the new arena's ice time was heavily booked for hockey at all levels.

In 1959, an inaugural two-day, twelve-team Peewee hockey tournament took place at the coliseum immediately after Christmas. Compared to later editions, this first Chilliwack Peewee Hockey Jamboree was small in scale and support. But the popularity and scope of the event soared in subsequent years, expanding to three days in 1962 and four in 1964. Thirty-two teams participated in 1964, representing eight hundred players, coaches and parents. In addition to squads from the Lower Mainland, teams travelled from Prince George, Kelowna, and Vancouver Island, as well as from Washington and Oregon, which sent six teams. The tournament soon became a much-anticipated Christmas tradition in the community, with thousands of fans cheering for as many as forty teams from western Canada and the US. It was also the annual highlight for many young hockey-playing boys.

The players were assigned to one of three ability levels (known as the "A," "B," and "C" Divisions), with each team competing for the coveted championship in its group. Winning the "A" Championship was considered the most prestigious accomplishment. By the mid-1960s, the jamboree was the biggest minor sports event in western Canada. The coliseum was packed with enthusiastic family members and hockey fans alike for the entire tournament, with games starting at 6 a.m. and ending at 11 p.m. Each year the event required considerable planning, support, and co-operation to transport, feed, schedule, and provide accommodation for hundreds of young players (and their parents and team officials) over four days. For months in advance, upwards of two hundred volunteers and officials made preparations for the jamboree, ensuring the event was well organized and successfully staged. Out-of-town players were billeted at the old Agricultural Hall (see chapter 3) across from the coliseum, the Drill Hall / Armoury on Princess Avenue, and fans' homes. Three meals a day were dished up at the Agricultural Hall and Riding Club Hall to anyone involved in the tourney, with Canadian Forces Base Chilliwack often supplying the chow.

Pee Wee
HOCKEY
JAMBOREE
DEC. 27 - 28 - 29 and 30th
Games from 6 a.m. to 11 p.m. continuously

TICKETS

ADULTS: 4 day pass — includes Finals $2.00
This is the best buy for your money.
STUDENTS — 1 day pass 50c per day
ADULTS — 1 day pass $1.00 per day
All players registered in Minor Hockey in Chilliwack and producing '71 - '72 membership card — **FREE**
Children under 6 and accompanied by parent—FREE

Tickets may be purchased at the Evergreen Hall and any member of the Hockey Executive or Jamboree.
Support local hockey — This is the main fund raising campaign to keep hockey costs at a minimum.

Backed by upwards of two hundred volunteers and officials, the Peewee Hockey Jamboree was well planned and publicized, contributing to its success and steady growth. *Chilliwack Progress* Archive

The opening of the city's new hockey rink in 1958 coincided with the emergence of a generation of particularly talented homegrown kids who would realize the ultimate prize of their young lives seven years later. In 1953 and '54, a number of boys were born in the community who went on to form the nucleus of Chilliwack's "A" Division entry in the 1965 jamboree. To that point, Chilliwack had never won the elusive "A" Championship, but its team that year appeared poised to advance through the tournament's four rounds. In the team's first game, it defeated Capilano Winter Club by a score of 8–2, followed by a narrow 4–3 victory in the quarter-finals over a strong North Shore team (its first loss in eighteen games). On December 28, in the semifinal game, Chilliwack's "A" squad dominated Coquitlam 10–2. Two evenings later, at eight o'clock on December 30, Chilliwack faced off in the final against

As the scope, reputation and prestige of the Chilliwack Peewee Hockey Jamboree grew over the years, so did fan support and crowd size. Games took place non-stop between 6 a.m. and 11 p.m. at the coliseum, and the stands were often full. If a team from Chilliwack was playing, crowds were even bigger and more vocal. *Chilliwack Progress* Archive

Esquimalt. Chilliwack won this extremely tight game 2–1, with Dale Martin scoring in the first period and captain Greg Robinson netting the winner with seven minutes left in the third. Robinson was also voted the outstanding player of the "A" Division. The coliseum was packed to the rafters with extremely loud crowds for this jamboree, particularly for the "A" Division final. Indicative of the calibre of this vintage of local hockey talent, several members of the 1965 "A" team went on to play hockey at the major junior, college, and professional levels.

Since its inception in 1959, only once was Chilliwack's annual jamboree cancelled, and that was in 1996 when a heavy snowfall blanketed the city in the last week of December. During the blizzard, some players were stranded for a week in local hotels, and most of the 1,100 out-of-town fans, players and officials spent several nights in Evergreen Hall. After the turn of the twenty-first century, perhaps reflecting the trend with other long-time traditions, interest in the annual jamboree began to wane. The opening of the modern Prospera Centre (with two ice rinks) in 2004 did little to stem the downturn.

A number of factors were cited as contributing to the tournament's decline. At one time, Chilliwack's was the only post-Christmas Peewee

Chilliwack's "A" Division team in the 1965 Peewee Hockey Jamboree was a team of destiny, winning the community's first "A" championship that year. Third from the right in the front row is team captain Greg Robinson, who scored the winning goal in the December 30, 1965, championship game and was named the outstanding player in the "A" Division. *Chilliwack Progress* Archive

hockey tournament in the region, but by the early 2000s, there were over a dozen such events in the week between Christmas and New Year's. Also, while the jamboree had long operated on a not-for-profit basis, the new tournaments were profit-oriented—viewed as a means for their respective minor hockey associations to raise revenue—and this dynamic had its effect. Another complicating issue was inconsistent year-to-year continuity of volunteers running the tournament, exacerbated by an overall decline in volunteerism. Finally, life had become busier in late December, with numerous other entertainment options making it difficult for the jamboree to attract interest.

After a string of indifferent jamborees, the event hit its nadir in 2019 when it was cancelled for the year. The stated reason was that the board of the Chilliwack Minor Hockey Association (CMHA) was being pressured by dues-paying minor hockey players for more ice time during the last week of December, instead of the jamboree being staged then. The CMHA announced that the city's long-time Christmas season fixture would take a one-year hiatus to allow the association to brainstorm a solution to the worsening problem, but then the COVID-19 pandemic ensured there was no jamboree in 2020 or 2021. After a three-year absence, the event returned in 2022; the sixtieth version of the jamboree was smaller-scale than it had been, however, with only sixteen teams participating, all in the "C" Division.

The days of loud crowds cheering Peewee hockey players at Chilliwack Coliseum in the last week of December are long gone. In its heyday, the jamboree was widely viewed as *the* event to participate in and attend—a seasonal tradition and a source of local pride. Of all the tournaments staged over the decades, none was more exciting than the seventh annual edition in 1965, when a team of talented local boys destined for greatness won the community's first Chilliwack Peewee Hockey Jamboree "A" Championship.

ACKNOWLEDGEMENTS

AS I WAS SOON TO FIND OUT, WRITING A BOOK (LET ALONE GETTING ONE published) can be a lengthy and challenging undertaking. In my case, it would not have happened when and how it did had I not had the support, co-operation, and faith of certain people. I would like to acknowledge them and express my gratitude for their role in this exciting process. In particular:

Janine, for your patience, love, and constant support through what was a long journey. Instead of being a sports widow, you were a book widow for a while, but that's behind us now (book number two will be a breeze!).

Naomi Pauls, for your invaluable and spot-on advice, insights, and coaching. Without you, I doubt this would have all happened.

Tristan Evans and his staff at the Chilliwack Archives, for unfailingly (and in a timely fashion) fielding my questions about local history and sourcing images that I sometimes did not know existed.

My grandmother, Irene Bunt (née Knight, 1891–1988), the granddaughter of Isaac Kipp, who did her best to interest me in Chilliwack history and left me a treasure trove of books, photos, letters, and memories.

The group of writers who produced *The Chilliwack Story* in 2007. This book lit a fire in me, showing me what could be done in terms of chronicling our great city's history.

And lastly, the literally thousands of followers of Chilliwack History Perspectives, who for the past decade have given me weekly appreciation, validation, motivation, and feedback. And for those followers reading this book, I thank you again.

CHRONOLOGY

Sep. 1872	First Chilliwack Agricultural Exhibition
1873	Incorporation of Township of Chilliwhack
1881	Centreville developed
1887	Ashwell store established downtown, the name Chilliwack replaces Centreville
Oct. 1906	Royal Bank moves to new building
Feb. 21, 1908	Incorporation of City of Chilliwack
May 5, 1913	Opening of brick post office
May 21, 1913	Chilliwack High School opens on Yale Road East
Dec. 1, 1915	CN train station opens
Mar. 19, 1926	Spencer's department store opens downtown
Jun. 23, 1927	CHWK Radio goes live
1928	Safeway chain established in Chilliwack
Mar. 21, 1929	Chilliwack High School gymnasium opens
1931	CHWK Radio moves to second location
1933	Meadowlands Golf Course opens
May 10, 1935	Safeway moves to bigger premises on Wellington
Dec. 21, 1935	The Peaks restaurant opens, Yale Road West
Apr. 24, 1936	Opening of new Ag Hall
Apr. 17, 1939	Addition to Chilliwack High School opens
Aug. 23, 1941	Chilliwack Bowling Alley opens on Young Road
Nov. 1941	Pringle Electric Hatcheries opens
1944	Opening of Shangri-La Apartments
Nov. 15, 1944	The Twin Peaks opens, Yale Road East
1946	Doug Hartley purchases Chilliwack Bowling Alley
1946	Fashion Bakery opens in the Turpin Block
May 11, 1947	Opening of Chilliwack Airport's terminal
May 20, 1947	First baseball game played at future Monarch Park
Jun. 1947	CHWK Radio moves to third location
Mar. 1948	Construction of Menzies Subdivision begins
Dec. 1948	T. Eaton Co. acquires Spencer's chain
1949	Doug Hartley expands his bowling alley
Jun. 9, 1949	Opening of Paramount Theatre

Jun. 22, 1949	Opening of Fire Hall No. 1
Dec. 14, 1949	Opening of Chilliwack Library building
Jan. 9, 1950	New Chilliwack High School opens
Jun. 12, 1950	Liquor store on Victoria Avenue opens
Jul. 1, 1950	Opening of Chilliwack Drive-In Theatre
Jul. 10, 1950	Opening of Royal Bank Building at Five Corners
Sep. 30, 1950	Last run of BC Electric Railway interurban car to Chilliwack
Oct. 10, 1950	Opening of Pacific Stage Lines bus depot
Nov. 9, 1950	Safeway opens new, larger store on Mill Street
1951	Record-breaking rainfall and damaging flood
1952	Eaton's opens new premises downtown
Feb. 1952	Gymnasium opens at Chilliwack Senior High School
Sep. 11, 1952	Woolworth's opens on Wellington Avenue
Sep. 17, 1952	Opening of second Chilliwack courthouse
Jul. 24, 1953	Marilyn Monroe makes quick visit to Chilliwack
Summer 1954	Construction of Berkeley Subdivision begins
Sep. 1954	Little Mountain Elementary opens
May 13, 1955	First official function at the Chilliwack Coliseum
Aug. 13, 1955	Dairy Queen opens
Sep. 1955	J. Y. Halcrow begins career as principal of Chilliwack Senior High
Nov. 1955	Opening of Solange Apartments
May 1956	Bill Bunt appointed principal of Little Mountain Elementary
Sep. 20, 1956	Dari-Lou drive-in restaurant opens
Dec. 12, 1956	Work begins on Chilliwack Bypass
1958	Ronal TV-Electric started by Hiebert brothers
Jul. 29, 1958	Royal Hotel fire
Sep. 5, 1958	Park Lanes Recreation bowling alley opens
Oct. 16, 1958	Southgate Shopping Centre opens
Nov. 1, 1958	First hockey game at the Chilliwack Coliseum
Dec. 27, 1958	Official opening of the Chilliwack Coliseum
Jul. 14, 1959	Royal visit of Queen Elizabeth II and Prince Philip
Dec. 1959	Chilliwack Peewee Hockey Jamboree established
Aug. 1, 1960	Opening of Chilliwack Bypass (Highway 1)
Summer 1961	A&W drive-in restaurant opens, Yale Road West
Oct. 1, 1961	Detroit Red Wings first NHL team to play in city
Oct. 24, 1961	Safeway opens new store at 115 Main Street
1962	Building begins in Mount Shannon Estates
Sep. 25, 1962	Toronto Maple Leafs play exhibition game at Chilliwack Coliseum
1963	Ronal's record store opens on Wellington
Apr. 2, 1963	Overwaitea opens in former Safeway store

Nov. 9, 1963	Roy Orbison performs at the Agricultural Hall
Feb. 9, 1964	Beatles make debut on *The Ed Sullivan Show*
Sep. 25, 1965	Dog n Suds drive-in restaurant opens
Nov. 25, 1965	Eaton's opens remodelled store
Dec. 1, 1965	Liquor store opens on Kipp Avenue
Dec. 30, 1965	Chilliwack wins Peewee "A" Championship
1966	Haunting of Hetty Fredrickson house
Oct. 1966	Dunc Sutherland sells Meadowlands Golf Course
Oct. 9, 1969	Woolworth's officially opens new, larger store
May 1, 1970	Meadowlands becomes eighteen-hole golf course
May 15, 1970	Opening of new post office
Oct. 1971	First Dairy Queen closes
Jan. 5, 1972	Demolition of brick post office
Apr. 1972	Second Dairy Queen opens
1975	Twinning of Paramount Theatre
May 1976	Opening of Zen Building on old post office site
Aug. 1976	Ronal's record store goes out of business
Jan. 22, 1977	Eaton's permanently closes downtown
1977	CHWK 1270 moves to fourth location
Jun. 1977	J. Y. Halcrow retires from Chilliwack Secondary
1978	Fashion Bakery closes
Jan. 1, 1980	Merger of city and township into district of Chilliwack
1980	Fraser Park baseball diamond constructed
Sep. 4, 1981	Chillibowl Lanes opens on Wellington Avenue
1984	Dog n Suds drive-in restaurant shuts down
May 12, 1984	CN freight train derails in Chilliwack
Sep. 22, 1984	CN train station gutted by suspicious fire
Oct. 15, 1984	CN train station razed
Jul. 5, 1986	Opening of Chilliwack Airport's new terminal
Oct. 29, 1986	Chilliwack Airport's old terminal burns down
1987	A&W drive-in restaurant shuts down
Feb. 25, 1987	Fire destroys top floor of Meadowlands clubhouse
1988	Dari-Lou drive-in restaurant shuts down
Feb. 15, 1988	Save-On-Foods and liquor store open at new Salish Plaza
Apr. 1996	Chilliwack Junior Secondary torn down
Feb. 22, 2001	Monarch and Fraser Park ball diamonds dug up
2011–13	Chilliwack Senior Secondary replaced
Feb. 2013	Demolition of Paramount Theatre
Nov. 9, 2015	Demolition of former Safeway store on Main
Mar. 19, 2024	Opening of Paramount Building

SELECTED SOURCES

For a more complete set of endnotes and chapter-by-chapter citations, please visit harbourpublishing.com/pages/boom-times-in-chilliwack.

In researching this book, I relied heavily on two main sources for my stories—one private and subjective, the other accessible to all, verifiable, and objective. As I have referenced elsewhere, given my age I have a connection, direct or otherwise, to most all of the topics covered in *Boom Times in Chilliwack: Memories from the Post-war Years*. This first-hand experience and knowledge, coupled with an increasing sense of nostalgia for old Chilliwack, gave me the inspiration to put my memories on paper. It also afforded me storylines and facts not necessarily found elsewhere.

My other prime source was the online *Chilliwack Progress* archive (theprogress.newspapers.com). This resource goes back to literally the newspaper's first issue in 1891, and one can search any time period for any topic and obtain much insight to how the item was reported on over the years—sometimes with varying degrees of accuracy and completeness.

Other resources that I utilized included my grandmother, Irene Bunt (née Knight, 1891–1988), who was born in Popkum and moved to downtown Chilliwack in 1897. She loved Chilliwack and its history, and she would often tell me stories of the old days (including how she and her friends enjoyed meeting folk hero / train robber Billy Miner in 1904 as he regaled them with tales while he sat in front of the Dominion Hotel at Five Corners). She also left me left much historical material.

There are numerous books on Chilliwack history out there, and three in particular that I found useful were *The Chilliwack Story* (edited by Ron Denman, Chilliwack Museum and Archives, 2007), *Five Corners: The Story of Chilliwack* (Bruce Ramsey, Chilliwack Historical Society, 1975), and *Floodland and Forest: Memories of the Chilliwack Valley* (Imbert Orchard, Provincial Archives of British Columbia, 1983). Although they were not primary sources for my book and largely cover pre-1945 Chilliwack, they did serve to corroborate my understanding of facts and circumstances.

Finally, the Chilliwack Archives, and its user-friendly staff, provided much information that I could not confirm elsewhere.

Regarding the various images in *Boom Times in Chilliwack*, I employed three main sources:

The *Chilliwack Progress* Archive has a wealth of photographs taken over the years, most after the 1940s, when newspaper photography techniques and technology improved. However, only a relatively small portion of these original prints are accounted for, and they belong to the Chilliwack Museum and Archives. The whereabouts of the rest of the collection is unknown. Nevertheless, I do include numerous low-resolution scans from historical *Chilliwack Progress* editions to illustrate my stories, and while the quality is not as good as others', their grittiness conveys the historic spirit of a Chilliwack place or event from long ago.

The Chilliwack Archives has an extensive collection of images of higher quality/resolution of which I availed myself.

To convey how aspects of historical Chilliwack look in a current context, *Boom Times in Chilliwack: Memories from the Post-war Years* also includes some current-day images from my personal collection.

Other image sources include the City of Chilliwack, the 1948 Chilliwack Board of Trade publication titled *Chilliwack, British Columbia*, the Provincial Archives of British Columbia, and miscellaneous other smaller publications and personal collections.

ADDITIONAL IMAGE CREDITS

CHAPTER 1

p. 6 Photograph courtesy of the Chilliwack Museum and Archives, Photo Number 1981.021.035

p. 11 Photograph courtesy of the Chilliwack Museum and Archives, Photo Number 1981.021.018

p. 17 Photograph courtesy of the Chilliwack Museum and Archives, Photo Number 1987.048.002

p. 19 Scott Taylor / City of Chilliwack

p. 20 Photograph courtesy of the Chilliwack Museum and Archives, Photo Number 2009.017.038.004

p. 22 Photograph courtesy of the Chilliwack Museum and Archives, Photo Number 1971.002.011

CHAPTER 2

p. 31 Photograph courtesy of the Chilliwack Museum and Archives, Photo Number 1981.021.032

p. 33 Photograph courtesy of the Chilliwack Museum & Archives, Photo Number: P5644

p. 37 Image courtesy of the BC Archives (I-27734)

p. 40 Photograph courtesy of the Chilliwack Museum and Archives / Norman Williams, Photo Number: 2010.005.1302

CHAPTER 3

p. 43 Photograph courtesy of the Chilliwack Museum & Archives, Photo Number: PP501098

p. 50 PicClick // Grant-Mann Lithographers

p. 55 Chilliwack Board of Trade

p. 57 Photograph courtesy of the Chilliwack Museum & Archives, Photo Number: 1999.029.064.027 and the *Chilliwack Progress*

p. 59 Image courtesy of the BC Archives (I-27722)

p. 62 Photograph courtesy of the Chilliwack Museum & Archives, Photo Number: 1999.029.084.050 and the *Chilliwack Progress*

p. 63 Photograph courtesy of the Chilliwack Museum & Archives Photo Number: 2013.109.001

p. 65 Photograph courtesy of the Chilliwack Museum & Archives, Photo Number: 1999.029.175.119 and the *Chilliwack Progress*

CHAPTER 4

p. 73 Image courtesy of the BC Archives (I-27722)

p. 80 Photograph courtesy of the Chilliwack Museum & Archives, Photo Number: 1999.029.088.001 and the *Chilliwack Progress*

p. 86 Photograph courtesy of the Chilliwack Museum and Archives, Photo Number 1989.042.001

CHAPTER 5

p. 97 Photograph courtesy of the Chilliwack Museum & Archives, Photo Number: 1999.029.010.023 and the *Chilliwack Progress*

p. 100 Chilliwack Museum & Archives / Norman Williams

p. 105 Photograph courtesy of the Chilliwack Museum & Archives Photo Number: 2010.005.0683

p. 111 Photograph courtesy of the Chilliwack Museum and Archives, Photo Number 1998.041.012

CHAPTER 6

p. 134 Photograph courtesy of the Chilliwack Museum & Archives, Photo Number: 1999.029.022.034 and the *Chilliwack Progress*

p. 137 Photograph courtesy of the Chilliwack Museum & Archives and Norman Williams, photographer, Photo Number: 1995.023.003.006

p. 139 Image courtesy of the BC Archives (I-27725)

p. 142 Photograph courtesy of the Chilliwack Museum and Archives / Norman Williams, Photo Number: 1995.023.005.020 (1)

CHAPTER 7

p. 151 Photograph courtesy of the Chilliwack Museum & Archives Photo Number: 2018.053.004

p. 152 Photograph courtesy of the Chilliwack Museum & Archives Photo Number: 2018.053.003

p. 153 Photograph courtesy of the Chilliwack Museum & Archives Photo Number: 2007.010.016

p. 157 From the Collection of Rick Horne, photographed by Don Horne

p. 160 Photograph courtesy of the Chilliwack Museum & Archives, Photo Number: P. Coll 106, unnumbered

p. 161 Photograph courtesy of the Chilliwack Museum and Archives Photo Number: 2018.010.009 (2)

p. 163 Photograph courtesy of the Chilliwack Museum and Archives Photo Number: 2018.010.009 (1)

p. 169 Photograph courtesy of the Chilliwack Museum & Archives, Photo Number: 1996.040.025

p. 171 CBC // Red Robinson Collection

p. 173 Photograph courtesy of the Chilliwack Museum & Archives, Photo Number: 1983.095.001

p. 178 Photograph courtesy of the Chilliwack Museum & Archives, Photo Number: 1999.029.059.046 and the *Chilliwack Progress*

CHAPTER 8

p. 191 Photograph courtesy of the Chilliwack Museum & Archives, Photo Number: 1998.041.021

p. 194 Photograph courtesy of the Chilliwack Museum & Archives, Photo Number: 1989.060.001

p. 195 Photograph courtesy of the Chilliwack Museum & Archives Photo Number: 1999.029.028.052 and the *Chilliwack Progress*

CHAPTER 9

p. 211 Photograph courtesy of the Chilliwack Museum & Archives, Photo Number: P3857

p. 213 Photograph courtesy of the Chilliwack Museum & Archives, Photo Number: 2009.017.054.005

p. 218 Photograph courtesy of the Chilliwack Museum & Archives, Photo Number: P3863

p. 224 Image courtesy of the BC Archives (I-27732)

CHAPTER 10

p. 251 Photograph courtesy of the Chilliwack Museum and Archives [Photo number 2022.009.001]

INDEX